W9-BKT-917

The corporate greenhouse

The corporate greenhouse

CLIMATE CHANGE POLICY IN A GLOBALIZING WORLD

YDA SCHREUDER

DISCARDED

ZED BOOKS
London & New York

The Corporate Greenhouse: Climate Change Policy in a Globalizing World was first published in 2009 by Zed Books Ltd,
7 Cynthia Street, London N1 9JF, UK and Room 400, 175 Fifth Avenue, New York, NY 10010, USA

www.zedbooks.co.uk

Designed and typeset in Monotype Garamond
by illuminati, www.illuminatibooks.co.uk
Cover designed by Rogue Four Design
Printed and bound in Great Britain by CPI
Antony Rowe, Chippenham and Eastbourne

Distributed in the USA exclusively by Palgrave Macmillan, a division of St Martin's Press, LLC, 175 Fifth Avenue, New York, NY 10010, USA

A catalogue record for this book is available from the British Library
Library of Congress Cataloging in Publication Data available

ISBN   978 1 84277 957 6 Hb
ISBN   978 1 84277 958 3 Pb

Contents

Figures, tables and boxes

Acknowledgements

This book has been a long time in the making. The concerns expressed and the ideas presented have been discussed and debated in several courses that I have taught over the years. As part of course assignments on climate-change policy in a globalizing world, we conducted so-called North/South Debates which engaged students in discussion on often contested issues of sustainable development and social justice. On several occasions I had the opportunity to work with some highly motivated students on climate-change policy issues. Some of the research on transformational accounting practices and the early joint implementation projects was conducted by Christopher Sherry, to whom I owe a huge debt. Subsequently, other students contributed to the project and I am grateful for their help. I would like to mention Carolyn Luttrell and Jo Anne Tobin in particular. I also thank Linda Parrish for help with tables and figures, and Colleen Leithren for cleaning up the book manuscript. I would also like to acknowledge the editors at Zed Books and project editors Lucy Morton and Robin Gable. While in the Netherlands at the University of Groningen, during my sabbatical year in 2006, I received valuable support from colleagues at the Centre for Energy and Environmental Studies. I would like to thank Ton Schoot Uiterkamp, director of the

Centre, in particular. At the University of Delaware my colleagues at the Center for Energy and Environmental Policy have been a great inspiration, and were the motivation for writing the book. John Byrne, director of the Center, tirelessly rallied to my cause; without his encouragement, I might not have finished the project. In my home Department of Geography, I have been blessed with some good friends who provided great support following the death of my husband. I would like to mention four colleagues in particular: Edmunds Bunkše, whom I sometimes call my soulmate; Dan Leathers, who as chair of the department arranged for leave time during my husband's illness; Peter Rees, who has been my mentor and confidant; and April Veness, with whom I lament the burdens of life. Finally, I dedicate this book to my daughter Aafke Klara Lazar, and to the memory of her father, my husband, Joseph Lazar.

Newark, Delaware, 2008

Introduction

On 23 January 2008 the European Commission put forward a far-reaching package of proposals on the European Union's ambitious commitments to fight climate change and promote renewable energy. Central is an expansion of the Emissions Trading Scheme – the EU's key tool for cutting emissions – and implementation of a binding national renewable energy targets package. The EU is committed to reducing its emissions by 20 per cent by 2020 and has pledged to cut them by 30 per cent by 2020 if a new global climate-change agreement is implemented in Copenhagen in 2009. The EU also seeks to promote the development and safe use of carbon capture and storage (CCS).

Meanwhile, in the United States, inaction on climate-change policy within the context of the United Nations Framework Convention on Climate Change (UNFCCC) negotiations is notable, and except for the 2007 Energy Independence and Security Act – which mandates production and use of 36 billion gallons of biofuels per year by 2022 – most initiatives lack binding target agreements. States and cities are now coordinating efforts to fill the void left by the federal government. However, the new US administration will hopefully be more proactive on climate change and renewable energy policy, and we anticipate the implementation of some kind of cap-and-trade system. The outcome of the 2008 US elections suggests that there may be change in the air in terms of energy and environmental policy. In his election campaign, Barack Obama promised to support an economy-wide cap on greenhouse-gas emissions and to invest US$15 billion a year in renewable energy. While Obama acknowledges that under the current financial crisis and economic recession some of his proposed policy recommendations may require more time to implement, it is likely that at the December 2009 UNFCCC climate-change negotiations in Copenhagen, the Obama administration's position on global climate-change policy will be different from that of the Bush administration.

As the EU has had mixed success so far in 'going it alone' in terms of compliance with the Kyoto Protocol's binding emissions-reduction targets, the endorsement of an ambitious energy and climate-change policy by the European Commission was received with some apprehension. European business organizations were the most critical of the Commission's initiative. Ever since the EU implemented an emissions trading scheme in 2005, business leaders have warned that the EU's competitive position in the global economy might be threatened. Their concern is that more effort should be made to improve the EU's CO_2 emissions trading scheme, which in its current form has contributed to large and unjustified windfall profits for energy and electricity producers at the expense of energy-intensive industries. Several industry leaders have warned that EU industrial competitiveness is at stake and that further corporate investment in the EU may stall. The very ambitious goals on renewable energy and greenhouse gas (GHG) emissions-reduction targets should be checked against the economic and technological capabilities of European industry, they argued.

European industry leaders claim that energy-intensive industry is too heavily exposed to global competition, and with the EU's ambitious Lisbon Strategy, adopted in 2000 – emphasizing competitive economic growth objectives – the turmoil in the global financial markets, and increased pressure for liberalization of European energy and electricity markets, the scope for productive cooperation among EU member states is in question. EU member states have made numerous public calls for tough action on climate change, and the

Council and Parliament have applauded the Commission's push for binding CO_2 emissions-reduction targets and renewable energy standards, but concern about relocation of energy-intensive industries and 'carbon leakage' have member states' environment ministers now calling for more flexible climate-change action. It is not in the best interests of the European Union, they argue, that production moves to countries with less strict emissions limits, and the Commission notes in a recent communication that Europe 'going it alone' may not have been the best strategy. EU business organizations confirm that their members complain about the lack of clarity and certainty in climate-change policy under the Kyoto Protocol.

With this example of recent developments in EU energy and climate-change policy, we are presented with the broader problems associated with the Kyoto Protocol. From the ongoing debates in climate-change policy and the apparent ineffectiveness of the current Kyoto regime dealing with GHG-reduction schemes to halt or reverse climate change, it is obvious that something is wrong with the way the world order is dealing with global environmental problems. Much debated now, but not considered at the time the Kyoto Protocol was signed, is the recognition that national emissions-reduction commitments have little effect in a global economy that is driven by intense competition and organized around transnational corporations and international production networks. Ever since the United States withdrew from the commitment to comply with binding emissions-reduction targets as stipulated under the Kyoto Protocol, the success of the EU's climate-change policies have been in doubt. Furthermore, the emergence on the world economic scene of, in particular, China and India has rekindled the debate on who is to blame and who is to pay. That development and environmental concerns are closely related is no longer in question, but how to deal with the reality of the global marketplace and tackle the urgent problems associated with climate change remain major issues of debate.

This book addresses the political economy of the climate-change debate in the context of the changing geopolitical order and the geographic shift in production that is occurring. The text is organized around these two recurrent themes, which have been played out against each other over the past few decades. The book starts out with a discussion of the attempts to come to terms with GHG emissions reduction under the UNFCCC and the emergence of a world economic order that seriously challenges the role of the nation-state in emissions-reduction strategies. While our political leaders recognize the challenges of addressing global environmental problems, they offer little in the way of solving the problems and ending the stalemate that exist in the UNFCCC today.

Conceptually, the book derives from a series of papers I have co-authored and published on the 'corporate greenhouse'.[1] In two papers published a decade ago, we asked 'How can we reach a more sustained North–South cooperation in solving global environmental problems like climate change in a globalizing world?' and 'How can we develop more effective agreements and more equitable burden-sharing in order to reach such agreements?' By analysing the dynamics and impacts of foreign trade and foreign direct investment (FDI) on GHG emissions, we suggested a more equitable and just way of accounting for them in the context of the growing importance of privatization, market liberalization and the role of the multinational corporation. As these forces have changed since the late 1990s, when these papers were published, the current text is updated and rewritten to include the emergence of China and India on the global economic scene, and there is extensive discussion devoted to the role of the EU in assuming leadership in climate-change negotiations and policy implementation. In 2005, when I wrote the paper on the EU Emissions Trading Scheme (ETS) and the impact of carbon constraints on the geographical shift in location of energy-intensive industries, there were no data to substantiate my projection of what might happen after the scheme's implementation. I suggested a likely course of events based on past corporate investment strategies and reports from, in particular, energy-intensive industries in the EU at the time. In 2006, while on sabbatical leave at the University of Groningen in the Netherlands, I had the opportunity to research the corporate response and to document global shifts in production.

The topic is timely as the UNFCCC begins the negotiations for the post-Kyoto climate-change policy regime, in which the EU is trying to persuade the United States, China and India (among other countries) to sign up to binding emissions-reduction targets. EU policymakers and business leaders realize that they cannot 'go it alone': for the Kyoto process to succeed, it is necessary to bring other major economic powers, in particular the United States, on board. The fact that American public opinion with respect to climate change/global warming and the Kyoto Protocol is changing, and that several states – including California and the northeastern and mid-Atlantic states – are signing up to an emissions trading scheme, suggests that state governments, the public, and perhaps even US corporations, are closer to committing to the climate change/global warming strategies of the Kyoto Protocol than the US federal government. The book should serve as a stimulus in further discussions and negotiations on climate change policy.

I anticipate that the book will be used primarily as a text for graduate courses in development and environmental policy studies and upper-level or graduate courses in international relations, political economy and economic geography. The text may also serve a non-scholarly or more policy- or diplomatic-oriented readership. In writing the text I have assumed that the reader has a general knowledge of the history of the climate-change negotiations, the Kyoto Protocol, and other international global governance issues. I have also taken for granted the reader's awareness of the dynamic forces in the global economy, capitalist market principles, and international corporate business strategic decision-making.

Whereas there are several texts that address economic globalization and global environmental concerns, few specifically address climate-change policy in the context of the changing geopolitical order and the global geographic shift in production that is occurring at the present time. The text relates particular Kyoto Protocol implementation strategies (the EU Emissions Trading Scheme and the Clean Development Mechanism) to the forces of economic globalization to illustrate the challenges of climate-change policy as we approach the end of the commitment period of the UNFCCC Kyoto Protocol. It places the climate-change debate in the context of the ongoing North–South debates where the global partnership for development meets equity and environmental sustainability concerns.

Chapter 1 introduces the reader to the ongoing debates in climate-change negotiations and treaty-making with as background the UN

Conference on Environment and Development (Rio de Janeiro 1992) and the Kyoto Protocol (1997). The chapter gives a brief overview of the Kyoto Protocol and introduces the reader to the various aspects that explain the GHG emissions record in different parts of the world. The data pose the question of whether any climate-change policy would be effective in reducing GHGs in the atmosphere if the United States, China, India and other rapidly developing countries do not commit to binding emissions reductions.

Chapter 2 places the UN Framework Convention on Climate Change within the context of the ongoing United Nations development dialogue and addresses the climate-change negotiations within the framework of the political economy of globalization in the North–South context. The reader is introduced to the issues of equity and sustainability and learns about the UN as the forum for international debates on environment and development issues.

Chapter 3 introduces the reader to the debate about the neo-liberal economic and political agenda and its global implications. Trade liberalization under the Washington Consensus, the IMF and World Bank Structural Adjustment Programmes, and the WTO trade regime are the main foci of discussion. The chapter concludes with a general discussion of the impact of trade liberalization on the global environment.

Chapter 4 further discusses the contradictions and unresolved tensions between economic globalization and climate-change negotiations, and looks at the growing concern about the role of multinational or transnational corporations (TNCs). We consider intra-firm patterns of trade that diverge from traditional foreign trade, which calls national economic and emissions accounting practices into question.

Chapter 5 analyses the impact of the EU Emissions Trading Scheme on corporate investment strategies and global production shifts of energy-intensive manufacturing. Under conditions of 'carbon constraint', energy-intensive industries in the EU began the debate about the wisdom of the EU 'going it alone'. The chapter also presents a discussion about the expansion of energy-intensive production in China.

Chapter 6 examines the intent and practice of using the 'Flexible Mechanism' under the Kyoto Protocol. Attention focuses on the

Clean Development Mechanism (CDM), which encourages investment in GHG emissions-reduction projects in developing countries. Case studies reveal, however, that in fact strategic manipulation by major oil and energy companies leads to serious misuse of the CDM as a mechanism to reduce GHG emissions.

Chapter 7 returns to the question of equity, sustainability and burden-sharing in the 'global atmospheric commons' in a globalizing world and suggests some alternative approaches to mitigating climate change. Recognizing that multinational or transnational corporations play a major role in fostering a fossil-fuel-based development course in developing countries, the chapter concludes with a call to restructure GHG emissions accounting to give greater weight to TNCs' share of the global pool of emissions.

1

Climate-change policy
in a globalizing world

The Corporate Greenhouse explores the most pressing issue confronting the world community in our time. As the scientific basis of climate change appears to be no longer in doubt, discussions about climate-change policy and the Kyoto Protocol have re-emerged in public debate. The Intergovernmental Panel on Climate Change Fourth Assessment Report, issued in February 2007, states that 'most of the observed increase in globally averaged temperatures since the mid-20th century is very likely due to the observed increase in anthropogenic greenhouse gas concentrations'.[1] Based on current model simulations, projections are that continued greenhouse-gas emissions at or above current rates would cause substantial warming of the atmosphere and induce many changes in the global climate system during the twenty-first century that would very likely be larger than those observed during the twentieth century.[2] There is much evidence in the report to support the thesis not only that climate change will occur if no action is taken but also that it really is human activity that is induc-ing the change. The Report embodies substantial new research and addresses gaps that existed in our knowledge hitherto. Also, it has practically eliminated earlier uncertainty. With this assessment and with the realization that so far under the Kyoto Protocol, greenhouse-gas emissions worldwide have increased rather than diminished, the effectiveness of the Protocol and the commitment on the part of the industrialized countries to combat human-induced climate change are called into question.

Measures against global warming had been dominating the international arena of climate-change negotiations under the auspices of the UNFCCC since the Earth Summit in Rio de Janeiro in 1992, and nation-states had agreed to confront dangerous anthropogenic interference with the earth's climate system and to achieve stabilization of GHG concentrations in the atmosphere low enough so that climate change could be prevented. The actions were aimed primarily at industrialized countries with the intention of stabilizing their emissions of greenhouse gases at 1990 levels by the year 2000 and below 1990 levels in years following. Participating parties agreed that they would recognize 'common but differentiated responsibilities', with greater responsibility for reducing GHG emissions in the near term assumed by developed industrialized countries, which were listed and identified in Annex I of the UNFCCC (hereafter referred to as Annex I countries).

Since 1992 – when the UNFCCC was first introduced – a significant number of international climate-change meetings have been held through the annual Conferences of the Parties (COPs), resulting in the adoption of the Kyoto Protocol in 1997. The Protocol committed Annex I countries to binding GHG emissions reductions of 5.2 per cent relative to 1990 emissions by the period 2008–12. Technically, they are listed as Annex B in the Kyoto Protocol, but since they roughly coincide with the Annex I group under the UNFCCC, we will refer to both as Annex I.[3] Each country had its emissions-reduction target; ranging from an 8 per cent reduction to a 10 per cent increase. (GHG emissions reductions are measured in tonnes (metric tons) and all the protocol documents refer to the European measure, not to the US 'short' ton. In the remainder of the text we will refer to the international (metric) tonne unless otherwise noted.) The United States, the world's largest producer of anthropogenic greenhouse-gas emissions, agreed to a 7 per cent reduction relative to 1990 levels. The European Union agreed to an 8 per cent reduction while countries in central and eastern Europe agreed to a 6–8 per cent reduction, and Russia and the Ukraine each agreed not to exceed 1990 levels of emissions. Developing countries, also known as non-Annex I countries, were not required to sign on to the Protocol to meet binding emissions-reduction targets.

The Protocol languished in Washington and Brussels for some time until 2001 when, shortly after President Bush took office, the US administration decided to withdraw from the agreement as the Senate would not ratify the Protocol. During the final years of the Clinton administration the Senate repeatedly called for the full participation of the main developing countries (like India and China) in the Protocol's emissions-cutting requirements, but no negotiations to that effect were ever undertaken. In declining to support the Kyoto Protocol, President Bush referred to three concerns or conditions that any future agreement should address. First, the main developing countries would need to adhere to binding emissions-reduction targets and become full participants in any climate-change agreement, as the Senate had earlier resolved. Second, the uncertainty about the relationship between GHG emissions and climate change or global warming had to be established more firmly by the scientific community. And, third, Americans would prefer voluntary rather than regulatory action to be taken.[4] Meanwhile, the European Union went ahead with the ratification process, which passed, and in October 2001 the EU Commission and the European Parliament presented a proposal for establishing an emissions trading scheme. The EU Emissions Trading Scheme took effect on 1 January 2005.[5]

As Europe is 'going it alone', it is doubtful that the EU Emissions Trading Scheme will have any lasting impact on global climate change. The major reason being that the simultaneous effort to institutionalize global trade policy and economic development policy through the World Trade Organization (WTO), the World Bank and the International Monetary Fund (IMF), and the opening up of markets in developing countries and countries in transition in central and eastern Europe through privatization and liberalization, encouraged rapid economic growth and a carbon-intensive development which runs counter to any effort made through the UNFCCC to combat the build-up of GHGs in the atmosphere and avert global warming and/or climate change. Later in this chapter I elaborate on this, but first we need a more detailed discussion of the Kyoto

Protocol and the particular mechanisms set up to accomplish the task of reduction of GHG concentrations in the atmosphere, and of the actual GHG emissions reductions and increases measured since 1990.

The Kyoto Protocol

The Kyoto Protocol, signed in 1997, is an amendment to the United Nations Framework Convention on Climate Change agreed to at the Earth Summit in 1992, which assigned mandatory emissions reductions of greenhouse gases to signatory nations (Box 1.1). The Protocol was concluded at the Third Conference of the Parties (COP3) under the UNFCCC in Kyoto, Japan, in 1997. Countries that ratified the Protocol commit to reduce their emissions of carbon dioxide and five other gases – methane, nitrous oxide, sulphur hexafluoride, HFCs and PFCs; collectively known as greenhouse gases – or engage in emissions trading if they increase their emissions.[6] Since carbon dioxide (CO_2) contributes more than 75 per cent of human-induced GHG emissions and since more than 95 per cent of global CO_2 emissions are due to fossil-fuel burning and land-use change, most of the attention in the Kyoto Protocol is devoted to fossil-fuel-based CO_2 emissions reduction. The Kyoto Protocol entered into force on 16 February 2005 after 55 Annex I countries covering at least 55 per cent of 1990 GHG emissions had ratified the treaty. The Kyoto Protocol now covers more than 160 countries globally, including developing countries that subscribe to the global emissions-reduction efforts.

The objective of the Kyoto Protocol is the stabilization of GHG concentrations in the atmosphere at a level that will prevent dangerous anthropogenic interference with the climate system. The Intergovernmental Panel on Climate Change (IPCC) has predicted a likely average global rise in temperature of 1.8 to 4.0°C between 1990 and 2100 based on trends and projections of increased GHG concentrations in the atmosphere.[7] The Kyoto Protocol is seen as the first step towards stabilizing these concentrations in the atmosphere, while its goal is to lower overall emissions of the six GHGs calculated as

BOX 1.1   **The Kyoto Protocol**

- The Protocol is underwritten by governments and is governed by global legislation enacted under the UN's aegis.

- Governments are separated into two general categories: developed countries, referred to as Annex I countries, that have accepted GHG emissions-reduction obligations and must submit an annual greenhouse-gas inventory; and developing countries, referred to as non-Annex I countries, that have no GHG emissions-reduction obligations but may participate in the Clean Development Mechanism.

- Any Annex I country that fails to meet its Kyoto Protocol obligation will be penalized by having to submit 1.3 emission allowances in a second commitment period for every tonne of GHG emissions they exceed their cap in the first commitment period (2008–12).

- By 2008–12, Annex I countries must reduce their GHG emissions by an average of 5 per cent below their 1990 levels. For many countries, such as the EU member states, this corresponds to some 15 per cent below their expected GHG emissions in 2008. While the average emissions reduction is 5 per cent, national limitations range from 8 per cent reductions for the European Union to a 10 per cent emissions increase for Iceland. Reduction limitations expire in 2013.

- The Kyoto Protocol includes 'Flexible Mechanisms' which allow Annex I economies to meet their GHG emission limitation by purchasing GHG emissions-reduction credits from elsewhere. These can be bought either through financial exchanges such as the new EU Emissions Trading Scheme allows, or from projects which reduce emissions in non-Annex I economies under the CDM, or in other Annex I countries under the Joint Implementation (JI) clause.

- Only CDM Executive Board-accredited Certified Emission Reductions (CERs) can be bought and sold in this manner. Under the aegis of the UN, the Kyoto Protocol Clean Development Mechanism Executive Board (EB) which assesses and approves projects in non-Annex I countries prior to awarding CERs, certifies and validates projects for CERs. A similar scheme applies to Joint Implementation for countries in transition which are Annex I countries and include the former Soviet Union and countries in central and eastern Europe. What this means in practice is that non-Annex I countries have no GHG emissions restrictions, but when a GHG emissions-reduction project is implemented in these countries, that project will receive carbon credits which can be sold to Annex I buyers.

- To facilitate this process, the Kyoto 'Linking Mechanism' was adopted as part of the Protocol. Since the cost of complying with the Protocol can be quite expensive for those Annex I countries which already have highly energy efficient and low-emission industries, it allows for the purchase of carbon credits instead of reducing GHG emissions domestically. To engage and encourage non-Annex I developing countries to reduce GHG emissions – since doing so is now economically viable because of the sale of carbon credits – CDM is viewed as the mechanism by which developing countries would come on board in support of the Kyoto Protocol, and eventually may commit to binding emissions-reduction targets.

Source: Adapted from *The Kyoto Protocol to the UN Framework Convention on Climate Change*: www:unfccc.int/kyoto_protocol.

an average over the five-year period of 2008–12. The parties agreed that since the largest share of historical and current global emissions of greenhouse gases originated in developed countries and since per capita emissions in developing countries were still relatively low, developing countries would not have to commit to binding emissions-reduction targets during the Protocol's commitment period (2008–12). The Protocol treaty negotiated in Kyoto, Japan, in December 1997 opened for signature on 16 March 1998 and closed on 15 March 1999. Signatory countries first had to ratify the Kyoto Protocol, and on 16 February 2005, the agreement came into force following ratification by Russia on 18 November 2004. As of December 2006, a total of 169 countries and other governmental entities had ratified the agreement, representing 61.6 per cent of emissions from Annex I countries. The notable exception is the United States; Australia – another long time hold-out – ratified the treaty in March 2008. Other countries, such as India, China and Brazil, have ratified the

Protocol but are not presently required to reduce their domestic carbon emissions, although they do take advantage of CERs earned through the Clean Development Mechanism.

All committed Annex I countries have established designated national authorities to manage their GHG portfolios under the Protocol. Japan, Canada, Italy, the Netherlands, Germany, France, Spain and many more are actively promoting government carbon funds and supporting multilateral carbon funds intent on purchasing carbon credits from non-Annex I countries. These government organizations are working closely with their major utility, energy and chemicals conglomerates to acquire as many Certified Emissions Reductions as cheaply as possible. Virtually all of the non-Annex I countries have also set up their own designated national authorities to manage the Kyoto Protocol process – specifically the CDM process – whereby host governments decide which GHG reduction projects they do or do not wish to support for accreditation by the CDM Executive Board. The objectives of the two parties in the CDM process are quite different. Annex I countries want carbon credits as cheaply as possible, while non-Annex I countries want to maximize the value of carbon credits generated from their domestic GHG reduction projects.

From the beginning of the negotiations in Rio de Janeiro (1992) it was understood that the share of global emissions originating in developing countries would grow as these countries implemented economic development policies to meet their social and development needs. Annex I countries agreed that, as developing countries develop industrial capacity, they will help pay for and supply technologies to them for climate-change-related projects in order to encourage a more energy-efficient and low-emission development path. This clause in the Kyoto Protocol was an affirmation of Article 4 in the UNFCCC and has been applied through the CDM and through the linking of the EU Emissions Trading Scheme with the CDM. Critics of the Protocol argue that since China already is, and India and other developing countries soon will be, among those countries contributing most to global GHG emissions, they should therefore come on board with binding GHG emissions-reduction commitments for the post-Kyoto negotiations. Without carbon constraints on these countries, they argue, corporate industries in developed countries might lose their competitive position and will likely expand production in non-carbon-constraint countries like China, India, Brazil, or any other country competitively positioned for FDI or foreign trade. In that case, there would be no net reduction of GHG emissions concentrations in the atmosphere but just a shift in the geographical distribution of the source of emissions due to expanding manufacturing capacity in the developing non-Annex I countries.

The Kyoto Protocol left several issues unresolved and undecided. In November 2000, the Sixth Conference of the Parties (COP6), held in The Hague in the Netherlands, was to address remaining unresolved details of implementation of the Protocol. The key objectives of COP6 to the UNFCCC were to reach agreement on the development of an efficient and effective verification and compliance system, on what kind of instruments or mechanisms to use to arrive at the agreed-to emissions-reduction targets, and how to dissuade developing countries from following a carbon-intensive development path while helping small island nations to overcome the negative impacts of climate change.[8] The parties agreed to find the cheapest possible solutions with the least possible political risk involved. Under the terms of the Protocol, the industrialized nations would have two options for meeting their obligations. The first would be to cut domestic GHG emissions with the choice to sequester atmospheric CO_2 in forest 'sinks' through reforestation programmes and/or projects to control deforestation, as favoured by the United States, Canada and Australia. The second option was to earn credits towards the emission targets agreed to in the Protocol by using the 'flexible mechanism' clause (see Box 1.1). The flexible mechanisms would include trade in emissions with other industrialized countries and investments in emissions-reduction projects in other Annex I countries (referred to as Joint Implementation) or in non-Annex I countries (referred to as the Clean Development Mechanism). Joint Implementation, in effect, would most likely involve investment in central and eastern Europe while the Clean Development Mechanism was aimed at emissions reduction in developing countries.

The Climate Change Convention in The Hague (COP6) in 2000 was unable to reach an agreement on the first issue due to disputes between the European Union, on the one hand, and the United States, Canada, Japan and Australia, on the other. In 2001, a continuation of the previous meeting (COP6-bis) was held in Bonn, where the required decisions were adopted. After some concessions, the supporters of the flexible mechanisms of the Protocol, led by the European Union, which favoured tougher standards and measures, managed to get Japan and Russia on board by allowing greater use of 'carbon sinks'.

It had been the position of the EU that at least 50 per cent of the reduction of GHGs should be derived from cuts in domestic emissions. On the other hand, the United States had maintained that there should be no limitation to the use of the flexible mechanisms and that for those countries with large forests, carbon sinks should be counted as credits. In fact, the United States, along with Australia and Canada, claimed that they could possibly meet their commitments that way. Still other countries wanted to include nuclear power as an option to solve the GHG problem. Besides agreements on flexible mechanisms and carbon sinks, COP6-bis also addressed compliance measures which were agreed to at COP7 in Marrakesh in Morocco the following year (2002). Countries that did not meet their agreed-to emissions-reduction target would have to make up for the shortfall during the next (post-2012) commitment period at a rate of 1.3 tonnes to 1 tonne missed emissions reduction. COP7 also established the terms under which the Protocol would take effect.[9]

The fundamental premiss behind the flexible mechanisms is that the costs of emissions reduction are substantially lower in developing countries and in countries with economies in transition in central and eastern Europe than in highly developed industrialized economies. It therefore stands to reason that expenditures on emissions reduction will have more effect in developing countries and in transition economies than in industrialized countries. By investing in these countries, committed industrialized countries can earn carbon credits to offset lack of progress in meeting domestic reduction targets. With the COP6-bis agreement to include emissions trading as one of the primary means to comply with the Kyoto agreed-to emissions-reduction targets and timetables, a cap-and-trade system was introduced and later implemented by the EU Emissions Trading Scheme in 2005 to reach the goals. Emissions trading imposes national caps on the emissions of Annex I countries. On average, the cap requires countries to reduce their emissions a certain percentage below their 1990 baseline over the 2008 to 2012 period. Although the caps are national-level commitments, in practice participants are expected to transfer their emissions targets to individual industrial entities such as power plants or energy-intensive industries, which each received a certain number of allowances or carbon credits. This means that the ultimate buyers of emissions credits are individual companies that expect their emissions to exceed their quota or allowance. Typically, they will purchase credits directly from another party with excess allowances, from a broker, from a JI/CDM developer, or on an exchange. Countries that do not assign primary responsibility for meeting Kyoto obligations to industry but that have a net deficit of allowances will have to buy credits on their own government account. This occurs mainly via JI/CDM developers, for which purpose a national fund or agency is established, or via collective funds such as the World Bank's Prototype Carbon Fund (PCF).[10] Since carbon credits are tradable instruments with a transparent price, financial investors have started buying them for trading purposes. This market is expected to grow substantially, with banks, brokers, funds, arbitrageurs and private traders eventually participating in emissions trading. Chapters 5 and 6 address the particular strategies of emissions trading in greater detail.

Although Kyoto created a framework and a set of rules for a global carbon market, there are in practice several distinct schemes or markets in operation today with varying degrees of linkages among them. Kyoto enables a group of several Annex I countries to join together to create a so-called 'bubble', a cluster of countries that is given an overall emissions cap and is treated as a single entity for compliance purposes. The EU elected to be treated as a bubble, and created the EU Emissions Trading Scheme as a market within a market. The ETS's currency is a EUA (EU Allowance).

The UK established its own 'learning by doing' voluntary scheme, the UK ETS. The UK scheme exists alongside the EU's scheme and participants in the UK scheme had the option of applying to opt out of the first phase of the EU ETS, which lasted through 2007. Canada and Japan established their internal markets in 2008 and it is very likely that they will link directly into the EU ETS. Canada's scheme will probably include a trading system for large point sources of emissions and for the purchase of large numbers of outside credits. The Japanese plan will probably not include mandatory targets for companies but will rely on large-scale purchases of external credits. Furthermore, in the United States several regional consortia are experimenting with their own emissions trading schemes.

Next to the EU ETS, the most important sources of credits are the Clean Development Mechanism and Joint Implementation. The CDM allows the creation of new carbon credits by developing emissions-reduction projects in non-Annex I countries, while JI allows project-specific credits to be converted from existing credits in Annex I countries. CDM projects produce Certified Emission Reductions (CERs), and JI projects produce Emission Reduction Units (ERUs). CERs have been valid for meeting EU ETS obligations since 2005, and ERUs are valid from 2008 until 2012 (covering the Kyoto Protocol commitment period). Although individual countries may choose to limit the number and sources of CERs or ERUs they will allow for compliance purposes starting in 2008. CERs and ERUs are overwhelmingly bought from project developers by funds or individual entities rather than being exchange-traded like EUAs. Since the creation of these instruments is subject to a lengthy process of registration and certification by the UNFCCC, and the projects themselves require several years to develop, this market is at present almost completely a forward market where purchases are made at a deep discount to their equivalent currency, the EUA, and are almost always subject to certification and delivery, although up-front payments are sometimes made. According to the International Emissions Trading Association (IETA), the market value of CDM/JI credits transacted in 2004 was €245 million and it is estimated that more than €620 million worth of credits were transacted in 2005.[11] Further details of credits transacted in 2006 and 2007 are discussed in Chapter 6.

Several non-Kyoto Protocol carbon markets are starting up or are in an early phase of development and are likely to grow in importance in the coming years. They include the New South Wales Greenhouse Gas Abatement Scheme (Australia), and in the United States the Regional Greenhouse Gas Initiative (RGGI), the Chicago Climate Exchange, the State of California's recent initiative to reduce emissions, the commitment of hundreds of US mayors to adopt Kyoto targets for their cities, and the State of Oregon's emissions abatement programme. Taken together, these non-Kyoto initiatives could form a series of linked markets rather than single carbon markets. The common theme is the adoption of market-based mechanisms centred on carbon credits that represent a reduction of CO_2 emissions. The fact that most of these initiatives have similar approaches to certifying their carbon credits makes it conceivable that carbon credits in one market may in the long run be tradable in most other schemes. This would broaden the carbon market far beyond the current focus on the CDM/JI and EU ETS domains. An obvious precondition, however, is harmonization of different trading schemes so that credits in one market have an exchange value in another. For this to happen a system of penalties and fines for not meeting agreed-to emissions reductions has to be established.

Greenhouse gas emissions: the record[12]

The record of GHG emissions for 2005 – the latest year for which compiled data for all forty industrialized countries that have signed and ratified the UNFCCC is available – shows the percentage increase or decrease of GHG emissions compared to a specific base year (usually 1990).[13] Comparing total GHG emissions in 2005 to 1990 levels by region reveals some interesting patterns (See Appendix 1). US emissions were up by 16.3 per cent over 1990 levels while the EU group of 27 – including the new members from east and central Europe, admitted to the EU since 2004 – are now 7.4 per cent below their base-year emissions. The EU15 group of nations, which had been members of the EU before 2005 when central and eastern European countries joined, reduced their emissions 2.7 per cent below 1990 levels. Within the EU, only four countries of the pre-enlargement EU15 (Britain, France, Germany and Sweden) are on course to meet their 2012 targets. Portugal, Ireland and Spain – the fast-growth countries in the EU – and Austria and Italy were well above their Kyoto targets in 2005. While the statistics indicate that, as a group, the EU signatory countries – including the newly admitted central and eastern European members – are likely to meet their agreed-to reduction target by 2012, most of the progress in GHG reduction has come from the stark decline in central and eastern European countries' emissions following the fall of Communism in the 1990s. The USA, meanwhile, has so far taken no nationwide action to reduce greenhouse-gas emissions and has seen a continuous increase from year to year.

At a global scale, GHG emissions are increasing at an alarming rate. The Global Carbon Project[14] summarized the latest findings on global and regional CO_2 emissions increases in the following way:

> CO_2 emissions from fossil-fuel burning and industrial processes have been accelerating at a global scale, with their growth rate increasing from 1.1 per cent per year for 1990–1999 and 3 per cent per year for 2000–2004. The emissions growth rate since 2000 was greater than for the most fossil-fuel intensive of the Intergovernmental Panel on Climate Change emissions scenarios developed in the late 1990s. Global emissions growth since 2000 was driven by a cessation or reversal of earlier declining trends in the energy intensity of gross domestic product (GDP) (energy/GDP) and the carbon intensity of energy (emissions/energy), coupled with continuing increases in population and per-capita GDP. Nearly constant or slightly increasing trends in the carbon intensity of energy have been recently observed in both developed and developing regions. No region is de-carbonizing its energy supply. The growth rate in emissions is strongest in rapidly developing economies, particularly China. Together, the developing and least-developed economies (forming 80 per cent of the world's population) accounted for 73 percent of global emissions growth in 2004 but only 41 percent of global emissions and only 23 percent of global cumulative emissions since the mid-18th century. The results have implications for global equity.[15]

The Global Carbon Project was formed in 2001 to assist the international science community to establish a common, mutually agreed upon, knowledge base supporting policy debate and action to slow the rate of increase of greenhouse gases in the atmosphere.[16]

Fossil fuel emissions have increased exponentially in the past decades with a clear acceleration in growth rates over the last few years.[17] In fact, growth in CO_2 emissions over the last five years resembles 'Scenario A1B' which the IPCC uses to predict how much the global climate will change with increased greenhouse-gas emissions. The 'A1B' scenario assumes that 50 per cent of energy over the next century will come from fossil fuels, resulting in atmospheric carbon dioxide concentrations that will likely have climatic change consequences. The IPCC concludes that if we stay on the current path then it will be extremely difficult to reduce carbon emissions enough to stabilize the atmospheric CO_2 concentration at 450 parts per million (ppm), and even 550 ppm will be a challenge. Research suggests that stabilizing carbon dioxide concentrations at 450 ppm could limit global warming to 2 degrees Celsius, but 550 ppm would likely cause an increase of between 4 and 5 degrees Celsius.[18] All this naturally leads to questions about the merits of a market-based regulatory approach to curbing emissions as adopted and implemented by the EU, as we will discuss in Chapters 5 and 6. Indeed, the data raise the question of whether any climate-change policy would be effective in reducing GHGs in the atmosphere if the United States, China, India, and other developing countries do not commit to binding emissions reductions. A lively debate has emerged between the EU and the USA as to the most effective measures with which to pursue a plan of action for the period after 2012 when current Kyoto Protocol commitments expire. As stated in the Introduction, in January 2008 the European Commission put forward an EU energy policy that included a unilateral 20 per cent reduction in GHG emissions by 2020. The EU has consistently been one of the major supporters of the Kyoto Protocol, negotiating hard to get wavering countries on board, while the United States, although a signatory to the UNFCCC, has not ratified the Protocol and officially withdrew when President Bush came into office. As a result the USA is not committing to binding emissions reductions targets. While the USA was until recently the largest single emitter of carbon dioxide from the burning of fossil fuels and is still by far the largest per capita CO_2 emitter, it would seem paramount that the USA comes on board. Meanwhile, China has now become the world's largest emitter of CO_2

TABLE I.I   **Carbon emissions in China, India, Europe, Japan and the United States 2004, and increase 1990–2004**

Country/region	Emissions (m tonnes)	Emissions/ capita (tonnes)	Emissions/ PPP GDP (tonnes/$m)	Increase in emissions (%)
China	1,021	0.8	158	67
India	301	0.3	99	88
Europe	955	2.5	94	6
Japan	338	2.7	95	23
United States	1,616	5.5	147	19

Source: Christopher Flavin, *State of the World; Special Focus: China and India*, World Watch Institute, Norton, New York, 2006: 8–9, Box 1–1.

and its rapid economic development suggests that rising emissions will continue.[19]

To evaluate the implications of these rising emissions in China and other countries in the context of the climate-change debate, other aspects must be taken into account such as economic development, energy intensity levels, and per capita emissions. Obviously, countries with larger populations and larger economies will use more energy and emit more CO_2 and, therefore, it is not surprising that large countries or regions such as the United States, China, the European Union, Russia, India and Japan are the top six of CO_2 emitters. A more meaningful comparison would be emissions based on energy intensity of unit of production or GDP, or per capita CO_2 emissions (Table 1.1). The implications of these different ways of measuring and comparing emissions rates between countries are far-reaching. Comparing CO_2 emissions between nations based on emissions per unit of production or GDP suggests that technologically more advanced economies display greater energy efficiency compared to developing economies or economies in transition, as the latter operate manufacturing units with often inefficient or outdated equipment. Measuring and comparing emissions per capita are based on equity and sustainability considerations and the principle of the 'right to the global commons'. An equity- and sustainability-based policy response to global climate change would require that upper-income countries reduce emissions to the GHG stabilization rate first and that lower-income countries should be allowed to further expand their emissions as they pursue an economic development course. The distinction between Annex I and non-Annex I under the Kyoto Protocol is based on this principle. To reach per capita parity in the year 2050 we can then project trajectories for both developed and developing countries.[20] This is sometimes referred to as 'contraction and convergence'.[21] It is generally acknowledged that since industrialized countries emit more CO_2 per capita than developing countries and have emitted more CO_2 and other greenhouse gases in the past, they therefore should be held responsible for accumulated GHG/CO_2 emissions in the atmosphere. Further discussion of this issue is presented in Chapter 2.

Another complicating factor in comparing emission rates between countries derives from the conditions in the global market with respect to foreign trade and FDI. In newly industrializing developing countries such as China, Malaysia, Mexico and South Korea, a large fraction of the goods produced by the manufacturing industry is subsequently exported – particularly to high-income industrialized countries – and a substantial part of this production is manufactured by multinational or transnational corporations. Thus, China's emissions growth is being driven to a large extent by consumers in industrialized countries buying Chinese goods.[22] This means that the fast increase of these countries' emissions is partly due to their increasing share in the global production of goods for the global market. Although we have not seen any studies that are conclusive on the fraction of national greenhouse-gas emissions directly related to these exported goods, what is clear is that for countries like China this is not an insignificant part of their national emissions. It should be observed though that the UNFCCC does not take account of these so-called 'embedded emissions' in exported goods. Neither does the UNFCCC take into account that countries like China and India, but also Brazil, Mexico or South Korea, under conditions of the 'global division of labour' assume a far greater share of manufacturing capacity while the more mature economies of the EU, Japan and the United States become 'global service economies' with relatively much lower emissions rates per GDP.

According to the Global Carbon Project, far from slowing down, global carbon dioxide emissions are rising faster than before. Between 2000 and 2005, global greenhouse-gas emissions grew four times faster than in the preceding ten years.[23] Annual global GHG emissions growth reached 3.2 per cent per annum during the period 2000–2005 as economic growth rates in China and India reached double digits. As has been stated by the USA and agreed to by the EU, it is important that China, India and other rapidly developing countries come on board 'in some meaningful way', in the words of US policymakers, in order to curb global GHG emissions. As China and India are among the fastest growing economies in the developing world and as their emissions rates have increased substantially, their commitment to some kind of future energy-efficiency and emissions-reduction plan is particularly important.

Economic growth, energy use and GHG emissions in China and India

Since 2000, both India and China have entered a period of rapid economic growth. In the case of India, outsourcing of IT and financial services played an important role in the growth spurt. In China, rapid growth occurred in industrial production, much of it through investments by multinational corporations for export production. China's real gross domestic product (GDP) is estimated to have grown at around 10 per cent per year for the last couple of years and economic forecasts for further growth remain strong. Together with strong economic growth, which increases energy demand, consumer demand is surging in both India in China, in part because of the growing affluence of an emerging urban middle class. With China's entry into the World Trade Organization in November 2001, the Chinese government made a number of specific commitments to trade and investment liberalization, which has substantially opened up the Chinese economy to investment by foreign firms through FDI and foreign trade, and China is now the largest recipient of FDI in the world with a total of US$72.4 billion invested in 2005.[24] Much of the investment has occurred in the energy-intensive sector which has contributed to the rapid increase in GHG emissions.[25]

In both India and China, manufacturing capacity is fuelled mostly by direct combustion of coal. The US Agency for International Development predicts that the growing energy demand could drive a fourfold increase in the use of coal by 2030, which could result in a greatly increased annual emissions total.[26] Between 2004 and 2005, the world's coal consumption increased by 5 per cent, 80 per cent of which growth derived from China's increased use alone. China's and India's combined share of the total world coal use (expressed in millions of tonnes oil equivalent) is now larger than all of North America's and all of Europe's combined share.[27]

Together with strong economic growth, China's demand for fluid fuels is surging as well. The Energy Information Administration of the US government (EIA) forecasts that China's oil consumption will increase by almost half a million barrels per day, or over 40 per cent of the total growth in world oil demand. At present, China is the world's third largest net importer of oil behind the United States and Japan.[28] Accordingly, carbon dioxide emissions from China and India have increased at an alarming rate. But, whereas the total amount of carbon emitted by China and India is approaching levels of the traditional industrialized countries like Europe, Japan and the United States, the per capita carbon emissions rates are still far behind those of the mature industrialized economies (Table 1.1).[29] Other rapidly growing developing countries in Latin America, such as Brazil and Argentina, or Mexico and Chile, are also fast becoming large energy users and carbon emitters.

In terms of the increase in pressure on the carrying capacity of the earth's ecological system as a result of the rapidly growing global economy, important questions arise as to how the world's ecosystems can withstand the ongoing increase in carbon emissions in the atmosphere. The IPCC alerts us to the fact that carbon dioxide is the most important anthropogenic greenhouse gas and that its global atmospheric concentration has increased from a pre-industrial value of about 280 ppm to 379 ppm in 2005.[30] The atmospheric concentration of carbon dioxide in 2005 exceeded by far the natural range (180–300 ppm). The 2005 Millennium Ecosystem Assessment, conducted under the auspices of the United Nations, concluded that the world's ecosystems, ranging from water, soils, the biosphere and the atmosphere, are seriously undermined as the world's two most populous nations (India and China) are moving to centre stage of the global economy.[31]

In the energy sector, FDI in power plants and the fossil fuel infrastructure is already occurring on a large scale, and coal mining and energy-intensive industries are expanding rapidly. As carbon-emitting industries multiply at a rapid rate, China is building on average one coal-fired power plant every week and plans to continue to do so for many years to come. Coal makes up approximately 70 per cent of China's total primary energy consumption and the country is both the largest consumer and the largest producer of coal in the world.[32] It is estimated that China has 126.2 billion tonnes of recoverable coal reserves, which places it third in the world behind the United States and Russia. In 2004, the country consumed 2.1 billion tonnes of coal, representing more than one-third of the world total, which amounts to a 46 per cent increase since 2002.

Coal consumption has been on the rise in China over the last five years, reversing the decline seen from 1997 to 2000. China's rapid economic growth has brought with it several energy-related environmental problems. Environmental pollution from fossil fuel combustion is damaging human health, air and water quality and agriculture, and many of China's cities are now among the most polluted in the world. Forecasts predict that China will experience the largest growth in carbon dioxide emissions between now and 2030.[33] The Chinese government has taken several steps to improve environmental conditions in the country. Chief among these is the Law on Renewable Energy, which took effect on 1 January 2006. The new law seeks to promote cleaner energy technologies, with the stated goal of increasing the use of renewable energy to 10 per cent of the country's electricity consumption by 2010 (up from roughly 3 per cent in 2003).[34]

China insists, along with other developing countries, that its GHG emissions levels should be considered as a multiplication of its per capita emission and its population size and not calculated in terms of its total national GHG emissions increase. China is a non-Annex I country under the UNFCCC, meaning that it is not bound to any GHG emissions-reduction targets set under the Kyoto Protocol. However, this raises questions about how effective Kyoto or a similar

FIGURE I.I **The global economy and climate-change policy**

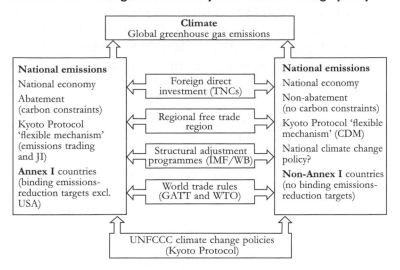

type of protocol will ever be in reducing GHG emissions in the atmosphere. As the example of China illustrates, energy use and GHG emissions sharply increased after China became a member of the World Trade Organization. Opening up to FDI and foreign trade gave China a competitive advantage over the more mature economies of the EU and North America. In fact, corporations headquartered in industrialized countries are becoming increasingly integrated in the economies of the developing world as markets open up and as state-owned enterprises are privatized. Global institutionalized trade policy as promoted by the General Agreement on Tariffs and Trade (GATT), the WTO, the World Bank and the IMF has made so-called free trade the model pursued in most parts of the world. At the same time, the current greenhouse-gas accounting and reduction regime based on emissions by nation-states ignores the fact that multinational enterprises or transnational corporations (TNCs) dominate the global economy and that their activities are not bound by national borders. Considering the complex web of relationships between global energy and resource use, production and throughput, economic growth and trade activity, we must begin to conceptualize global environmental impacts in the same manner. Assigning primary responsibility to nation-states in managing global environmental problems like climate change under the UNFCCC Kyoto Protocol raises the question, 'Whose emissions are they anyway?' To illustrate, I will use British Petroleum (BP) as a case study of how TNC investment abroad drives intensive fossil-fuel-based production and may render national CO_2 emissions-reduction commitments as defined under the Protocol ineffective.[35]

BP is probably one of the more environmentally conscious multi-national oil companies, but nonetheless, reading the promotional literature of its Annual Report, addressed to shareholders, one cannot escape the impression that energy savings and GHG emissions reductions have greater weight in BP's portfolio in the developed industrialized world than in its China portfolio.[36] In its 2006 Annual Report, BP claims that it had achieved 1.2 million tonnes of GHG emissions reductions through various projects worldwide and that it plans to invest in new technologies to give society new sources of energy that are both low-carbon and local. For this purpose, BP established a subsidiary, Alternative Energy, in November 2005, with a focus on low-carbon power generation and an ambitious agenda on achieving a threefold increase in manufacturing capacity of solar photovoltaic (PV) panels, expanding wind power production to 450 MW, advancing development of the world's leading commercial hydrogen power plant, and the construction of gas co-generation power plants with a total capacity of more than 700MW, and reducing projected carbon dioxide emissions on a per unit basis as a consequence. But for China, BP projects a different approach. BP China is a subsidiary of BP–Amoco, which heads its business in China. In its promotional literature the company states:[37]

> The scope of BP China includes hydrocarbon resources exploration and development, the petrochemical sector, natural gas, and oil products distribution. BP is deeply committed to growing its business in China and in helping China address its energy security issues. We are working with Chinese partners now to advance the cooperation we have begun. We believe that the steps we've taken so far are just the beginning.

In a speech presented by Dr Gary Dirks, BP Group vice president and Asia regional president, at an international symposium on energy

BOX 1.2   **Whose emissions are they anyway?**
The case of BP

- One of the largest foreign investors in China is British Petroleum.
  BP arrived in China over thirty years ago. In the beginning BP's
  activities included chemicals licensing and marketing. During the
  1980s its investment shifted to onshore and offshore exploration, and by the 1990s BP became involved in large-scale FDI
  in China. To date, with a total investment of US$3.4 billion, BP
  is one of the largest foreign investors. BP China's investment
  is varied and ranges from constructing the liquefied natural gas
  infrastructure, to importing and distributing liquefied petroleum
  gas, aviation fuel and lubricants. In addition, BP owns many gas
  stations and solar power installations. Some of the investment
  is through joint ventures with major chemical plants.

- BP was the first foreign company in China to explore oil and gas
  fields offshore and onshore and is playing a big role in bringing liquefied natural gas (LNG) to consumers in Guangzhou
  and Fujian provinces. Large-scale investment in chemicals
  joint ventures include the Shanghai Ethylene Cracker complex,
  Zhuhai PTA plant, and Chongqing and Nanjing Acetic Acid
  Plant. In the retail market in which BP works with PetroChina
  and Sinopec, it has built and operates 1,000 retail stations in
  Guangdong and Zhejiang provinces. BP is also China's leading
  liquefied petroleum gas (LPG) importer and operator and the
  only foreign company participating in the aviation fuels market.
  BP's lubricants are marketed throughout China.

- To be sure, BP is also working with Chinese partners to develop
  sustainable energy solutions to support Chinese economic
  development, such as 'Clean Energy Facing the Future', a ten-
  year R&D initiative in partnership with the Chinese Academy
  of Science and Sun Oasis, joint venture to manufacture and
  supply solar PV panels to the Chinese market. BP presently
  employs 3,000 workers in China, most of whom are Chinese
  nationals, and has helped establish the Centre for China in the
  World Economy (CCWE) at Tsinghua University, which supports
  China's future economic growth. CCWE aims to become an
  internationally recognized centre of research and training for
  governments and corporations to deepen their understanding
  of China in the world economy.

- In its 2006 Annual Report, BP states that it intends to build production in China with improving returns by focusing on locating the largest oil and gas fields and concentrating involvement in a limited number of the most prolific hydrocarbon basins and building leadership positions in these areas. Furthermore, BP plans to manage the decline of existing producing assets and divesting itself of them when they no longer compete in BP's portfolio, and focus exploration in locations with potentially large oil and natural gas fields. In terms of refining and marketing capacity, China offers very lucrative business opportunities. BP operates in various retail markets and endeavours to capture market share by increasing brand and product loyalty and by building strong strategic relationships in the business-to-business sector. Clearly, BP operates in a world in which increasing demand for energy and the potential risks of climate change create significant – and often intricately connected – challenges.

- BP claims that it applies advances in science and engineering to make the world's relationship with energy more diverse, more responsible, and more sustainable; according to its 2006 Annual Report, contributing to the future of energy means pursuing proved technologies that make the planet's hydrocarbon assets last longer, enabling more efficient production with less environmental impact, and also helping to strengthen the communities from which they are sourced.

Source: www.bp.com/sectiongenericarticle.do?categoryId=9004963&contentId=7010305.

security 'China and the World', held in Beijing on 24 May 2006, the company promoted the view that China should look for international partnerships to tackle its energy security challenges. BP projected an important role for itself along with other energy companies in offering China a commitment to look for new energy resources worldwide and to develop these resources in the most efficient way to fuel its economic growth and meet its domestic demand. These goals could only be achieved through the opening up of the energy sector to all eligible participants, according to the BP director and former CEO of BP China. Opening up of the domestic refinery sector would allow the building of world-class refineries that could process a greater variety of crude oil; opening up the shipping and logistics sectors, building a modern and efficient oil transportation system, and diversifying wholesale and retail activities would make the energy distribution sector more competitive. In the case of China, BP saw a greater need for closer collaboration between the Chinese oil companies and international energy corporations in terms of technology research and development, and of co-investment in energy projects worldwide.[38]

The global economy and climate-change policy

The example presented is intended to illustrate how the global economy driven by intensive competition organized around TNCs and international production networks may render national reduction commitments as defined under the Kyoto Protocol rather ineffective in reducing global GHG emissions in the atmosphere as a way to counter climate change/global warming (see Figure 1.1). Indeed, reconciling the impact of foreign trade and FDI with the UNFCCC is perhaps the greatest challenge in international diplomacy in our times. As we notice in the examples presented, trade liberalization has brought a vastly increased energy demand in China, in particular, as a result of increased manufacturing and the emergence of a vastly populous emerging middle class. As the demand for energy has put China on the fossil-fuel-based development path, the investments made and the infrastructure being developed now will shape the manufacturing economy for at least two decades. For example, a major transnational oil company like BP is actively involved in developing the oil and gas fossil fuel infrastructure to capture the demand for gasoline and natural gas in the rapidly developing private transportation and residential sectors. Thus, the structure of the emerging industrial economy and urban society of China will determine the air pollution and GHG emissions levels in the immediate future, rather than local or national environmental regulatory regimes that China may develop or any sustainability projects that major international corporations may sponsor in their host society.[39] In fact, globalization poses very serious challenges to traditional governance structures as national governments are ill-suited to managing environmental problems that transcend borders, whether through air flow and water currents or through global commerce. Furthermore, as experience has taught, international environmental treaties and institutions are mostly too weak to manage global environmental problems of the sort we now encounter with climate change/global warming. At the same time, national governments around the world are granting significant and growing powers to economic institutions such as the WTO, the World Bank and the IMF, for whom environmental issues are mostly secondary considerations or an afterthought. At the same time, TNCs are the main players in the field, driven by competitive pressures to please shareholders in the developed world, and to guarantee that consumers at Wal-Mart and the like can buy products cheaply.

Considering these circumstances, we must ask ourselves what the likelihood is that the nations of the world will gather to agree to a set of international regulations and governance structures that will render greater success than has been achieved so far under the Kyoto Protocol. In *Vanishing Borders* (2000), Hilary French from the World Watch Institute projected that, given the fact that emissions from developing countries are not limited by the Protocol, CO_2 levels could reach as high as 30 per cent above 1990 levels by 2015, while, at the same time, climate scientists estimate that emission cuts in the order of 60–80 per cent below current levels will be required to eventually stabilize CO_2 concentrations in the atmosphere.[40] Based on 2006 emissions data for non-OECD countries, total emissions of developing countries are projected to increase more than 50 per cent by 2015 from 1990 levels (21.2 million tonnes of CO_2 in 1990 projected to increase to 33.7 million tonnes in 2015).[41] At this rate of increase – as the IPCC reports indicate – climate change is certainly going to occur.

2

From Rio to Kyoto and beyond

The UN North–South debates

As the nations of the world gather to negotiate, and hopefully agree to, a post-Kyoto global climate-change policy, and as GHG emissions continue to rise, it is perhaps time to stand still for a moment and remind ourselves how we arrived at where we are now. This chapter, therefore, is meant to set the stage to understand how the negotiations under the UNFCCC proceeded and how the governance structures dealing with climate change were developed. To do this, we need to go back to the UN deliberations in the North–South context and the dynamics of the debates as they occurred in the past few decades. As negotiations about post-Kyoto global climate-change policy appear to be at a stalemate, this chapter addresses the geopolitical divisions between 'North' and 'South', between developed and developing countries, in historical context. The geopolitical division between 'North' and 'South' presents a serious challenge to the effectiveness and success of the UNFCCC and the Kyoto Protocol. To understand why it is (or appears to be) so difficult to arrive at a satisfactory negotiated agreement on climate-change policy, it helps to know the history of negotiations within the context of the UN as the primary international organization dealing with global problems.

The United Nations Conference on Environment and Development (UNCED) – the Earth Summit, held in Rio de Janeiro, Brazil, in June 1992, where the UNFCCC was signed – was perhaps the largest and was certainly the most publicized gathering of heads of state and delegates from national governments, representatives of non-governmental organizations (NGOs), journalists, youth groups, indigenous people, and other interested parties, to have discussed environmental and development issues – but it was not the first! Whereas the Earth Summit was referred to as a new beginning by Maurice Strong, UNCED's secretary-general, so far as the developing countries were concerned the Earth Summit reflected a short memory that ignored the failed attempts at improving the plight of the developing world. As we reflect on the outcome of the Earth Summit fifteen years later, doubts remain about the sincerity of the negotiating partners and the intention to reach agreement on solving major global environmental problems, which have subsequently compounded in severity. Several treaties were signed and specific actions were agreed to, but how effective the Earth Summit ultimately was remains an issue of debate. Whether the UNCED was cause for hope or for disappointment remains to be seen. At the start of the conference, Strong said in his opening address:

> The Earth Summit is not an end in itself but a new beginning. The measures you agree on here will be but first steps on a new pathway to our common future. Thus, the results of this conference will ultimately depend on the credibility and effectiveness of its follow-up.... The preparatory process has provided the basis for this and the momentum which has brought us to Rio must be maintained. And institutional changes, to be made within the United Nations must provide an effective and credible basis for its continued leadership of this process.... The road beyond Rio will be a long and difficult one; but it will also be a journey of renewed hope, of excitement, challenge and opportunity, leading as we move into the 21st century to the dawning of a new world in which the hopes and aspirations of all the world's children for a more secure and hospitable future can be fulfilled.[1]

International conferences and institutions are only as effective as governments choose to make them.[2] So UNCED was called in order to harmonize the many disparate paths of environmental protection that countries had pursued since the UN Conference on the Human Environment held in Stockholm in 1972. Many industrialized countries had incorporated environmental protection into their policymaking, but in the developing world change had been much slower. Few developing countries had any capacity to respond to environmental threats and still fewer had any intention to build capacity to do so. The major reason for this perceived discrepancy was that for countries of the South environmental protection was inseparable from economic issues, whereas in the North environmental protection was a more or less autonomous issue. Because of the persistence of severe poverty and perceived injustice in the South, environmental protection never reached the level of public concern in the North. This realization convinced the World Commission on Environment and Development, which issued the Brundtland Report in 1987, that it was 'futile to attempt to deal with environmental problems without a broader perspective that encompasses the factors underlying world poverty and international inequality'.[3] Thus, when the Commission presented its report to the UN General Assembly in 1987, among its recommendations was a call for the United Nations to prepare a universal declaration and a convention on environmental protection and sustainable development. The official and stated purpose of UNCED was to 'elaborate strategies and measures to halt and reverse the effects of environmental degradation in the context of increased national and international efforts to promote sustainable and environmentally sound development in all countries'.[4] As a result, the mandate of the Rio Conference – environment and development – was extremely broad.

Much of the preliminary work for the conference was conducted by the Preparatory Committee, which held an organizational meeting in March 1990 and four substantive sessions before the Earth Summit in 1992. Consensus was reached on the Rio Declaration and on most of the text of Agenda 21. Two more controversial environmental treaties on climate change and biodiversity had been negotiated separately and were presented for signature at the Earth Summit. Several new international institutions were created at the same time; these included the Sustainable Development Commission, the Convention on Climate Change, and the Convention on Biodiversity. Furthermore, several informal councils and NGOs were formed; these included the Planet Earth Council and the Business Council for Sustainable Development. The Rio Declaration proclaimed a number of very ambitious general principles, which are summarized in Box 2.1.[5]

BOX 2.1   **The Rio Declaration**

- Human beings are at the centre of concerns for sustainable development. They are entitled to a healthy and productive life in harmony with nature.
- States have, in accordance with the Charter of the United Nations and the principles of international law, the sovereign right to exploit their own resources pursuant to their own environmental and developmental policies, and the responsibility to ensure that activities within their jurisdiction or control do not cause damage to the environment of other States or of areas beyond the limits of national jurisdiction.
- The right to development must be fulfilled so as to equitably meet developmental and environmental needs of present and future generations.
- In order to achieve sustainable development, environmental protection shall constitute an integral part of the development process and cannot be considered in isolation from it.
- All States and all people shall cooperate in the essential task of eradicating poverty as an indispensable requirement for sustainable development, in order to decrease the disparities in standards of living and better meet the needs of the majority of the people of the world.
- The special situation and needs of developing countries, particularly the least developed and those most environmentally vulnerable, shall be given special priority. International actions in the field of environment and development should also address the interests and needs of all countries.
- States shall cooperate in a spirit of global partnership to conserve, protect and restore the health and integrity of the Earth's ecosystem. In view of the different contributions to global environmental degradation, States have common but differentiated responsibilities. The developed countries acknowledge the responsibility that they bear in the international pursuit of

---

sustainable development in view of the pressures their societies place on the global environment and of the technologies and financial resources they command.

- To achieve sustainable development and a higher quality of life for all people, States should reduce and eliminate unsustainable patterns of production and consumption and promote appropriate demographic policies.

- States should cooperate to strengthen endogenous capacity-building for sustainable development by improving scientific understanding through exchanges of scientific and technological knowledge, and by enhancing the development, adaptation, diffusion and transfer of technologies, including new and innovative technologies.

- Environmental issues are best handled with the participation of all concerned citizens, at the relevant level. At the national level, each individual shall have appropriate access to information concerning the environment that is held by public authorities, including information on hazardous materials and activities in their communities, and the opportunity to participate in decision-making processes. States shall facilitate and encourage public awareness and participation by making information widely available. Effective access to judicial and administrative proceedings, including redress and remedy, shall be provided.

- States shall enact effective environmental legislation. Environmental standards, management objectives and priorities should reflect the environmental and developmental context to which they apply. Standards applied by some countries may be inappropriate and of unwarranted economic and social cost to other countries, in particular developing countries.

- States should cooperate to promote a supportive and open international economic system that would lead to economic growth and sustainable development in all countries, better to address the problems of environmental degradation. Trade policy measures for environmental purposes should not constitute a means of arbitrary or unjustifiable discrimination or a disguised restriction on international trade. Unilateral actions to deal with environmental challenges outside the jurisdiction of the importing country should be avoided. Environmental measures addressing trans-boundary or global environmental problems should, as far as possible, be based on an international consensus.

- States shall develop national law regarding liability and compensation for the victims of pollution and other environmental damage. States shall also cooperate in an expeditious and more determined manner to develop further international law regarding liability and compensation for adverse effects of environmental damage caused by activities within their jurisdiction or control to areas beyond their jurisdiction.

- States should effectively cooperate to discourage or prevent the relocation and transfer to other States of any activities and substances that cause severe environmental degradation or are found to be harmful to human health.

- In order to protect the environment, the precautionary approach shall be widely applied by States according to their capabilities. Where there are threats of serious or irreversible damage, lack of full scientific certainty shall not be used as a reason for postponing cost-effective measures to prevent environmental degradation.

- National authorities should endeavour to promote the internalization of environmental costs and the use of economic instruments, taking into account the approach that the polluter should, in principle, bear the cost of pollution, with due regard to the public interest and without distorting international trade and investment.

- Environmental impact assessment, as a national instrument, shall be undertaken for proposed activities that are likely to have a significant adverse impact on the environment and are subject to a decision of a competent national authority.

- States shall immediately notify other States of any natural disasters or other emergencies that are likely to produce sudden harmful effects on the environment of those States. Every effort shall be made by the international community to help States so afflicted.

- States shall provide prior and timely notification and relevant information to potentially affected States on activities that may have a significant adverse trans-boundary environmental effect and shall consult with those States at an early stage and in good faith.

- Women have a vital role in environmental management and development. Their full participation is therefore essential to achieve sustainable development. The creativity, ideals and

courage of the youth of the world should be mobilized to forge
a global partnership in order to achieve sustainable development
and ensure a better future for all.

- Indigenous people and their communities and other local
communities have a vital role in environmental management
and development because of their knowledge and traditional
practices. States should recognize and duly support their identity,
culture and interests and enable their effective participation in
the achievement of sustainable development.
- The environment and natural resources of people under oppres-
sion, domination and occupation shall be protected.
- Warfare is inherently destructive of sustainable development.
States shall therefore respect international law providing protection for the environment in times of armed conflict and
cooperate in its further development, as necessary.
- Peace, development and environmental protection are interdependent and indivisible.
- States shall resolve all their environmental disputes peacefully
and by appropriate means in accordance with the Charter of
the United Nations.
- States and people shall cooperate in good faith and in a spirit
of partnership in the fulfilment of the principles embodied in
this Declaration and in the further development of international
law in the field of sustainable development.

Source: Adapted from the UNCED Report (Rio de Janeiro, 3–14 June 1992) Annex I: Rio
Declaration on Environment and Development; www.un.org/documents/ga/conf151/
aconf15126–1annex1.htm.

Agenda 21 set out to formulate a blueprint for implementation and
detail on the UN's other agencies' sector-specific activities relevant to
environmental and development issues and monitoring progress on
UNCED's agenda. Integration and monitoring were considered vital
because of the vast scope of the measures specified in Agenda 21.

The Business Council for Sustainable Development, an international group of forty-eight companies' chief executive officers, was
formed to advise UNCED on business and industry issues and to
stimulate involvement by business in UNCED. Environmentalists saw

the formation of the Business Council as representative of business interests in policymaking and as evidence of corporate hijacking of UNCED. Supporters, including Secretary-General Maurice Strong, its leader, argued that its goal was to persuade business leaders to recognize the importance of sustainable development. The Planet Earth Council, a privately financed NGO – also led by Secretary-General Strong – formed a committee of twenty-eight internationally known scientists who would monitor the environment and report to the Sustainable Development Commission. UNCED adopted a number of reporting commitments for national governments. Participating countries were invited to submit national reports on the environment and development as part of their preparations for UNCED, and since then the UNFCCC has required governments to report on their efforts to monitor and control anthropogenic emissions of greenhouse gases as well as on the likely net impact of control policies.

Financial measures to support these efforts fell far short, and implementation of Agenda 21 was threatened with deadlock almost from the start. The Secretariat estimated that the full cost of implementing Agenda 21 in developing countries would require at least US$600 billion per year, of which US$125 billion would have to come from industrial-country sources. Developing countries' representatives had hoped to obtain substantial funds in the form of subsidized technology transfer, debt relief and an increase in official development assistance. Discussion of using existing aid agencies to finance Agenda 21 focused on the World Bank's Global Environmental Facility (GEF), which was created in 1990 to finance projects related to global warming, biodiversity, international waters and ozone depletion. The developing countries' 'Group of 77' took the initiative to establish an independent green fund in lieu of GEF, which was dismissed by the industrialized countries. Many developing countries distrust the World Bank because they perceive it as intrusive in domestic policymaking and dominated by developed countries. On the other hand, donor countries feared that inefficient economic policies and corrupt public officials would likely lead to waste, and thus they viewed the transfer of funds with great suspicion.

A common future?

Within a year of the Earth Summit, the authors of *The Ecologist*'s edited volume *Whose Common Future?* (1993) questioned the success and credibility of the UNCED talks.[6] Even though the meetings were perceived as all-inclusive and broad-ranging, it was clear that the corporate sector was a major player both in the formulation of the various conventions and as actor in the negotiations. In the battle to save the planet, free-market environmentalism was promoted and the corporate sponsors were given special access to the Secretariat. The philosophy of the Business Council on Sustainable Development prevailed throughout most of the deliberations. The desirability of economic growth, the market economy, and the Western development model were never questioned, and UNCED thus never had a chance of addressing the real problems of the environment and development relationship, according to the critics. The Earth Summit's action plan, Agenda 21, suggested ways to enable poor nations to achieve sustainable development, but never questioned the desirability of the rich nations' pursuit of the same. So, the authors of *Whose Common Future?* asked the question, in whose interest are we promoting sustainable development, and who is to manage it? In fact, the stage was set for a conflict of interests between the North and the South, and climate-change negotiations under the UNFCCC proved difficult.

In *Planet Dialectics* (1999), Wolfgang Sachs questions the desirability of the Western development model as it is at odds with both equity (or fair share) and sustainability of the earth resource base and carrying capacity.[7] Sachs poses that in a fundamental way sustainability is about global citizenship and argues that the principles of equity and sustainability derive from equal access to resources and the global commons.[8] In his critique of the Earth Summit he questions the recommendations for sustainable development offered in the Brundtland Report sponsored by the World Commission on Environment and Development (WCED) in 1987.[9] The Report formed the foundation for the Earth Summit and its definition of sustainable development: 'development that meets the needs of the present without compromising the ability of future generations to meet their own needs' in which economic growth was never questioned. Thus, according to Sachs, the

Commission called for action of justice towards future generations, but was unable to deal with equity demands of the South in a sustainable way at the present time. The call from the developing countries for a more equitable share in wealth and resources was translated in terms of the 'right to development'. At the Earth Summit, the leaders from the South aligned with the North in their praise for economic development as the solution to all global environmental problems. With higher levels of economic development would come greater care for the environment and more efficient use of energy, thus lower pollution and GHG emission levels.[10] As Sachs states: 'the quest for justice was firmly wedded to the idea of development, nobody had to profoundly change and all parties could turn to business-as-usual' – a position amply borne out in recent years.[11]

The 1992 *World Development Report* opened with the assertion that 'the achievement of sustained and equitable development remains the greatest challenge facing the human race'.[12] In its assessment following the outcome of the Earth Summit in 1992 there were claims that this had been the UN conference that reflected a global consensus and political commitment at the highest level on development and environmental cooperation.[13] A more critical view was that the conference had failed to live up to the expectation that had preceded it and had failed to bring about a new economic and environmental world order. In *Whose Common Future?* the authors suggest that the UN-sponsored Earth Summit was nothing more than a repeat of the development debates of the 1960s and 1970s.[14] They maintain that mainstream solutions proposed at the Earth Summit would be counterproductive because the Western economic development model was never questioned. The US and EU proposals presented at the Earth Summit for combating global environmental crises recommended limiting population growth, stimulating free-market enterprise, and the application of Western technology, know-how and capital. The recommendations (according to the authors of *Whose Common Future?*) did not sound terribly convincing after decades-long efforts to fight poverty, famine and starvation by the same means. Repeated efforts to make life for the majority of the population of the South better through programmes such as basic needs fulfilment, human resources development and education, and now sustainable development, obscure the real issue, which is that the introduction of the Western economic development model has more often than not resulted in increased poverty levels and environmental degradation, and has also often contributed to geopolitical instability.[15] Under these circumstances, critics believe, it is hard to imagine that 'improved environmental management is to be achieved through greater integration with the global economy' and that 'liberated trade fosters greater efficiency and higher productivity and may actually reduce pollution by encouraging the growth of less polluting industries and the adoption and diffusion of cleaner technologies'.[16]

The UN as forum for international debate on the environment and development

To understand the role of the UN in international debates on global economic and environmental problems it helps to be reminded of the foundations of the international order following World War II.[17] In July 1944, representatives of forty-five countries met at Bretton Woods, New Hampshire, to discuss how to build the new world order after World War II and how to avoid the mistakes made after World War I when the League of Nations was founded. As was the case following World War I, financial and economic concerns were an important part of the negotiations. Instead of burdening the defeated nations with war debts and repayments, the Bretton Woods meetings established the organizations that would help rebuild the countries that were devastated by war. The International Monetary Fund, and the International Bank for Reconstruction and Development (IBRD), together with the International Finance Corporation (IFC) and the International Development Association (IDA) – known later as the World Bank – became the designated international financial institutions to accomplish the task. When the United Nations (UN) was formed in 1945, the Bretton Woods institutions became an integral part of the UN system, although in practice they are only loosely connected to the rest of the UN and they maintain some distinction due to membership criteria. The Bretton Woods institutions are subject to financial subscription, and voting is weighted according to member financial shares, unlike the one country, one vote principle assigned to UN membership. Later, the Bretton Woods institutions would become the leading financial institutions to help the developing world in terms of financial need (IMF) or in terms of development efforts (World Bank). A key UN initiative was the General Agreement on Tariffs and Trade (GATT), set up in Geneva, Switzerland, in 1947. The GATT was intended to ensure open trade regimes in order to avoid the mistake of protectionism as was the case and source of conflict before the outbreak of World War II. As most of the rest of the world was still under colonial rule, African and Southeast Asian countries took no part in the negotiations or formulation of policies at the time. The GATT later became the World Trade Organization, which is discussed in the next chapter.

The UN currently has 192 member states. Its most important decision-making entities are the General Assembly and the Security Council. All UN countries belong to the General Assembly and each has a vote. The Security Council comprises 5 permanent and 10 non-permanent members with one vote each. The non-permanent members are elected by a two-thirds majority of the General Assembly and serve a two-year term. The permanent members are the victors of the Second World War: France, Russia, the UK, the USA and China. As the power of the UN and the Bretton Woods institutions remains firmly in the hands of the Western world, developing nations have begun to view the institution as a handmaiden of the wealthy industrialized countries, in particular in so far as financial and economic functions are concerned. Many in the South argue that the institutions do not represent their interests and that the programmes and treaties negotiated under the auspices of the UN and related institutions are not fair and equal. Lately, the UN and related bodies, including the World Bank, the IMF and the WTO, have become contested territory and there is considerable criticism of their roles in the world economy.[18] The most pervasive criticism is that they reflect and reinforce the highly uneven global distribution of political and economic power. For instance, many critics argue that the IMF's response to problems of developing countries' indebtedness has been to advocate and enforce economic reform through structural adjustment programmes which often worsen rather than ameliorate the living conditions of the poor. Similarly, the WTO has come under attack as it is seen as the instrument of the USA, in particular, to open up world markets for US trade.

As stated, the Earth Summit was not the first UN conference to incorporate economic development and environmental concerns. In the 1960s and 1970s links between ecology and development were fostered by the International Biological Program (IBP), established in 1964. In 1969 the Scientific Committee for Problems of the Environment (SCOPE) was established, and in 1971 the Man and the Biosphere Program (MAB) was launched by UNESCO. This latter initiative came from the Intergovernmental Conference of Experts on a Scientific Basis for Rational Use and Conservation of the Biosphere, held in Paris in 1968, and led to the growing engagement of researchers, conservationists and environmentalists in economic development projects in the developing world.[19] Through the 1960s, international aid organizations became increasingly aware that they could not influence decisions about the use of natural resources and the environment unless they addressed development issues at the same time.[20] And in 1968 the International Union for Conservation of Nature and Natural Resources (IUCN) joined UNESCO, the Food and Agriculture Organization (FAO), the UN Development Programme (UNDP), the Conservation Foundation, and the World Bank in organizing a conference at George Washington University in Virginia on ecology and international development.[21]

On the economic development front, developing countries' demands for a New International Economic Order (NIEO), was the most important initiative.[22] In 1964, the first UN Conference on Trade and Development (UNCTAD) was held in Geneva, and a year later (1965) the UN Development Program was formed. During the conferences that followed it became clear that there were stark differences between the North and the South with respect to perceptions or viewpoints on the benefits of Western-style economic development.[23] Through UNCTAD, the developing countries' 'Group of 77' insisted that the industrialized countries should change their pattern of trading and manufacturing in the interests of the developing world, and in doing so the developing countries would become more fully integrated in the world economy. In 1968, the developing countries won a partial success at the UNCTAD conference in New Delhi, India, in so far as the industrialized countries agreed to work for the establishment of a system of special tariff preferences for the developing countries through the General System of Preferences (GSP). Although the implementation was more limited in scope than the demands of the Group of 77, some concessions were made by the industrialized countries through the Organisation for Economic Co-operation and Development (OECD) in subsequent years. However, only manu-factured goods and semi-manufactured goods were included in the preference system and several products were excluded because of the industrialized countries' interest in protecting domestic production. Only very limited trade preferences were granted for agricultural products, the mainstay of export production of most developing countries.

At the meeting of foreign ministers of the Non-Aligned Move-ment (formerly the Group of 77), in Georgetown, Guyana, in 1972, a programme for further action for economic cooperation was adopted. A great deal of emphasis was given to the pursuit of self-reliance and more concrete measures to improve trade opportunities and economic cooperation and development were agreed to. In addition, industrialized countries were asked to increase their foreign aid. Encouraged by the growing power of the Organization of Petroleum Exporting Countries (OPEC), the Non-Aligned Movement at its meeting of heads of state in Algiers in 1973 began to make even bolder demands. Then, in 1974, at the Sixth Special Session of the General Assembly of the UN, the Declaration of Programme of Action for the Establishment of a New International Economic Order was adopted. The NIEO was to achieve a more even distribution of wealth between developing and developed countries, and was seen as a guarantee to economic and social progress in the developing world by the Brandt Commission Report (1980).[24] Previously, many of the demands had been rejected by the industrialized countries, but the declaration and resolutions on three documents were adopted without a vote. Among the most fundamental principles are those listed in Box 2.2.[25]

BOX 2.2 **The New International Economic Order**

- Sovereign equality of States, self-determination of all peoples, inadmissibility of the acquisition of territories by force, and territorial integrity and non-interference in the internal affairs of other States.
- The broadest cooperation of all the States of the international community, based on equity, whereby the prevailing disparities in the world should be banished and prosperity secured for all.
- The right of every country to adopt the economic and social system that it deems the most appropriate for its own development and not to be subjected to discrimination of any kind as a result.
- Full permanent sovereignty of every State over its natural resources and all economic activities.
- Regulation and supervision of the activities of transnational corporations by taking measures in the interest of the national economies of the countries where such transnational corporations operate on the basis of the full sovereignty of those countries.
- Just and equitable relationship between the prices of raw materials, primary commodities, manufactured and semi-manufactured goods exported by developing countries and the prices of raw materials, primary commodities, manufactures, capital goods and equipment imported by them with the aim of bringing about sustained improvement in their unsatisfactory terms of trade and the expansion of the world economy.
- Ensuring that one of the main aims of the reformed international monetary system shall be the promotion of the development of the developing countries and the adequate flow of real resources to them.
- Preferential and non-reciprocal treatment for developing countries, wherever feasible, in all fields of international economic cooperation whenever possible.
- Facilitating the role which producer's associations may play within the framework of international cooperation.

Source: Adapted and summarized from: Declaration for the Establishment of a New International Economic Order, adopted by the UN General Assembly in 1974; www.un-documents.net/s6r3201.htm.

The similarities between the Rio Declaration and the principles adopted at the Sixth Special Session of the General Assembly of the UN and the Declaration for the Establishment of a New International Economic Order in 1974 are striking. Is it surprising, therefore, that the Rio Declaration and Agenda 21 were received with some suspicion by the developing nations of the South? The New International Economic Order in 1974 was an ambitious plan, to say the least, and one that would remain in the planning stages.

In the meantime, the UN Conference on the Human Environment, held in Stockholm in 1972, had set an equally ambitious agenda for global sustainable development.[26] The growing concern about the environmental aspects of economic development by the experts from UN organizations and allied foundations from the North had been received with some alarm by developing countries. In fact, developing countries saw discussions of global resource management as an attempt by industrialized countries to take away control over their resources as they had just begun to address these issues in the North–South debate on economic development.[27] Agreement was eventually reached on 26 principles, which included Principle 11, that development need not be impaired by environmental protection; and Principle 8, that development was needed to improve the environment. Of the 109 recommendations for action recommended at the Stockholm Conference on the Human Environment, only 8 specifically addressed the question of development and the environment.[28] The most noteworthy accomplishment of the Stockholm Conference was probably the creation of the UN Environment Programme (UNEP), which organized several environmental conferences during the 1970s and 1980s.

Sustainable development was first codified in the World Conservation Strategy (WCS), prepared by the International Union for Conservation of Nature (IUCN) with financial support from UNEP and the World Wildlife Fund (WWF) in 1980. Since then it has received more publicity with the report of the World Commission on Environment and Development, known as the Brundtland Report, or *Our Common Future* (1987) and *Caring for the Earth* (1991).[29] Discussions and debates following these landmark publications culminated in the Agenda 21 at the Rio Conference in 1992. As we trace the evolution of thought in these documents, it becomes evident that there is a remarkable consistency between Stockholm (1972) and Rio (1992).[30] In the recommendations presented, we find a strong belief in science and technology, the free-trade regime, and rational or technological management of resources. The elements of the sustainable development ideas in *Our Common Future* include the need to achieve a sustainable level of population growth and resource use, while at the same time economic growth is seen as the only way to tackle poverty and to achieve environmental objectives. The Brundtland Report's vision of sustainable development rests firmly on the need to stimulate more rapid economic growth in both industrial and developing countries. Free-market economies are seen as the means towards that end. This, as is argued in the Brundtland Report,[31] can be accomplished by opening markets, by lowering interest rates, by promoting technology transfer and by allowing significantly larger capital flows from the developed to the developing countries. Clearly, these recommendations reflect mainstream Western ideas of development, which do not always square with the interests of developing countries or the environment.

In the midst of the debates about sustainable economic development came the first warnings about global warming. Faced with growing concerns about climate change, the UN General Assembly organized a panel to advise governments on the issue. The Intergovernmental Panel on Climate Change – or the IPCC, as it became known – represented a large body of scientists and policy experts from a multitude of countries that were charged with the task to write consensus reports on the science of global warming, the probable impacts of climate change, and the potential policy responses. The first Scientific Assessment Report was published in 1990, which formed the basis for discussion of the first World Climate Conference, held in Geneva, Switzerland, in November 1990. At this conference the groundwork was laid for the Framework Convention on Climate Change Treaty that was to be signed in Rio de Janeiro during the 1992 Earth Summit.

The climate change treaty: the Rio conference and the Kyoto Protocol

The road to Rio had been difficult for the UN Framework Convention on Climate Change. Whereas a climate treaty was agreed to in principle at the World Climate Conference in November 1990 in Geneva – to be ready for signature by heads of state at the Earth Summit in Rio de Janeiro in June 1992 – the various opponents had been most effective in putting up roadblocks, including the US government, OPEC, and fossil fuel business lobbyists.[32] Only during the final stages of preparation prior to the Earth Summit, at the UN Conference in New York in May 1992, did the USA agree to participate. During the deliberations in preparation for presentation, extensive efforts were made by the US delegation to water down the wording of the document to be signed. Whereas the original document made reference to the need to stabilize atmospheric greenhouse gas concentrations at levels which pose no danger to the global climate system, the USA wanted to change the wording to the need to control the rate of increase in the concentrations from human emissions. In the end, the USA gave in and the first article of the UNFCCC to be agreed to commits governments to the ultimate goal of stabilizing atmospheric concentrations of greenhouse gases, and therefore to deep cuts in emissions.

The signing of the Framework Convention on Climate Change took place at the Rio Conference, but the fact that no legally binding targets were agreed to left the UNFCCC mostly ineffective. In other words, the UNFCCC committed signatory governments to reduce their levels of GHG emissions but binding emissions targets were not agreed to until 1997 in Kyoto. An earlier climate conference, held in Berlin in 1995, had issued a statement in which the nations of the world had agreed to strengthen their commitments to curb GHG emissions. Known as the Berlin Mandate, it called for continuing negotiations and quantified reduction targets to be set within specified time frames. At the Berlin conference, the US delegation proved to be non-cooperative once again, whereas major developing nations, like India, China, Indonesia, Malaysia and Brazil had joined the group of small island nations in agreeing to a 20 per cent reduction target for CO_2 emissions.

Two years later in December 1997 in Kyoto, Japan, 24 members of the OECD, the European countries of the former Soviet Union, and central and east European countries – a total of 34, known as the Annex I countries – agreed to emissions-reduction targets within specified time frames. The USA had tried to stall the Kyoto Protocol one more time in Bonn in October 1997, just prior to the Kyoto Conference. At the Bonn Conference, the USA had announced its proposal for a Kyoto Protocol, asking Annex I countries to freeze GHG emissions at 1990 levels averaged over a period ranging from 2008 to 2010. At the same time, under urging from the US delegation, developing countries should agree to 'meaningful participation', although the position had been all along that the South should not be held responsible for solving the GHG problem during the first phase of the Kyoto Protocol (2008–12). The Bonn Conference also uncovered various loopholes that were under consideration by negotiators such as inclusion of three fluorine-bearing greenhouse gases, 'hot air' trading with Russia, and the counting of national 'carbon sinks' as credit against CO_2 emissions.[33] In fact, it seemed just two months before the Kyoto Conference that the Protocol was dead upon arrival.

And then, against all odds, at the eleventh hour, an agreement was reached in Kyoto. During the negotiations in Kyoto, the USA had held to its position that all greenhouse gases (including CO_2, methane, nitrous oxide and CFCs) plus carbon sinks should be included in the Protocol, along with emissions trading and investment in joint implementation projects for credit as legitimate means to meet the agreed-to emissions-reduction targets. The general impression was that the US negotiators tried to find ever more loopholes in the agreement.[34] In the end, after intensive final negotiation sessions, the USA agreed to sign on to the Protocol under pressure of public opinion. Had the USA stalled and ended the negotiations as the sole opponent of a climate change treaty, it would no doubt have isolated itself from the company of nations that had agreed to the UNFCCC terms in Rio de Janeiro in 1992.

Between 1997 and 2000 (the year COP6 was held in The Hague, the Netherlands), two more COP meetings were called. At COP4 in Buenos Aires in 1998 and COP5 in Bonn in 1999, market-based mechanisms were first discussed in detail. These so-called 'Flexibility Mechanisms' in the Kyoto Protocol would assist industrialized developed nations in lowering their GHG emissions at the least cost and would permit CO_2 reduction targets to be met through emissions trading. Certified Emission Reductions from project activities in developing countries could count towards emissions-reduction targets in Annex I countries in the future once the Kyoto Protocol was implemented through ratification. By March 1999, one year after the Kyoto Protocol opened for signature, 84 countries had signed it but only 7 had taken the far more important step of ratifying it; 55 countries would have to do so before the Kyoto Protocol could come into force. President Clinton signed the Kyoto Protocol during the Buenos Aires talks, but there was little sign the US Senate would ratify it.

In November 2000, the Sixth Conference of the Parties (COP6) was held in The Hague. The key objective of COP6 to the Convention on Climate Change was to reach agreement on a number of unresolved issues, which included the development of an efficient and effective verification and compliance system for the Kyoto Protocol, agreement among the parties on what kind of instruments or mechanisms to use to arrive at the agreed-to emissions-reduction targets, how to help prevent developing countries from following a carbon-intensive development path, and how to help small island nations to overcome the negative impacts of climate change. When COP6 convened, discussions evolved rapidly into a high-level negotiation over a number of very politically charged issues. These included major controversy over a US proposal to allow for essentially unlimited credit for carbon sinks in forests and agricultural lands in order to satisfy a major proportion of the US emissions reductions in this way, disagreements over consequences for non-compliance by countries that did not meet their emissions-reduction targets, and difficulties in resolving how developing countries could obtain financial assistance to deal with adverse effects of climate change and meet their obligations to plan for measuring and possibly reducing greenhouse-gas emissions. In the final hours of COP6, despite some compromises agreed to between the United States and some EU countries, notably the United Kingdom, the EU as a whole, led by Denmark and Germany, rejected the compromise positions and the talks in The Hague collapsed. In other words, difficult issues remained, which included the use of the

BOX 2.3 **Agreements reached at COP6-bis, Bonn 2001**

- *Flexible Mechanisms* The 'flexibility' mechanisms which the
  United States had strongly favoured as the Protocol was initially
  put together, including Emissions Trading, Joint Implementation and the Clean Development Mechanism, which allow
  industrialized countries to fund emissions-reduction activities
  in developing countries as an alternative to domestic emissions
  reductions. One of the key elements of this agreement was that
  there would be no quantitative limit on the credit a country
  could claim from use of these mechanisms, but that domestic
  action must constitute a significant element of the efforts of
  each Annex B country to meet their targets (Annex B parties
  to the Kyoto Protocol have legally binding emissions reduction
  obligations).[35]
- *Carbon sinks* Credit was agreed for broad activities that absorb
  carbon from the atmosphere or store it, including forest and
  cropland management, and re-vegetation, with no overall cap
  on the amount of credit that a country could claim for sinks
  activities. In the case of forest management, an Appendix Z
  establishes country-specific caps for each Annex I country, for
  example, a cap of 13 million tonnes could be credited to Japan
  (which represents about 4 per cent of its base-year emissions).
  For cropland management, countries could receive credit only
  for carbon sequestration increases above 1990 levels.
- *Compliance* Final action on compliance procedures and mechanisms that would address non-compliance with Protocol provisions was deferred to COP7, but included broad outlines of
  consequences for failing to meet emissions targets that would
  include a requirement to 'make up' shortfalls at 1.3 tonnes to
  1; suspension of the right to sell credits for surplus emissions
  reductions; and a required compliance action plan for those
  not meeting their targets.
- *Financing* Three new funds were agreed upon to provide assistance for needs associated with climate change; a least-developed-
  country fund to support National Adaptation Programs of
  Action; and a Kyoto Protocol adaptation fund supported by a
  CDM levy and voluntary contributions.

Source: Adapted from *Earth Negotiations Bulletin* 12(176), 30 July 2001; www.iisd.ca/climate/
cop6bis/.

flexible mechanism as agreed to under the Kyoto Protocol, the role of carbon sinks, and the compliance and verification regimes.

As the COP6-bis negotiations resumed in July 2001, in Bonn, Germany, little progress had been made on resolving the differences that had produced an impasse in The Hague. The COP6-bis Bonn meeting took place after President George W. Bush had become US president and had rejected the Kyoto Protocol in March of that year. As a result the US delegation to this meeting declined to participate in the negotiations related to the Protocol and chose to act as observers. As the remaining parties negotiated the key issues, agreement was reached on most of the major political issues, to the surprise of most observers given the low level of expectations that preceded the meeting (see Box 2.3.)

At the COP7 meeting in Marrakesh in October 2001, negotiators in effect completed the work of the Buenos Aires Plan of Action, finalizing most of the operational details and setting the stage for nations to ratify the Protocol. By this time, securing participation for ratification began to take priority over issues concerning effectiveness in terms of sustainability and equity.[36] The US delegation continued to act as observers, declining to participate in active negotiations. Other parties continued to express their hope that the United States would re-engage in the process at some point, but indicated their intention to seek ratification of the requisite number of countries to bring the Protocol into force (55 countries representing 55 per cent of developed country emissions of carbon dioxide in 1990). As target date for bringing the Protocol into force, the August 2002 World Summit on Sustainable Development (WSSD), to be held in Johannesburg, South Africa, was proposed.

As the United States showed no inclination to re-engage with the Kyoto Protocol, the remaining parties sought to find the cheapest possible solution to implementing the Protocol with the least possible political risk involved. Under the terms of the Kyoto Protocol, the industrialized nations had two options for meeting their obligations. The first was to cut domestic GHG emissions and/or sequester atmospheric CO_2 in forest sinks through reforestation programmes and/or projects to control deforestation. The second option was to earn credits towards the emission targets agreed to in Kyoto by use of

---

BOX 2.4 **The main decisions made at COP7, Marrakesh 2001**

- Operational rules for international emissions trading among parties to the Protocol and for the CDM and joint implementation.
- A compliance regime that outlines consequences for failure to meet emissions targets but defers to the parties to the Protocol after it is in force to decide whether these consequences are legally binding.
- Accounting procedures for the flexibility mechanisms.
- A decision to consider at COP8 how to achieve to a review of the adequacy of commitments that might move towards discussions of future developing country commitments.

Source: Adapted from *Earth Negotiations Bulletin* 12(178), 29 October 2001; www.iisd. ca/climate/cop7/.

---

the 'Flexibility Mechanism' clause in the Protocol. These included trade in emissions reduction with other industrialized countries ('Emissions Trading'), investments in emissions-reduction projects in other Annex I countries, referred to as 'Joint Implementation' (in practice, these would be countries in central and eastern Europe), and investments in emissions-reduction projects in non-Annex I countries, referred to as 'Clean Development Mechanism'. It had been the position of the EU all along that at least 50 per cent of the reduction of GHG emissions should be derived from cuts in domestic emissions, and in order to reach this objective the EU countries began to think in terms of bundling their efforts and proposed to form a cooperative entity with a common emissions-reduction target.[37]

From the start of the UNFCCC negotiations, in the early 1990s, the EU had positioned itself as one body acting in the interest of its member states. However, as member states agreed to widely varying national emissions targets, it became paramount that the EU negotiate some kind of overall EU target at the Kyoto meeting in 1997. At Kyoto, the EU managed to get an agreement for the so-called 'bubble', where countries could pool their emissions and reallocate them internally.[38] In the Kyoto Protocol, all then fifteen members of the EU accepted a target of 8 per cent emissions reduction overall. In 2004, ten new members from central and eastern Europe joined the EU and two more joined in 2005, all of whom will participate in the 'bubble' in a post-Kyoto climate change treaty.[39] Meanwhile, as we will see in Chapter 5, the EU ETS treats the new members to the EU as full participants in its emissions trading scheme during the second phase of the EU ETS which covers the first Kyoto Protocol commitment period 2008–12.

COP8 in New Delhi, in 2002, addressed seriously for the first time the issue of adaptation to climate change. Sensing that the UNFCCC might have little effect on emissions reduction during the first commitment period of the Kyoto Protocol, several developing countries began to request relief funds that would assist the poor in their adaptation to and relief from disasters like flooding or droughts that might result from climate change. The principal outcome of COP8 was the commitment to such a fund. Meanwhile, the EU busied itself with the preparations for the implementation to the Kyoto Protocol in the hope that it would be implemented after full ratification at the Johannesburg Summit on Sustainable Development in 2002. The EU decision to pursue GHG emissions reduction through use of the 'Flexibility Mechanisms' clause under the Kyoto Protocol and CO_2 emissions trading under the EU ETS was a fundamental decision that derived from the uncertainty surrounding the US position on climate-change policy at the time. The current EU climate-change policy reflects to a large extent a least-cost solution to climate-change policy through 'Climate Shopping', which is discussed in Chapter 6.[40] As the EU policymakers got bogged down in the details of their plans to find least-cost solutions to their commitment to reduce GHG emissions, the issues that mattered most to developing countries, like equity and sustainability, were never addressed and resolved.

Equity and sustainability: the North–South divide

As discussions and negotiations shifted from social equity and ecological sustainability to cost–benefit and profitability considerations among politicians and policymakers, academics and NGOs continued to emphasize equal rights to the 'global commons' and the bio-physical limits of the earth. In the process, concerns about transfer of technology from the North to the South and emissions trading between industrialized countries took centre stage among policymakers, and members of the academy and NGOs began to question the sincerity of political and government leaders in dealing with climate change and sustainability problems. In the course of the delibera-tions, the fundamental flaws of Rio and Kyoto became increasingly clear. Principles of equity and sustainable development had been fundamental themes of the climate change debate from the very beginning and were, at least in principle, agreed to at the Earth Summit in Rio in 1992. These principles had provided the guidelines upon which the UNFCCC had formulated its objectives, as for instance Article 12 of the Kyoto Protocol, which specified the contribution to sustainable development as a requirement for the eligibility of CDM projects. Two points underscore these principles. First, the 'atmospheric commons' in the form of carbon-absorbing capacity are finite. Second, 'business as usual' is not an option. Even though under present technological conditions, the right of access to the atmospheric commons (i.e. the right to emit greenhouse gases) is a necessary condition for economic development, conventional paths to development are unsustainable. The resources required are too vast and the damage to the global ecosystems too great. The UN World Summit on Sustainable Development, held in Johannesburg in the Republic of South Africa in 2002, recognized this and promoted sustainability and equity in access to resources and wealth as the principles under which to pursue future economic development.[41] The Johannesburg Declaration on Sustainable Development sets down a number of principles (see Box 2.5).

Efforts to meet the objective of the ambitious agenda of the Johan-nesburg Declaration would require that the rich reduce their footprint in order for the poor to ensure their sustainable livelihood rights.[42] Productive ecosystems are core assets for sustainable livelihoods. Securing community rights to natural resources is an important part of livelihood strategies, which means that the demand for resources of corporate-driven capitalist interests needs to be curtailed. Thus the demands for easily available and cheap resources will have to be limited in order to secure the poor communities around the world their livelihoods. However, these resource conflicts will not be resolved unless the economically well-off change their patterns of production and consumption.

BOX 2.5   **Johannesburg Declaration on Sustainable Development**

- Commitment to build a humane, equitable and caring global society cognizant of the need for human dignity for all.
- All of us, coming from every corner of the world, informed by different life experiences, are united and moved by a deeply felt sense that we urgently need to create a new and brighter world of hope.
- Accordingly, we assume a collective responsibility to advance and strengthen the interdependent and mutually reinforcing pillars of sustainable development – economic development, social development and environmental protection – at local, national, regional and global levels.
- Recognizing that humankind is at a crossroads, we have united in a common resolve to make a determined effort to respond positively to the need to produce a practical and visible plan that should bring about poverty eradication and human development.
- Poverty eradication, changing consumption and production patterns, and protection and management of the natural resource base for economic and social development are overarching objectives, and essential requirements for sustainable development.
- Globalization has added a new dimension to these challenges. The rapid integration of markets, mobility of capital and significant increases in investment flows around the world has opened new challenges and opportunities for the pursuit of sustainable development. But the benefits and costs of globalization are unevenly distributed, with developing countries facing special difficulties in meeting this challenge.

Source: Adapted from the Johannesburg Declaration on Sustainable Development, adopted at the 17th Plenary Meeting of the World Summit on Sustainable Development, 4 September 2002.

Rio failed to bid farewell to the conventional pattern of production and consumption. Government delegates at the Earth Summit, while acknowledging the declining state of the environment, insisted on a business-as-usual pattern of development. The right to Western-style development was paramount and without carbon-emitting rights (or access to alternative technological options) developing countries would be unable to pursue their socio-economic goals to catch up with the developed countries. The right of developing countries to pursue their aspiration to become like us was seen as an implicit equity issue, and the incorporation of equity into climate-change negotiations meant that the UNFCCC held the highly developed industrialized countries primarily responsible for the climate change problem as the value-added from high energy use for development had benefited them more than the rest of the world.

In due course, the North backtracked from the Rio principles by putting the atmosphere up for sale while simultaneously pressuring the South to come on board. At the same time, the South continued to show little interest in global environmental affairs and remained aloof to proposals to commit to carbon constraints if it undermined their economic growth aspirations. Meanwhile, the health of the planet is deteriorating further and global income inequalities are increasing. Generally speaking, governments prioritized the WTO agenda over their Rio commitments. As Rio did not bid farewell to the development-as-growth philosophy and as the reach of Western capital established a fossil-fuel-based economy and society worldwide, it seems that we are further removed from social equity and ecological sustainability than ever before.[43] If business-as-usual development prevails, then atmospheric carbon concentrations will exceed 520 ppm in 2050 and 700 ppm in 2100, according to the IPCCC.[44]

If the climate change problem is taken seriously, it becomes clear that mitigation requires deep GHG emission cuts and that both Annex I and non-Annex I have to commit to reducing their carbon footprint. The necessary GHG emissions reduction to achieve long-term stabilization of atmospheric concentrations was estimated at over 60 per cent of CO_2 emitted in 1990 according to the IPCC *Second Assessment Report* issued in 1996.[45] Using the 1990 world population total, the Center for Energy and Environmental Policy (CEEP) at the

University of Delaware estimated at the time (1998) that in order to reach a climate stable level by 2050 a per capita allowance of CO_2 emissions of 3.3 tonnes would have been the global benchmark.[46] If we consider that every person should have equal access to and share equal responsibility for the global atmospheric commons, and if we project to achieve sustainable levels of 450 ppm by the year 2050 as the stabilization target year for per capita equity, then we can assign specific carbon budgets by country.[47] Recently, the Stern Review (2006) projected the need for cuts of 80 per cent or more in human-induced GHG emissions involving all nations.[48] Using the latest IPCC data the CEEP recently recalculated the 1998 model taking into account that a fossil-fuel-based business-as-usual development path had resulted in much higher CO_2 emissions worldwide and that global population growth had continued to increase.[49] CEEP now estimates that a safe level of emissions per person worldwide is 2.0 tonnes of CO_2 in 2050. Whereas most developing countries are currently well below a sustainable per person limit, Americans still emit over 20 tonnes of CO_2 per person per year, which means that substantial progress has to be made in the USA in order to reach both equitable and sustainable levels. The implications of this are far-reaching and it would seem that the longer we wait with implementing new energy systems the more difficult it will be to achieve a sustainable level of emissions in an equitable way in the future. As CEEP's 2008 calculated trajectory indicates (Figure 2.1), an equity- and sustainability-based policy response to global climate change will require that upper-income (Annex I) countries reduce their emissions to the GHG stabilization level of 2.0 tonnes of CO_2 per capita at a rapid rate and that lower-income (non-Annex I) countries should be allowed to further expand their emissions until about 2040 and then cut back their CO_2 emissions in order to reach equity and sustainability levels at around 2050.

Presently, under the existing economic world order, human welfare and income depend on the right to emit carbon, and restrictions on this right mean lowering development prospects. As stated in the Declaration for the Establishment of the New International Economic Order (NIEO, 1974), and reiterated at the Johannesburg World Summit on Sustainable Development in 2002, equity and

FIGURE 2.1   **CO₂ from fossil fuels under the CEEP scenario**

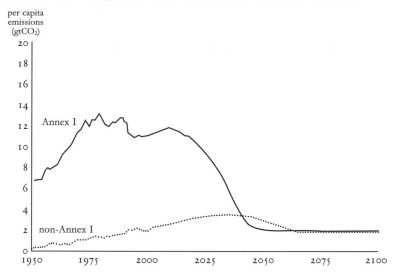

Source: J. Byrne et al., 'Undoing Atmospheric Harm: Civil Action to Shrink the Carbon Footprint', in P. Droege (ed.), *Urban Transition: From Fossil Fuels to Renewable Power*, Elsevier, Oxford, 2008: 33, Fig. 2.6.

prosperity for all were considered to be the basic rights upon which policies and actions should be based. The other important principle, as stated in NIEO, was the sovereign rights of states to decide on resource use. On both counts, the present climate-change policy falls far short.

As we consider the complexity of the debates on climate change and the difficulties associated with reduction of GHG emissions worldwide, it becomes clear that these are problems with specific political, economic and geographical contexts. In the UN debates on economic development culminating in the Declaration on the New International Economic Order in 1974, similar issues in similar contexts were discussed. In fact, the diverging opinions of North and South on economic development, sustainable development, and climate change, have a lot in common. So far, the Declaration and Program for Action for the Establishment of a New International Economic Order (NIEO, 1974), the Conference on Environment and

Development (Earth Summit, 1992), the Climate Change Treaty (Kyoto Protocol, 1997), and the World Summit for Sustainable Development (Johannesburg, 2002), have failed to deliver on their promises. Financial support necessary to implement Agenda 21 has fallen far short of what was needed and it never set a new agenda for development, let alone for a New International Economic Order.[50] The negotiations on international climate-change policy remain deadlocked, and if anything the global economic and environmental order has become more and more controlled by multinational or transnational corporations and UN institutions like the IMF, the World Bank and the WTO. As the atmosphere has gone up for sale and the business community has gained the upper hand in the climate-change negotiations, it is business-as-usual that seems to be the model for further deliberations on the future of the global community and global atmosphere.[51]

It took a while before business interests settled for a market-based climate-change policy. At the time of the Rio Earth Summit in 1992, following the signing of the UN Framework Convention on Climate Change, President George Bush proclaimed that climate change was an economic, not an environmental, issue. Actions to reduce greenhouse-gas emissions were presented as potentially damaging to national economic interests and employment. Based on studies conducted at the time, US business leaders and corporate lobbyists called for voluntary action to be taken in pursuit of a least-cost, efficient response to the demand for new technologies as part of a climate-change strategy.[49] Technology transfer was promoted and implemented on a limited scale through CDM, but only in as far as it served profit-motivated investments in countries that would serve transnational capital in the global marketplace. The idea of 'leapfrogging' into a future of alternative energy strategies on the part of developing countries did not really figure into these schemes, and thus that opportunity has passed now that FDI and international trade have firmly established a business-as-usual pattern of development for the developing world. Creative accounting schemes have also been part of the corporate strategy in dealing with climate-change policy through carbon seques-tration, which allows Annex I countries to count carbon sinks in the form of reforestation and forest protection in developing countries as credits towards meeting GHG reduction targets.[53]

The contradictions and unresolved tensions between, on the one hand, the pursuit of economic growth and business interests in a globalizing world and, on the other, the realization and recognition that the earth and atmosphere are ultimately finite have added urgency to the debates and negotiations over the last few decades.[54] In fact, the dynamics of globalization and the removal of barriers to the free flow of capital and goods have laid the foundations for a relentless expansion of the impact of multinational/transnational corporations (TNCs) and foreign trade, and the introduction of a fossil-fuel-based economy and society in the developing world. Economic globalization is a fact of life in major parts of the world today, which has left one wondering if the world order can still be perceived of as a community of nation-states in which national governments negotiate international treaties, or if it should be conceived of as a world of TNCs.

Disengaged from any particular country or any particular community, TNCs have become the major players in the global economy. The economic power inherent in many TNCs today is greater than the GDP or GNP of many national economies; therefore questions arise as to the effectiveness of implementation of international treaties dealing with environmental or climate-change issues. Ten years ago, when the Kyoto Protocol was concluded, over 70 per cent of world trade was controlled by just 500 corporations which also controlled 80 per cent of foreign investment and approximately 40 per cent of world GDP.[55] These figures speak for themselves. That almost all of the world's largest corporations are headquartered in OECD countries, and that only a few of the largest global corporations are headquartered within the developing world, suggests that practically all global economic decision-making is controlled by shareholders and CEOs in company headquarters in the developed countries. Thus, the consolidation of strategic political-economic power in the hands of the wealthy well-positioned business interest groups is such that it should make us wonder how sincere proposals about a new international economic order, sustainable development and climate-change policy really are.[56] In fact, the liberalization of international investment and global trade policy and the rapidly expanding reach of the IMF, the World Bank and the WTO should force us to take a more critical look at the UN institutions dealing with economic development and global environmental issues (see Figure 1.1).

The formal structures of the post-World War II international regulatory bodies like the UN, the IMF, the World Bank and GATT/ WTO were shaped by the interests of the USA as the dominant world power, and since the end of the Cold War, the USA, Japan and the EU have become the primary partners in international negotiations. At the same time, TNCs headquartered in the same parts of the world have become the primary actors in the global marketplace. In the past few decades the field of operation of the TNCs has expanded to include major parts of the developing world in South and East Asia and Latin America in particular. Most of the multinational business activities occur under the banner of 'free trade', which holds the promise – according to neoliberal principles – of generating economic growth in those parts of the world that previously were isolated or shielded from foreign investment. This phenomenon is referred to as economic globalization and is the context in which the climate-change negotiations take place. This reality of the world of the early twenty-first century forces us to take a closer look at the relationship between the dynamics of the world economy and the earth's biophysical limitations.

Globalization has been hailed as the new era for humanity with great promise for improvement of conditions in developing countries. Under the banner of 'levelling the playing field', globalization promises greater efficiency in the use of resources and competition for production capacity of developing countries. Through modern communications and transportation systems which facilitate transnational integration of production chains, developing countries with favourable investment 'climates' and a developed infrastructure stand to receive manufacturing production capacity through globalization. As transnational corporations tend to standardize technologies between countries at a more advanced level, foreign direct investment can be a force to 'leapfrog' technological change. On closer examination, however, transnational interaction and geographically extended chains of production networks show a different picture.

Transnational investment may reduce energy and material input per unit of output, but the total use of resources will likely grow as economic activity, overall, expands and as a fossil-fuel-based infra-structure is developed in newly industrializing countries. That is, FDI and the worldwide geographical expansion of chains of production by TNCs have enabled transnational corporations to choose the most profitable location for each stage of production, and a well-developed transportation system and centralized electricity network form part of the conditions for investment. Through the economic restructuring of some regions of the developing world (South and East Asia, in particular) and in the economies in transition in central and eastern Europe, it has become possible to further competition among TNCs, formerly based in OECD countries (USA, EU and Japan, in particular). Their markets were largely saturated by the end of the 1970s and expansion became imperative. Most of the world economic growth in the 1980s and 1990s, and in the early twenty-first century, has been accomplished through a geographical shift in production capacity and the incorporation of new markets.[57] The total value of world production nearly doubled between 1975 and 2000 and has been accelerating since China became a member of the WTO in 2001. As a result, the pressure on the earth's biosphere and atmosphere is without precedent.

With increased foreign trade and FDI, the fossil-fuel model of development has spread to several other parts of the world and countries in the developing world are rapidly entering a resource- and energy-intensive phase of economic development. Countries like China, India, Brazil and Mexico are recording a steep rise in CO_2 emissions as a result.[58] At the same time, some industrialized countries increased their emissions from manufacturing production only slightly due to deindustrialization. In fact, as many production facilities have relocated to South and East Asia and Latin America, the traditional industrial economies of the OECD have moved into the post-industrial phase of economic development. Simultaneously, the use of the automobile is rapidly replacing the bicycle and public transportation in many emerging economies, adding to fossil-fuel use and CO_2 emissions.[59] All in all, fossil-fuel use and CO_2 emissions have almost doubled in parts of South and East Asia since the 1980s.

Alongside the extended geographical reach of the transnational economy, national regulatory regimes have been dismantled, and deregulation and increased competition have made the global market-place free for all. Disengaged from the web of national norms, controls and standards, economic globalization has unleashed worldwide competition for labour, resources and unobstructed access to the global commons (the biosphere and atmosphere), with the subsequent result that TNCs can afford to ignore labour and environmental standards in their search for more profitable overseas locations of production and thus the environment is coming under increased pressure in many parts of the world. As the number of competitive economic actors on this levelled playing field increases, governments tend to attach more value to 'comparative advantage' or competitive strength than to environmental protection. The outcome of this condition in the global economy has led to great controversies within the OECD and WTO about equity and sustainability and has resulted in renewed calls for environmental and labour regulations and protection. Under current trade rules overseen by the WTO, national governments are entitled to enforce labour and environmental laws on production within their own countries, but they cannot keep products of their markets or discriminate against imported goods whose production process does not conform to their national environmental or labour standards. Since national or domestic producers are subsequently put under competitive pressure from outside, national governments often lose the political will to insist that production standards should conform to sustainability principles. This situation led Wolfgang Sachs to conclude that: 'So long as prices do not tell the ecological truth, deregulation will only take the market further down the ecologically slippery slope.'[60]

The ecologically slippery slope

One aspect of the ecologically slippery slope associated with economic globalization is the increased unequal ecological or environmental burden placed on developing countries. The international division of labour in the global production and supply chain now links the producer in developing countries in the South with the consumer and investor in the developed countries in the North. As a consequence the cost and benefits are unequally distributed throughout the chain.

Lower prices for consumers and higher profits for the investors in transnational corporations have benefited the developed world, while cheap labour, tax breaks and lax environmental standards have put a heavy burden on developing countries. Whereas the post-industrial society has the luxury to enjoy a cleaner environment and the benefit of low-priced consumer goods, the developing countries bear the burden of air and water pollution, soil erosion and deforestation.[61] In the international arena this translates into an increased pressure on the developing countries (often from well-meaning environmentalists of the developed countries) to clean up their act. From the perspective of the developing countries, this is global 'environmental imperialism', as global climate-change problems and other environmental problems are seen as the direct outcome of the resource- and energy-intensive global chain of production and consumption. In fact, if we attribute CO_2 emissions to consuming countries rather than producing countries, 90 per cent of the total would be the responsibility of the developed countries.[62]

In contrast to the New International Economic Order, which put forward demands by the developing world for a more equal access to global resources and wealth created, the new economic world order of globalization was unilaterally proclaimed by the leaders of the developed world. Whereas the new economic world order is a structural transformation directed from above which bears the stamp of US hegemony in the global economy, the NIEO was a transformation directed from below and was a collective effort by the majority of the countries in the South. As the NIEO was predicated on the principle of justice and equitable distribution of resources and wealth, the new economic world order reinforces the North–South inequity and dichotomy, which leads to opposition and political instability. These alone should be reasons to change direction in the global climate-change negotiations, and hopefully sooner rather than later we may be on the way to a more fruitful debate on how to meet the emissions targets agreed to in the Kyoto Protocol.

As the UN Framework Convention on Climate Change remains deadlocked, we have no credible proposal to avert the climate change problem in either an equitable or a sustainable fashion. Although there is a growing academic literature that recognizes the importance of alternative development pathways in achieving an environmentally and socio-economically sustainable development, the proposals remain largely closeted and considered non-realistic in the international debate or the global marketplace. However, in order to break out of the deadlock and to be positively engaged in climate change solutions, we need to consider constructive options.[63]

One of the options would be for Annex I countries to build more constructive alliances with developing countries and to follow through on the promise of the Kyoto Protocol without the use of loopholes. This means that there should not be any further pressure on developing countries to commit to emissions reduction through 'meaningful participation' within the present commitment period (2008–12). Furthermore, Annex I countries should indicate to non-Annex I countries that they are prepared for a full debate on equity and sustainability issues and that future proposals will include more equitable allocations of 'rights to the atmospheric commons' based on some kind of burden-sharing scheme. This strategy would inevitably lead to a debate on the disjuncture between the current climate change regime and the economic globalization regime. Without reconciliation between these two global arenas, further negotiations will be fruitless.

Equity and sustainability have been mostly academic constructs. In order to apply these principles in the real world, we need convincing schemes that make a real difference. As noted, the negotiations have mostly abandoned developing countries' interests and have moved from sustainability and equity concerns to cost–benefit and marketplace concerns. In addition, the options considered until now are near-term rather than long-term. For the long term, massive emissions reductions will be needed, which will be well beyond what technology transfer and financial transfer can accomplish. Without reconciliation and cooperation from the developing countries and a dramatic change in the global economic order, it is doubtful if much can be achieved.

3

Trade liberalization, economic development and the environment

Is capitalism sustainable?[1]

From the ongoing debates in climate-change policy and the apparent ineffectiveness of the current Kyoto regime dealing with GHG reduction schemes to halt/reverse climate change, it is obvious that something is wrong in the world order dealing with global environmental problems. Much debated presently but not considered at the time the Kyoto Protocol was first signed is the recognition that national emissions-reduction commitments have little effect in a global economy that is driven by intense competition in foreign trade and organized around multinational or transnational corporations and international production networks. Furthermore, the North–South divide – as discussed in the previous chapter – proved to be much more divisive than was anticipated and the emergence on the world economic scene of, in particular, China and India has rekindled the debate on 'Who is to Blame' and 'Who is to Pay'. That development and environmental concerns are closely related is no longer in question, but how to deal with the reality of the global marketplace and the foreign trade regime as it exists today and at the same time solve the problems associated with climate change requires a whole different set of principles and a quite different approach.

In his persuasive exposé, *Capitalism as if the World Matters* (2005), Jonathon Porritt charges that the bipolar challenges of biophysical limits to growth, on the one hand, and materialism and business-as-usual approaches to development, on the other, require profound transformations of contemporary capitalism sooner rather than later if we are to avoid dramatic disruptions to life on earth.[2] Arguing that capitalism in its present form is unsustainable, he asserts that only principles associated with sustainable development can provide the foundations upon which to base the transformations necessary to meet the bipolar challenges. He recommends that core values like interdependence, empathy, equity, personal responsibility and inter-generational justice should be the guiding principles for a new world vision. While all this may seem like a far-fetched idea, his message is well worth considering.

Economic globalization, foreign trade and climate change raise questions about how and to what extent environmental standards should be incorporated into international trade regulations. Should developing countries be expected to forgo development through industrialization because of strict environmental standards and regulations which industrialized countries were not themselves subjected to when they were at a similar stage in their development? If developing countries are forced or asked to impose and enforce strict environmental regulations, who should foot the bill? There is no doubt that lower standards of environmental regulation and enforcement in some instances entice industrial firms to expand or relocate production to developing countries, but how to level the playing field through standards that are developed in and enforced by developed countries remains a very tricky question.

Environmental concerns associated with global production and foreign trade question the validity of the neoliberal economic and political agenda as promoted by the USA, the WTO, the IMF and the World Bank. Since many negative effects of global production are not confined within national boundaries but spill over to affect other parts of the world (like greenhouse-gas emissions), the seriousness of global environmental problems associated with industrial production and other economic activities through FDI becomes all too clear.[3] But can or should developing countries like

India and China be expected to comply with emissions targets, as suggested by the Bush administration? If we consider that the average Chinese still only emits 16 per cent of that emitted by the average US citizen, and the average Indian emits only 6 per cent, then it is difficult to argue that they should be equally involved with the effort to reduce GHG emissions.[4] At the same time, according to the most recent IPCC Report (2007), greenhouse-gas emissions from developing countries will reach the levels of developed countries by 2015 or 2020, and emissions in developing countries, especially in East and South Asia, have been growing at a much faster rate than in developed countries.[5]

So, questions as to whether capitalism is sustainable, and who is to blame and who should pay, are very much with us today. The extra costs of production involved in introducing new clean technologies will be substantial, and, even with assistance from developed countries, developing countries' economies can hardly bear the loss of economic opportunity this will involve; therefore developing countries see the imposition of carbon emissions-reduction targets (or 'carbon constraints') as yet another form of protectionism or imperialism. Some in the developed countries, on the other hand, suggest that if a country allows lax environmental standards, then it should not be permitted to market and sell products overseas as they are produced more cheaply as a consequence. Here, one could argue that lax environmental standards are a form of subsidy on production in countries where firms locate in order to avoid dealing with 'carbon constraints', as some would say is the case under the Kyoto Protocol. The energy costs of transporting materials and goods across the world are not accounted for in foreign trade and are therefore heavily subsidized, at ever greater environmental cost. Some environmentalists and ecologists take this a step further and argue that under the more open international trade regime as promoted by the WTO, the IMF and the World Bank, free trade and the economic growth model associated with capitalism should be abandoned completely.[6]

In its stead, we should pursue a sustainable development course that would promote fair trade and fair-share principles. As Herman Daly and others have argued, economic growth is all about quantitative expansion and limitless transformation of natural capital into man-made capital.[7] Sustainable development, on the other hand, is about qualitative improvement, permitting increased economic activity only in so far as it does not exceed the capacity of the ecosystem. In pursuit of economic growth, mainstream economists put the emphasis on non-physical parameters of the economy (i.e. income, productivity, profit and competition). In pursuit of sustainable development, economists must put the emphasis on physical parameters such as resources and carrying capacity, and accept that the non-physical variables will have to be adjusted accordingly. For many it has become abundantly clear that the poor of the world will bear the brunt of unsustainable growth and of the damage to ecological systems and will carry most of the associated costs, while they are hardly to blame or in a position to make any changes themselves. Marginalized from the rest of the global marketplace, they will nonetheless be the major victims when climate change occurs.

In mainstream political and business discussions about sustainable development and climate-change policy, the question 'Is capitalism sustainable?' is never asked. In fact, no one really dares to ask the question because the premiss is that the benefits of free markets are all around us. But the question must be asked if we are to find support for international climate-change policy and treaty-making. Therefore this chapter sets out to ask the question if the neoliberal economic model of development, as promoted today under the auspices of the WTO, and USA and EU policies through the IMF and the World Bank, is compatible with climate-change policy as designed under the UNFCCC and the Kyoto Protocol. It is probably fair to say that the US-designed neoliberal economic and political agenda and the Bush administration's unilateralist ambitions have put a great deal of stress on the 'global partnership' ideal. Economic globalization and the changing global order since 9/11 have set us on a course that is not terribly conducive to international cooperation on global environmental problems. Widespread suspicion about the Western world's real intentions have intensified, and while the new geography of the world economy heralds 'the world is flat',[8] led by the growing interlinking of global and local production systems, the emergence of the growing power of multinational corporations defines another reality. The income gap between developed and developing countries is increasing and whereas some countries in South and East Asia, in particular, are experiencing remarkable growth, the distribution of the wealth created mostly benefits elite groups in these countries and Western consumers and investors rather than the majority of the population. The mobility of capital, goods, people, ideas, emissions and pollutants across borders increasingly challenges the capacity of individual governments to sustain their social-political and environmental laws and regulations within national borders, and new patterns of engagement have emerged as a result of increased divergence between the global reach of economic and social activity and the traditional nation-state-based mechanisms of political control. Globalization does not necessarily mean the death of the nation-state, as some want us to believe, but the regulatory capacity of states increasingly has to be matched by the development of collaborative mechanisms of governance at supranational, regional and global levels.

One of the issues brought up in discussions about climate-change negotiations is the effect of economic globalization on the environment. The impact of foreign trade and FDI by multinational or transnational corporations often forms part of these debates. This chapter introduces the reader to these debates, including discussions about trade liberalization, globalization and the impact on the environment. While there is no consensus about the overall extent to which the current level of global economic integration impacts on the environment, trends suggest that under conditions where the institutional framework or regulatory regime is missing, the forces of the global marketplace can lead to rapid degradation of the environment. This chapter first reviews how the neoliberal economic and political agenda of the USA and the EU, as well as the World Bank and IMF structural adjustment programmes (SAPs) and the WTO, changed the global economic arena, and then introduces the reader to the issue of the impact of economic globalization on the global environment. The chapter also provides detail on the competitive forces in the capitalist world economy and illustrates, with examples from the literature, the extent to which foreign trade and international economic production have challenged the effectiveness of the nation-state and international environmental treaty-making.

Neoliberalism and the Washington Consensus

Neoliberalism refers to an intellectual and political movement that espouses economic liberalism as a means of promoting economic development and securing political liberty. The movement is sometimes described as an effort to revert to the economic policies of nineteenth-century classical liberalism based on Adam Smith's and David Ricardo's ideas of national economic growth and the comparative advantage of nation-states. Neoliberalism also refers to a historically specific re-emergence of economic liberalism's influence among Western economists and policymakers during the 1970s through the 1990s. Often the term is used to denote a group of neoclassical-influenced economic theories, libertarian political philosophies and political rhetorics that portray government control over the economy as inefficient, corrupt or otherwise undesirable. Neoliberalism is not a unified economic theory or political philosophy: it is a label denoting a shift in social-scientific and political sentiments that is manifested in theories and political platforms supporting a reform of largely centralized post-war economic institutions in favour of decentralized ones. Arguments of this sort gained a great deal of currency after the oil and stagflation crises of the 1970s, the debt crisis of the 1980s in Latin America, and the collapse of the Soviet Union in the early 1990s.[9]

The term 'Washington Consensus' was initially coined in the late 1980s by John Williamson of the Institute for International Economics, a research institution devoted to the study of international economic policy to promote a relatively specific set of economic policy prescriptions that were considered to constitute a standard reform package promoted for countries in economic distress by Washington-based institutions such as the IMF, the World Bank and the US Treasury Department.[10] The policies the Washington Consensus promoted were the policies pursued in Chile after the fall of President Allende and the oil crises of the 1970s, but they became a set of quite specific prescriptive dictates during the 1980s with the debt crisis in Latin America when the IMF and the World Bank signed on to them.[11] The coup against Allende had been backed by the CIA and was supported by then US secretary of state Henry Kissinger.

Allende's successor, General Augusto Pinochet, called in a group of economic advisers who had been trained by Milton Friedman at the University of Chicago. They advised the general to transform the Chilean economy along free-market lines, privatizing public assets, opening up natural resources to private business, and facilitating FDI. Export-led growth was to replace 'import substitution', which until then had been the dominant model for development in Latin America.[12]

Although arguments that stress the economic benefits of unfettered markets are as old as Adam Smith's *The Wealth of Nations* (1776) and served to guide economic thought throughout the nineteenth century, at the onset of the Great Depression, many saw free markets as less benevolent and government control as important in order to secure economic recovery.[13] By the end of World War II, many countries decided to expand government control and influence over economic policy, and within the capitalist world John Maynard Keynes formulated the means by which governments could stabilize and fine-tune free markets, which became the dominant ideology of the day. Neoliberalism, associated with Friedrich Hayek and Milton Friedman, changed all that.[14] In essence, neoliberalism represents a move away from Keynesian economics and towards an economic and political agenda of global capitalism through government and military interventionism that protects and promotes the interests of multinational corporations through free-market policies.[15]

In the US and the UK, neoliberal principles began to take root in the policies of Ronald Reagan and Margaret Thatcher. The years of economic stagnation following the oil crises of the 1970s saw domestic policies introduced that turned capital against labour in opposition to trade-union power, and tackled inflation with fiscal and monetary policies that resulted in high interest rates and tax reform favouring the rich over the poor. Deregulation of everything from airlines and telecommunications to finance and corporate business was to restore the faith in capitalism and free markets. Big money contributions to the Republican Party consolidated neoliberal political power under Ronald Reagan in the USA.[16] In the UK, Margaret Thatcher busied herself with dismantling the welfare state and withdrew government support from health care, education and social services,

BOX 3.1   **Policy recommendations of the Washington Consensus**

- *Fiscal discipline*, meaning that governments should cut expenditures and/or raise taxes to maintain a budget surplus.
- *Competitive exchange rates*, whereby governments would accept market-determined exchange rates, as opposed to implemented government-fixed exchange rates, as had prevailed under the Bretton Woods system.
- *Free trade*, which means the removal of tariffs and regulatory trade barriers.
- *Privatization*, which means the transfer of previously public-owned enterprises to the private sector.
- *Undistorted market prices*, meaning that governments would refrain from policies that would alter market prices.
- *Limited intervention*, with the exception of intervention designed to promote exports, educational or infrastructural development.

Source: Dani Rodrik, 'Understanding Economic Policy Reform', *Journal of Economic Literature* 34(1), 1996: 9–41.

including public housing, by promoting public–private partnerships in which the public sector bears all of the risks and the corporate sector reaps all of the profit.[17] Globally, the Washington Consensus sought to reduce tariff barriers to movement of capital and goods across national borders and the opening up of markets abroad for both commodities and investments. It is in this sphere that TNCs' interests coincided with government power in policymaking and in the creation of new international institutional arrangements under the WTO, which received support from the IMF and the World Bank. The policy recommendations that gained consensus approval among the Washington-based international economic organizations are listed in Box 3.1.

In the view of those who adhere to the neoliberal economic and political agenda, economic growth will be most rapid when the movement of goods, services and capital is unimpeded by government regulations. The trickle-down effect will then take care of the rest. Neoliberalism thus presents itself as the cure-all for the world's social, economic and environmental problems. In essence, the USA had held this point of view ever since the end of World War II, but after the demise of the Soviet Union it became the guiding light of US foreign policy. US advisers prescribed unfettered capitalism for eastern and central Europe, even though Bill Clinton, Tony Blair and Gerhard Schröder had tried to offer an alternative in the form of the 'Third Way'. The Third Way is a philosophy of governance in the social-democratic tradition that embraces a mix of market and interventionist philosophies that rejects both top-down directives and laissez-faire economic approaches. It stresses technological development and education but recommends competitive mechanisms to pursue economic growth. At the time, the Third Way promoted a social-democratic economic and political agenda for societies in transition in eastern and central Europe and the former Soviet Union, but it had little influence on policymaking for debt-ridden economies in Latin America, where the Washington Consensus prevailed.[18] Some point out that it offered no strategy to achieve a more equitable distribution of wealth and made no reference to power relations, as it accepts the basic framework of neoliberalism, especially as it concerns the global marketplace. Ironically, it was Clinton and then Blair who from the centre-left did more to consolidate the neoliberal agenda abroad than their predecessors, by supporting the WTO as the police chief of international trade rules. Thus, the Third Way took globalization as a given and failed to contest inequalities of income, wealth and power.

There is still ongoing debate in Washington and elsewhere about the importance of implementing the neoliberal economic and political agenda. With almost missionary zeal, Washington politicians set out to spread the belief that leaving the forces of supply and demand unencumbered by restrictions and constraints would lead to economic benefits for all. If only all tariffs could be removed, if only entrepreneurs could be encouraged by low taxes, and if only wages could be set by demand and supply (and not by union contracts), then the result would be the perfect society. This perfect society would be a democratic state as free markets create free peoples, and, as George W. Bush saw it, people who operate in open economies eventually demand more open societies.

The conservative writer Michael Novak (1982) called the Washington Consensus 'democratic capitalism'.[19] In the early 1990s, President George H.W. Bush began to draw up a US–Mexican–Canadian free-trade proposal that came to be known as the North American Free Trade Agreement (NAFTA). NAFTA was later signed into law by Bush's successor, President Bill Clinton, and the three North American countries agreed to gradually phase out or sharply reduce tariffs on foreign goods, a policy perfectly in line with the ideals of the Washington Consensus. The administration of George W. Bush negotiated a similar agreement with Central America, known as the Central America Free Trade Agreement (CAFTA), which was approved by Congress in 2005.

There is no denying that US neoliberal advocates are sincere in their belief that today's pattern of globalization fosters democracy and that market-based economies are an essential feature of democratic societies. By extension, they believe that the bigger those markets are, the more open they are likely to be. Since 9/11 there has been an almost dogmatic promotion of corporate globalization in the war against terror and the need for increased liberalization. US trade representative in George W. Bush's first administration, Robert Zoellick (now World Bank president) was quite explicit in his linkage of the 'war against terror' and the need for increased liberalization of world trade in seeking to persuade the US Congress to give President Bush fast-track powers to negotiate new trade deals with Congress. Fast-track meant that Congress could either accept or reject but not change a negotiated trade deal. Zoellick argued that 'the values at the heart of free trade have become an essential part of the struggle against terrorism; open markets are an antidote to the terrorists' violent plot against us.'[20] Free trade has thus been conscripted into a latter-day crusade to open up closed societies and 'liberate' the people – as has been attempted in Afghanistan and Iraq.

The neoliberal philosophy of George W. Bush's US administration and the millenarian beliefs it entails has had a dramatic impact on political and social cohesion in the USA, and in the world community at large.[21] The US corporate elite has seen itself as engaged in a planetary war for the maintenance of American prosperity and way of life, and for directing all of humanity to American ends, according to Northcott in *An Angel Directs the Storm* (2004).[22] The increasingly indifferent attitude towards other cultures, religions and societies, as well as the self-interested assertion of American imperial power, is the hallmark of this trend. Joseph Stiglitz, the former chief economist at the World Bank, maintains that, whereas in theory the IMF supports democratic institutions in the nations it assists, in practice it undermines the democratic process by imposing its own policies.[23] At the same time, some of the world's largest multinational companies use their bargaining power as foreign direct investors to secure exemptions from rules and regulations and to strike special deals and agreements in which the interests of the local population are routinely set aside. Naomi Klein (2007) therefore argues that it is far-fetched to think that foreign trade and FDI in the global economy is a force of freedom and democracy in the developing world.[24] So today's Washington Consensus and neoliberal agenda are a far cry from some kind of emerging 'sustainability consensus' that is needed in order to deal with the climate change threat. Global capitalism as we know it today is inherently incompatible with the pursuit of either ecological sustainability or social justice. The task of conceptualizing an ecologically and socially sustainable model of globalization requires a great deal of imagination.[25]

Structural adjustment programmes

The high interest rates of the 1980s jeopardized the repayment of loans extended to developing countries – particularly Latin American countries – and threw extremely vulnerable economies into default. The first to default was Mexico in 1982–84. The Reagan administration, which had thought of withdrawing support for the IMF, was persuaded to align with the Fund in order to resolve the Mexican crisis by rolling over the debt in return for structural reforms including cuts in welfare expenditures, privatization of state properties, and the restructuring of labour laws. This and subsequent policy prescription and reform packages were termed structural adjustment programmes. Due to economic stagnation and loss of access to foreign credit, many governments in Latin America could no longer sustain high levels of public spending without igniting hyperinflation and therefore were put on notice that unless they made adjustments in government policy and restructured their national economies, they would not receive any further funding from the IMF or the World Bank. Thus the recommended policy changes became conditions ('Conditionalities') for getting new loans from the IMF or the Bank, or for obtaining lower interest rates on existing loans. Structural adjustment programmes were created with the ostensible goal of reducing a borrowing country's fiscal imbalances, but in fact loans from both the World Bank and the IMF were designed to promote economic growth and to smooth the way for foreign trade and FDI.

Structural adjustment programmes generally involve the implementation of free-market programmes and policies. The programmes include internal changes (notably privatization and deregulation) as well as external ones (especially the reduction of trade barriers). Since the late 1990s, after negative side effects on the poor became evident, 'structural adjustment' has emphasized poverty reduction as the main goal. SAPs were often criticized for implementing free-market policies without regard for local conditions. To increase engagement with a programme, developing countries are now encouraged to draw up Poverty Reduction Strategy Papers (PRSPs); these have essentially taken the place of SAPs. It is believed that an increase in local governments' participation in creating the policy will lead to greater ownership of loan programmes, but the content of PRSPs has in fact turned out to be quite similar to the original content of the SAPs. Critics argue that the similarities show that the banks and the countries that fund them under the Washington Consensus are still overly involved in the policymaking process.

Thus SAPs have become the target of sharp criticism by the same groups and individuals that criticized the Washington Consensus.[26] These parties argue that neoliberal policies were pursued in order to open up less developed countries to investments from large multinational corporations and their wealthy owners in advanced developed economies. Proponents of the Washington Consensus claim that the policies promote economic growth in the participating countries and are a boon to US consumers, providing them with less expensive foreign goods. Critics of both the left and the right – including activists and allies of the trade-union movement and the anti-global-ization movement, as well as conservatives who promote 'Made in America' traditions – accuse the Washington Consensus of crippling the working class of the United States by promoting the relocation of production to cheaper labour markets in developing countries, and allege that such shifts have, in addition, resulted in the exploitation of workers overseas. Increasingly, the critics also assert that global environmental problems relate to economic globalization and the relocation of production to developing countries.

Economic globalization through trade liberalization and FDI, according to Noam Chomsky (2004)[27] and Naomi Klein (2007),[28] is a way for TNCs to exploit developing countries for their human and natural resources. The prescribed reductions in tariffs and other trade barriers allow the free movement of goods and capital across borders, but labour is not permitted to move freely due to tough visa laws and border controls.[29] This creates an economic climate in which goods are manufactured using cheap labour in underdeveloped economies, which are then exported to rich developed economies for sale at huge mark-ups, with the balance accruing to large multinational corporations. The criticism is that workers in the developing world remain mostly poor, as any pay raises they may have received over what they made before trade liberalization is offset by a higher cost of living and inflation. Meanwhile, workers in the developed world become unemployed while corporate CEOs and shareholders grow more prosperous. Anti-globalization critics further argue that the Washington Consensus has not, in fact, led to any great economic boom in most countries in the developing world but rather to increased poverty and vulnerability.[30]

The influence and impact of the Washington-inspired structural adjustment programmes are most pronounced and best documented in the case of Latin America. The outcome of the policy prescriptions (e.g. the privatization of state industries, tax reform and deregulation) as implemented following the Latin American debt crises is now seen as the mechanism whereby wealthy elites in Latin American countries would rise to political power and gain a vested interest in maintaining the status quo of labour and environmental exploitation.[31] Defenders of the policies point out that workers in factories created by foreign investment typically receive higher wages and experience better working conditions than are standard in their own countries' domestically owned factories, and that economic growth in much of Latin America in the last few years has been at historically high rates while debt levels – relative to the size of these economies – are on average significantly lower than they were several years ago. In addition, inflation rates are now much lower than they were a decade or two ago. Despite these macroeconomic advances, however, poverty and income inequality remain at high levels and have increased in many countries in Latin America.[32]

Some socialist political leaders in Latin America, such as Venezuelan president Hugo Chávez, former Cuban president Fidel Castro, and Bolivian president Evo Morales, are vocal and well-known critics of the Washington Consensus, while Argentina's former Peronist government of Nestor Kirchner took measures that represent a repudiation of some Consensus policies.[33] Others on the Latin American left took a different approach. Governments led by the Socialist Party of Chile, by Alan Garcia in Peru, and by President Lula in Brazil maintained a high degree of continuity with the economic policies prescribed under the Washington Consensus, but simultaneously sought to supplement these policies by measures directly targeted at helping the poor, through educational reforms and subsidies to low-income families.

Neo-Keynesian and post-Keynesian critics of the Washington Consensus and SAPs have argued that the underlining policies were often too rigid to be able to succeed and did not take into account the economic and cultural differences between countries. Some have pointed out that Consensus policies should be implemented, if at all, during a period of rapid economic growth and not during an economic crisis. They argue that there have long been major differences in opinion between economists over what the correct economic policy prescriptions actually were or should have been. Thus, according to Joseph Stanislaw and Daniel Yergin, authors of *The Commanding Heights* (1998),[34] the policy prescriptions dictated by the Washington Consensus were in reality developed in Latin America in response to what was happening both within and outside the region and in response to efforts on the part of trade unions and revolutionary movements to seize power from traditional political elites.

Most Latin American countries continue to struggle with high poverty, unemployment and underemployment, but some – like Chile or Brazil – have performed much better. Indeed, Chile has often been presented as an example of a Consensus success story.[35] In fact, the Chilean success story owes a lot to state ownership of key industries, particularly the copper industry, and currency interventions to stabilize capital flows.[36] Many argue that Chile's economic success was largely due to its combination of sound macroeconomics, market-oriented policies and relatively strong public institutions, including one of the better state school systems in the region. Klein (2007) describes Chile under General Pinochet as not a 'capitalist' but a 'corporatist' state, in which the police and large corporations joined forces to wage war on the workers – a war of the rich against the poor and the middle class.

A number of economists and policymakers argue that what was wrong with the Washington Consensus as originally formulated by Williamson in 1990 had less to do with what was included than with what was missing.[37] This view asserts that countries such as Brazil, Chile, Peru and Uruguay, currently governed by parties of the left, have not abandoned most of the substantive elements of the Washington Consensus but have achieved macroeconomic stability through fiscal and monetary discipline and defeated hyperinflation, which represents one of the most important positive contributions of recent years to the welfare of the poor. Most countries in Latin America maintained a fairly open policy on global trade and international investment, except perhaps Venezuela under Hugo Chávez.

The same economists, policymakers and politicians would likely agree that the Washington Consensus was incomplete and that countries in Latin America and elsewhere need to move beyond macroeconomic and trade reforms to a stronger focus on productivity-boosting reforms and government programmes to support the poor.[38] This includes fighting poverty directly via cash transfer programmes and improving the quality of primary and secondary education, as well as addressing the special needs of historically disadvantaged groups including indigenous peoples and Afro-descendant populations across Latin America.

The World Trade Organization

Another important development in the global economy was the emergence of the World Trade Organization, designed to supervise and liberalize international trade. The WTO came into being on 1 January 1995, as a successor to the General Agreement on Tariffs and Trade (GATT), which was created in 1947. The World Trade Organization deals with the rules of trade between nations and is responsible for negotiating and implementing new trade agreements. It is also in charge of policing member countries' adherence to all the WTO agreements.[39] Most of the WTO's current work comes from the 1986–94 negotiations, called the Uruguay Round, and earlier negotiations under the GATT. The organization is currently host to new negotiations under the Doha Development Agenda, launched in 2001. The WTO is governed by a Ministerial Conference which meets every two years, a General Council which implements the conference's policy decisions and is responsible for day-to-day administration, and a director-general who is appointed by the Ministerial Conference. The WTO's headquarters are in Geneva, Switzerland. The WTO's stated goal is to improve the welfare of the peoples of its member countries, specifically by lowering trade barriers and providing a platform for negotiations on trade. Its main mission is to ensure that trade flows as smoothly, predictably and freely as possible. It is the WTO's duty to review national trade policies and to ensure the coherence and transparency of trade policies through surveillance in global economic policymaking.

A major priority of the WTO is to provide assistance to developing, least-developed and low-income countries in transition to adjusting to WTO rules and regulations through technical cooperation and training. Over three-quarters of the 150 WTO members are developing countries and countries in transition to a market economy. They play an increasingly important and active role in the WTO because they look to trade (in particular export trade) as a vital tool in their development efforts. Developing countries are a highly diverse group with very different views and concerns, and WTO agreements contain special provisions on developing countries which deal with specific topics such as trade, debt, currency stabilization and technology transfer. For instance, the Secretariat provides technical assistance (mainly training of various kinds) for developing countries, and WTO agreements include numerous provisions giving developing and least-developed countries special rights or extra leniency, so-called 'special and differential treatment'; among these are provisions that allow developed countries to treat developing countries more favourably than other WTO members.

For example, the GATT has a special section (Part 4) on Trade and Development which includes provisions on the concept of 'non-reciprocity' in trade negotiations between developed and developing countries. It means that when developed countries grant trade concessions to developing countries they should not expect those countries to make matching offers in return. Other measures concerning developing countries in the WTO agreements include the granting of extra time for economies in transition to fulfil their commitments, increased trading opportunities through greater market access, and provisions requiring WTO members to safeguard the interests of developing countries when adopting domestic or international trade measures and regulations. The least-developed countries receive extra attention: all agreements recognize that they must benefit from the greatest possible flexibility, and better-off members must make extra efforts to lower import barriers in the case of least-developed countries' exports.

Since the Uruguay Round agreements were signed in 1994, several decisions in favour of least-developed countries have been taken. At the Singapore meeting held in 1996, WTO ministers agreed on a 'Plan of Action for Least-Developed Countries'. This included technical assistance to enable them to participate better in the multilateral system and a pledge from developed countries to improve market access for least-developed countries' products. A year later, in October 1997, six international organizations – the IMF, the International Trade Centre (ITC), the United Nations Conference for Trade and Development, the United Nations Development Programme, the World Bank and the WTO – launched the 'Integrated Framework', a joint technical assistance programme exclusively for least-developed countries. In 2002, the WTO adopted a work programme for the least-developed countries. It contained several broad measures, including improved market access, more technical assistance, support for agencies working

on the diversification of least-developed countries' economies, help in
following the rules of the WTO, and a speedier membership process
for least-developed countries negotiating to join the WTO.[40] The WTO
established a framework for trade policies, in which five principles are
of particular importance in understanding both the pre-1994 GATT
and the post-1995 WTO.[41] These are set out in Box 3.2.

BOX 3.2 **WTO framework for trade policies**

* *Nondiscrimination* The WTO recognizes two major components:
  the 'most favoured nation' rule and the 'national treatment'
  policy. Both are embedded in the main WTO rules on goods,
  services and intellectual property, but their precise scope and
  nature differ across these areas. The 'most favoured nation' rule
  requires that a product made in one member country be treated
  no less favourably than a very similar good that originated in
  any other member country. In other words, grant a country a
  special favour and you have to do the same for all other WTO
  member countries. According to the 'national treatment' rule,
  imported and locally produced goods should be treated equally.
  National treatment ensures that liberalization commitments are
  not offset through the imposition of domestic taxes and similar
  measures.

* *Reciprocity* This principle reflects both a desire to limit the
  scope of freeriding – which may arise because of the 'most
  favoured treatment' rule – and a desire to obtain better access to
  foreign markets. A related point is that for a nation to negotiate
  a trade agreement, it is necessary that the gain from doing so
  be greater than the gain available from unilateral liberalization;
  reciprocal concessions intended to ensure that such gains will
  materialize.[42]

* *Binding and enforceable commitments* The tariff commitments made
  by WTO members in a multilateral trade negotiation and on
  accession are enumerated in a schedule (list) of concessions.
  These schedules establish 'ceiling bindings': a country can change
  its bindings, but only after negotiating with its trading partners,
  which could mean compensating them for loss of trade. If

satisfaction is not obtained, the complaining country may invoke WTO dispute settlement procedures.

- *Transparency*   WTO members are required to publish their trade regulations, to maintain institutions allowing for the review of administrative decisions affecting trade, to respond to requests for information by other members, and to notify changes in trade policies to the WTO. These internal transparency requirements are supplemented and facilitated by periodic country-specific reports (trade policy reviews) through the Trade Policy Review Mechanism (TPRM). The WTO system tries also to improve predictability and stability, discouraging the use of quotas and other measures used to set limits on quantities of imports.

- *Safety valves*   In specific circumstances, governments are able to restrict trade. There are three types of provision in this direction: articles allowing for the use of trade measures to attain non-economic objectives; articles aimed at ensuring 'fair competition'; and provisions permitting intervention in trade for economic reasons.

Source: Bernard Hoekman et al., *Development, Trade and the WTO: A Handbook* (World Bank Washington DC, 2002): 41–9.

The process of becoming a WTO member is unique to each applicant country and the terms of accession are dependent upon the country's stage of economic development and current trade regime. The process takes about five years, on average, but it can last longer if the country is less than fully committed to the process or if political issues interfere. As is typical of WTO procedures, an offer of accession is only given once consensus is reached among all interested parties.[43] During the seven and a half years of the Uruguay Round, over sixty developing countries or countries in transition to market economies implemented trade liberalization programmes.[44] The WTO operates on a one country, one vote system, but actual votes have never been taken. Decision-making is generally by consensus and relative market size is the primary source of bargaining power. The advantage of consensus decision-making is that it encourages efforts to find the most widely acceptable decision. Main disadvantages include large time requirements and many rounds of negotiation to develop a consensus decision, and the tendency for final agreements to use ambiguous language on contentious points, which makes future interpretation of treaties difficult. Of late, the stalemate in the Doha Round is a case in point.

Arguably, this latest round of trade negotiations has been the most important for developing countries, but unfortunately it also appears to be the most contentious. The Doha Round was dubbed the 'Development Round' and its agenda has been aimed specifically at developing countries' concerns about agricultural exports. It has incorporated negotiations already under way on agriculture and services and furthered the process of trade liberalization as mandated in the Uruguay Round Agreements in 1986. The Agreement on Agriculture was adopted at the conclusion of the Uruguay Round of multilateral trade talks on 15 April 1994. It introduced important new rules on the trade of agricultural products and asked for elimination/reduction of agricultural subsidies, but until now very few of these goals have been realized. Developing countries have been vocal critics of agricultural policies in developed countries. During the Fifth WTO Ministerial Conference in Cancún, Mexico, in September 2003, the G20 (now G33) coalition of developing countries, under the leadership of Brazil, was instrumental in opposing a framework agreement based loosely on a proposal submitted jointly by the European Union and the United States that in effect would preserve EU and US subsidies for agriculture in international trade. Since then, developing countries have emerged as a significant political force and have been successful in securing agricultural agreements that address a number of their concerns. Overall, though, the Doha Round of negotiations has stalled.[45]

The Doha Round also marks the round of negotiations where a commitment was made to deal with sustainable development and environmental issues. This is the first time in the history of multilateral trade talks that such negotiations have been introduced. Pascal Lamy, director general of the WTO, stated in an address to the UNEP Global Ministerial Environment forum in Nairobi on 5 February 2007 that a failure of the Doha negotiations 'would strengthen the hand of all those who argue that economic growth should proceed unchecked without regard for the environments', and that 'trade, and indeed the WTO, must be made to deliver sustainable development'.[46]

Recognizing that only very modest first steps have been taken, he stressed that proper pricing of resources and sound energy policy were among the issues that had to be addressed and that externalities would have to be internalized in order to arrive at a more sustainable development strategy. While the Doha Round offered an opportunity to expand environmental concerns within the WTO, no substantive actions have been taken so far. At the Cancún Ministerial Meeting in 2003, some developing countries, including Brazil, India, China and South Africa, called for the incorporation of environmental protection rules in the negotiations about the implementation of competition and investment policy, but developed nations led by the USA, the EU and Japan rejected these suggestions and the issues were subsequently dropped from the agenda of the Doha Round.[47] Other attempts by NGOs and policy institutes to incorporate environmental issues at the Cancún meeting also failed. However, although progress has been slow, and environmental concerns have been neglected during the Cancún Ministerial, some feel that there are good reasons for NGOs and civil society organizations to remain in discussion with the WTO on the reform of environmental rules and mechanisms within the world trade system.

On 22 May 2003, shortly before the onset of negotiations in Cancún in September, some eighty international civil society experts came together in Washington DC for a one-day symposium on 'Investment, Sustainable Development and the WTO'.[48] The symposium was co-organized by Friends of the Earth USA, Oxfam America, the Center for International Environmental Law, the Global Development and Environmental Institute at Tufts University, the National Wildlife Federation and the Heinrich Böll Foundation North America. Friends of the Earth had been sceptical about the real intentions of the WTO with respect to environmental concerns. In their view, the proposed agreement on Non-Agricultural Market Access (NAMA) as part of the Doha Round immediately threatened to harm the environment and developing country economies.[49] The WTO proposal included the requirement that all natural resources would be fair game for either partial or complete trade liberalization, and developing countries could lose their ability to use national policies to protect their resource base and to promote development, fight unemployment and poverty, and thus countries would be forced to rely more heavily on the unsustainable and harmful export of natural resources. The agreement would also put undue pressure on developing countries to open up their service sectors. Furthermore, Friends of the Earth believed that the negotiations posed a threat to the capacity of countries to regulate basic services in the pursuit of social and development goals such as reform of education, water, health and energy sectors.

Popular opposition is effectively now a significant counterforce pressuring many WTO member states to reject the agenda pushed by the world's largest multinational corporations, which have used the WTO Secretariat and negotiators of the world's most powerful countries to write the rules of the global economy in favour of FDI. To date, most press coverage of the Doha Round collapse has played the blame game – focusing on which countries have failed to make specific agricultural concessions. But the underlying cause of the breakdown is growing scepticism about the WTO's real intentions and, more broadly speaking, the rejection of the corporate-led globalization model. Since the Doha Round's 2001 launch, every deadline on issues from service-sector liberalization to industrial tariffs has passed without resolution. In 2004 half of the original Doha agenda – adding new foreign investor rights and imposing limits on countries' competition and procurement policies – was simply jettisoned after the Cancún WTO summit imploded. At issue throughout have been major differences regarding the WTO's objectives and direction.[50]

Instead of promised gains during the WTO decade, economic conditions for the majority of people in the developing world have deteriorated. The number of people living on less than $2 a day has increased. Indeed, there is a growing consensus among a majority of the WTO membership that the neoliberal economic and policy model has failed to deliver economic growth or a higher standard of living for most of the world's population. Meanwhile, electoral victories for political leaders who have made rejection of the neoliberal agenda a staple of their political agenda were secured. Nowhere is this more evident than in Bolivia, Argentina and Venezuela, whose economies all suffered under previous neoliberal governments. After adopting alternative domestic economic policies, Argentina and Venezuela now boast the highest economic growth and fastest poverty reduction in the region. Likewise, Bolivia's president Evo Morales was elected on a platform of opposition to flawed trade deals after previous neoliberal governments' policies resulted in a lower per capita GDP today in Bolivia than twenty-seven years ago. In Costa Rica, Peru and Mexico presidential elections have been dominated almost entirely by debate over trade liberalization.

Although the stated aim of the WTO is to promote free trade and stimulate economic growth, much public discourse and a considerable body of expert literature assert that global free trade results in the rich (both individuals and countries) becoming richer, while the poor get poorer. Martin Khor, director of the WTO watchdog Third World Network, maintains that the WTO does not manage the global economy impartially but has in its operation a systematic bias towards rich countries and multinational corporations, harming smaller countries with less negotiating power.[51] He argues that developing countries have not benefited from the WTO agreements of the Uruguay Round, because import quotas and non-tariff barriers still obstruct developing countries' export positions. Meanwhile, domestic support and export subsidies for agricultural products in the developed countries remain very high and the opening up of developed countries' agricultural markets has yet to materialize. Following protracted negotiations, the EU finally agreed, at the Hong Kong Ministerial in 2005, to eliminate export subsidies by the end of 2013. The USA, for its part, agreed to eliminate export subsidies for its cotton farmers in 2006, although it keeps US$3.8 billion in place for domestic subsidies.[52]

Some critics have characterized decision-making in the WTO as complicated, ineffective, unrepresentative, and non-inclusive. For instance, Third World Network has called the WTO the least transparent of international organizations because the vast majority of developing countries have very little real say in the WTO system. The Network stresses that civil society groups and institutions must be given genuine opportunities to express their views and to influence the outcome of WTO policies and decision-making. With respect to development issues crucial for the post-2012 climate regime, Third World Network reminds its audience that it is important to put forward proposals that promote the environment and development interests of developing countries, and insists that the impact of economic globalization on the environment be addressed; otherwise it would become much more difficult for developing countries to switch to an emission-stabilization pathway.[53]

Economic globalization and the environment

With regard to the debate about the impact of economic globalization on the environment, opinions are varied. The traditional neoliberal point of view is that competitive markets provide the most effective mechanism for the allocation of resources and that free trade makes every nation a player on a global scale and gives every person equal access to goods and services in the most efficient way. For as long as each country trades the commodities it is most suited to produce through 'comparative advantage' in exchange for commodities from other countries, optimal conditions for wealth and efficiency are created. Economic growth, in turn, increases the potential for nations to institute environmental protections, as it enables governments to tax and raise revenue for the abatement of pollution and the general protection of the environment.[54] Furthermore, FDI, trade liberalization and efficiency gains from economic integration allow developing countries to 'leapfrog' into a more technologically advanced stage of development and speed up the adoption of cleaner technologies and management methods.[55] Unfortunately, this economic vision – central to most modern theories of international trade – ignores the historical-political conditions under which commodities were traded. In fact 'competitive advantage', rather than comparative advantage established through market dominance and political power, is probably a more significant determinant of economic specialization and resource allocation.[56]

The optimistic neoliberal viewpoint appears to be supported by the environmental Kuznets curve for developed countries, where an inverted 'U' shape curve shows the relationship between national average income and the state of the environment (Figure 3.1).[57] In this conceptualization, an improvement in the environment is preceded by an earlier period of environmental deterioration concomitant with

FIGURE 3.1 **Environmental Kuznets curve**

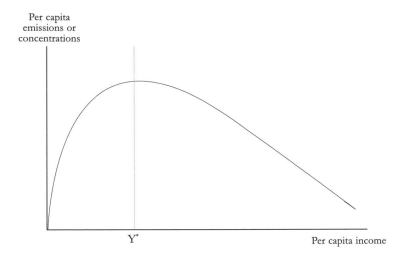

Per capita
emissions or
concentrations

Y*

Per capita income

Source: Stern Review on the Economics of Climate Change, Cambridge University Press, Cambridge, 2007: Annex 7A, Figure 7A.1

economic growth, but over the long term environmental conditions greatly improve. Some case studies have suggested that foreign trade and capital mobility through FDI have facilitated the transfer of green technologies and improvement in environmental management practices.[58] Other studies, however, suggest that with rapid global economic integration, irreversible environmental deterioration has occurred.[59] The different outcomes are likely related to the lack of institutional and/or regulatory control. The 'competitive advantage' through market dominance and political power on the part of TNCs lessens the control mechanisms available to developing countries and throws into question the integrity of capitalism as a system of production that protects the environment. Without the governing mechanisms in place to harness the 'invisible hand' of the marketplace, unsustainable development and widespread environmental deterioration may occur.

The question then arises of whether any of the optimistic thinking applies to CO_2 emissions. Some evidence suggests that whereas the inverted U-shaped relationship between per capita income and per capita emissions may apply to local pollutants like NO, SO_2 and

FIGURE 3.2 **Income effects on CO_2 emissions, USA 1990**

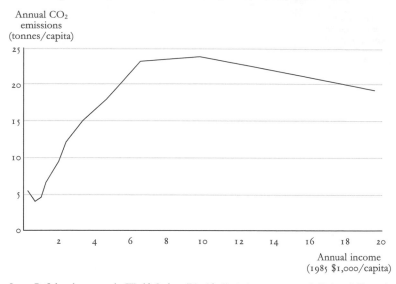

Source: R. Schmalensee et al., 'World Carbon Dioxide Emissions: 1950–2050', *Review of Economics and Statistics* 80(1), 1998: 15–27.

heavy metals, where well-to-do communities and political power elites demand cleaner air and water, in the case of greenhouse gases the argument is less convincing. As societies become wealthier, they may well want to improve their own environment, but there is little they can do about climate change by reducing CO_2 emissions on their own. This differs from the situation for local pollutants for which environmental Kuznets curves have been estimated (see Figure 3.1).[60] There is far greater incentive for communities affected by local air pollution to set up abatement programmes and political and regulatory mechanisms to control pollution than it is for them to deal with CO_2 emissions. Whereas income effects certainly have an impact on increases in CO_2 emissions, there does not seem to be a significant reduction with annual income increase per head as we see for local pollutants, and thus CO_2 emissions patterns relative to national per capita income seem to defy the validity of the environmental Kuznets curve (Figure 3.2).[61]

Add to this the fact that much energy-intensive production is shifting to lower-income countries as part of a 'new geographical division of labour' within the global economy and it seems clear that many developing countries will be in the upside of the environmental Kuznets curve for some time to come. Poor and middle-income countries will have to grow for a long time before they approach the levels of per capita income where Schmalensee et al. (1998) see a downturn in emissions.[62] If we use their data as the basis for projections of future emissions, emissions growth will likely be positive up to a forecast date well beyond 2050.

This leads us to the issue of 'pollution havens'.[63] This concept suggests that polluting industries tend to migrate towards poorer countries with weaker (or poorly enforced) environmental standards. Differences in national environmental standards would thus lead to an unequal distribution of environmental burdens between different regions of the world as environment, and/or energy-intensive industries and activities would seek out developing countries with lax or poorly enforced environmental standards. Empirical studies do not always support this hypothesis and sometimes suggest that environmental standards are just one factor among many other location factors and that environmental costs are negligible in comparison with other costs in location decisions.[64] While labour costs, political stability and the size of the internal market are often more important factors in decisions about location, free-trade regimes have led to rapidly deteriorating environmental conditions nonetheless in some parts of the world. A good example is Mexico after NAFTA took effect. While Mexico is perhaps not serving as a 'pollution haven' for American industries, environmental conditions have rapidly deteriorated nevertheless. This is likely explained by the lack of proper institutional mechanisms for preventing environmental impacts and systematic underinvestment in environmental protection and improvement.[65]

An even more pessimistic view of the globalization process argues that global competition by means of absolute – not comparative – advantage, allowed by the international mobility of capital, will lead to a deterioration of both environmental and labour standards at the global level.[66] In the 'race to the bottom', industrialized countries' labour forces will face an erosion of social contracts and a deterioration of standards driven by competition with unorganized labour in poorer countries in the world. Here too, the evidence in support of the hypothesis is mixed. Whereas many labour leaders in the USA and Europe would argue that this is true, evidence from developing countries often shows the opposite, in that more efficient technologies introduced by foreign firms improve the efficiency of production. Indeed, there is evidence to support the view that relocation of environmental-intensive industries to developing countries has improved the efficiency of production. Nevertheless – and because a fossil-fuel-based infrastructure is developed in support of foreign investment – FDI sets the stage for an energy-intensive development path, as suggested in Chapter 1.[67]

The development of a fossil-fuel-based infrastructure

With all the potential gains made in terms of greater efficiency per production unit, the net result of a shift in production from developed countries in the North to developing countries in the South points in the direction of expansion of a fossil-fuel-based infrastructure and production system. Unless this process is halted or at least more carefully controlled than is presently the case, FDI will have the effect of increasing CO_2 emissions. FDI typically occurs in those parts of the world that have not only opened up to free trade but have also made or are presently making investments in the physical infrastructure supporting such investments, including port facilities, airports, railways and highways, as well as oil refineries, oil and gas pipelines, the electric grid, and dedicating space to accommodate new plants, truck stops, parking facilities, and so on.[68] More recently, telecommunications networks have been added to the list. That this is an important consideration among WTO policy-makers is clear from recent statements made by Director-General Pascal Lamy at the Aid-for-Trade Conference held in Manila, the Philippines, in September 2007.[69] This initiative was launched at the 2005 Hong Kong Ministerial Conference, which focused on trade capacity and infrastructure-building in developing countries. It was presented as the way for developing countries to harness trade as an engine for growth. The initiative involves cooperation with the private sector and various international organizations, including the World Bank.

Data from the World Bank and public–private partnerships involved in investing in the infrastructure of developing countries are very revealing and show that expansion of foreign trade and FDI has been aided a great deal by investment in the improvement of telecommunications, energy, transportation and water/sewerage infrastructure.[70] Governments around the world have pursued policies that involve the private sector in the delivery and financing of these services. Private participation in infrastructure and reforms was often driven by high costs and the poor performance of state-owned network utilities and services. The scale of this move away from the dominant public-sector model was far more rapid than had been anticipated at the start of the 1990s, with investment flows at a peak at US$114 billion in 1997. Investments fell sharply after the 1997 Asian crises and followed a broadly declining trend for several years afterwards. In 2004 and 2005, investment in infrastructure projects bounced back and grew by 70 per cent to reach US$95 billion.

Earlier, in 1990, the World Bank's Infrastructure Economics and Finance Department formed a partnership with the Public–Private Infrastructure Advisory Facility in 1990. Its purpose was to stimulate private participation in infrastructure projects in low- and middle-income countries. The database that the World Bank partnership maintains highlights the contractual arrangements used to attract private investment, the sources and destinations of investment, and information on the main investors.[71] The World Bank's Private Participation in Infrastructure Project Database shows that in developing countries between 1990 and 2000, Latin America and East Asia captured the lion's share of investment, and that telecommunications and energy were by far the largest receiving sectors.[72] Investment over the period totalled nearly US$500 billion and private investment averaged about 40 per cent of the total for infrastructure in developing countries.[73] From 1990 to 1999 there were 700 energy projects in developing countries involving private investors, and investment in these projects totalled nearly US$190 billion, with foreign capital a major source of funding. Large foreign developers and multinational corporations were the top ten sponsors of private energy projects in developing countries, which accounted for just over a third of total investment.[74] Data for 2003 show that investment flows in the power sector increased by 44 per cent and grew fastest in East Asia and the Pacific region.[75]

Between 1990 and 1997 twenty-six developing countries introduced private participation in the transmission and distribution of natural gas.[76] The form of participation varied – ranging from greenfield projects to the export of natural gas from Algeria to Europe, to a natural gas distribution market in Mexico, to the privatization of existing assets in Argentina and Hungary. During the 1990s the private sector took on the operations and construction risks of seventy-seven natural gas transport projects with investments totalling US$18.9 billion. In transportation, airport management took up an important share of private investment. Airport projects involved eighty-nine locations in twenty-three developing countries, with investments total-ling US$5.4 billion. Some three-fifths of this investment was carried out in 1998 alone, and about two-fifths related to privatization of the Argentine airport system in that year. Analysis of the investment patterns shows that Latin America led in attracting foreign private investors for outsourcing operations and management of transporta-tion systems while governments were transferring networks to the private sector.[77] Long-term foreign concessions for airports, with governments taking a minority shareholding role in the venture, seemed to dominate in the effort to deliver efficient and effective airport infrastructure services to foreign business investors.[78] Also, developing countries turned to the private sector for construction, management and maintenance of toll roads. Between 1990 and 1999, US$61 billion of private investment was committed to 279 projects in twenty-six developing countries, comprising 34,369 kilometres of toll highways, bridges and tunnels.[79]

The private sector has also become increasingly involved in the operation of port facilities following public-sector dominance of the sector since the 1940s. During the past decade the reform of port administration has gained momentum in industrial and developing countries alike. Between 1990 and 1998, 112 port projects with private participation reached financial closure in twenty-eight developing countries, with investment commitments totalling more than US$9 billion. Most projects are in East Asia and Latin America, and are funded in order to sustain competition at a regional level, across networks, and with other transport sectors, such as road and rail.[80] As with airport public–private partnership, efforts to deliver an efficient and effective infrastructure to foreign business investors explains why private investment in the railway sector has increased significantly during the 1990s, with fourteen developing countries reaching financial closure on thirty-seven projects in the period 1990–97.[81]

These patterns and trends in public–private investment in developing countries' infrastructure suggest a rapid implementation of the fossil-fuel-based model of development common in the developed world. Given this trend, the prospect for a transition to an alternative energy provisioning system is not good. Investment decisions undertaken now are likely to set the pace of growth and development for some time to come. These are worrisome trends with respect to opportunities to leapfrog into a different kind of energy system in developing countries in the future. They are also the reason why we suspect that economic growth, energy use and CO_2 emissions trends will go hand in hand. For this reason we find that increase in GNP per capita is correlated with an increase in the use of fossil fuels and coal in particular, as in some parts of the world, such as China and India, coal is still available in great abundance. For, whereas the use of coal for energy is now often restricted through regulations or 'carbon constraints' in the developed world, elsewhere concerns about environmental conditions take a back seat to the need to develop the economy in order to improve living conditions for a largely poor population. Looking at foreign trade and FDI from this perspective can lead to a quite different conclusion about economic globalization and its impact on the environment.

4

The transnational corporation and the global economy

Foreign trade and the transnational corporation

The rapid growth of multinational, or transnational, corporations is one of the most significant developments of the past few decades.[1] Just as individual national economies are dominated by a small number of giant firms, so is the world economy dominated by large transnational corporations. This raises questions about the wisdom of considering solely national states or national governments responsible for emissions produced within their borders. To explain this, we will consider patterns of trade that have emerged with the activity of transnational corporations, which diverge considerably from the traditional international trade patterns established in a time when national governments held sway over economic affairs to a far greater degree than is the case today.

Conventional trade theory assumes that producers and consumers are confined within their respective national borders. Thus, international trade results from production in one country and consumption in another. The activities of multinational corporations significantly complicate this conventional model. Since TNCs are, by definition, located in more than one country and operate their own economic subsystems of spatial interaction, each functional unit of a multinational or transnational corporation is both a global producer and a consumer. This distinction severely complicates the tracking of international trade flows and the attendant material and energy flows and carbon emissions associated with the finished products.[2] The fact that these corporations are referred to as multinational or transnational indicates that they are viewed as enterprises that transcend and frequently compete with the interests of individual countries.[3]

Trade within TNCs, or intra-firm trade, has been increasing along with the global scope of transnational corporate activities. Within the context of the global corporate economy, the domestic product of an American-based firm is tallied as domestic production, as is the gross product of the domestic subsidiary of a foreign-based TNC. Correspondingly, the imports and exports of these firms are calculated on the basis of cross-border movement of goods and services, regardless of the geographic location of ownership, strategic managerial control, or the ultimate flow of economic benefits. As a result, national accounting systems obscure the real impacts and benefits of global economic activity. Thus the idea of an American or Chinese national economy is becoming meaningless given the role of the TNC and of FDI, and national economic accounting practices are called into question. It follows that emissions allocations tabulated solely on the basis of national accounts would need to be adjusted. Given an equitable economic playing field, such accounting nuances would be of little concern; however, within a polarized global political economy, the tracking of such flows is a fundamental precursor to an equitable international environmental management scheme.

A snapshot of the global economy demonstrates that the rhetoric in support of 'free trade' does not mesh with the ideal. Given the political and economic relationships just described, an increase in trade liberalization and economic integration will foster increased economic and political inequities and render more power to TNCs (Box 4.1).[4]

Indeed, it becomes obvious that some of the major global actors are not countries but companies and their shareholders. Thus, recognizing the consolidation of strategic economic resources and decision-making structures on the part of TNCs within the global economy is important. The ability of these economic actors to dictate national economic and environmental policies to the detriment of democratic civic society, in turn, is also a factor to consider as we

---

BOX 4.1   **Transnational corporations as global economic actors**

- According to the 2004 World Investment Report, at least 61,000 TNCs with over 900,000 foreign affiliates were registered with UNCTAD and these affiliates accounted for one-tenth of the world GDP and one-third of the world's exports.[5]
- The UNCTAD *World Investment Report* details the flow of capital of TNCs through FDI. In the Country Fact Sheet on China (2006), it reports for 2005 a total of US$72, 406 million of inward FDI and US$11,306 million of outward FDI. This amounts to 9.2 per cent of gross fixed capital formation for China's economy in 2005.[6] China's total FDI stock amounted to US$317,873 million, or 14.3 per cent of gross fixed capital formation.[7]
- It is estimated that trade among related parties (known as intra-firm trade) represented approximately half of all US imports and one-third of all US exports, and perhaps one-third of worldwide merchandise trade flows in 2000.[8]

Sources: UNCTAD, *World Investment Report*, 2004 and 2006, Geneva; L. Eden, 'Transfer Pricing, Intra-firm Trade and the Bureau of Labor Statistics', Working Paper 334, Bureau of Labor Statistics, Washington DC, January 2001.

---

move towards a more sustainable and equitable emissions-reduction scheme. As the leaders of the developed world constantly reiterate the need for developing countries to participate in global environmental negotiations – citing projections that demonstrate drastic increases in developing countries' economic output and greenhouse-gas emissions – TNCs based and headquartered in developed countries are banking on the exponential growth of developing economies to provide them with profitable business opportunities and expanded market share. With the removal of trade barriers, companies that hold the disproportionate share of the world's capital and control the flow of FDI will be able to exploit internal national markets, usually to the disadvantage or detriment of smaller domestic producers, undermining their economic livelihood and that of their communities. Thus, loss of control on the part of domestic producers in their own national economy has in some way to be recognized and accounted for in a more equitable emissions-reduction scheme.

Foreign direct investment and the transnational corporation

Foreign Direct Investment refers to an investment made to acquire lasting interest in enterprises operating outside of the home country of the investor.[9] The foreign entity or group of associated entities that makes the investment is termed the 'direct investor'. Very often a multinational or transnational corporation is the 'direct investor'. The components of FDI are equity capital, reinvested earnings and other capital – mainly intra-company loans. As countries do not always collect data for each of those components, reported data on FDI and investment strategies by TNCs are not fully comparable across countries. In particular, data on reinvested earnings are often not reported. The unincorporated or incorporated enterprise – a branch or subsidiary, respectively, in which direct investment is made – is referred to as a 'direct investment enterprise'. Some degree of equity ownership is almost always considered to be associated with an effective voice in the management of an enterprise, and a threshold of 10 per cent of equity ownership is usually considered to qualify an investor as a foreign direct investor. For FDI to be profitable, the investor needs to gain an effective voice in the management of the enterprise, but how to define a controlling interest and effective voice in management remains a tricky question.

Other than having an equity stake in an enterprise, there are many other ways in which foreign investors may acquire an effective voice. These include subcontracting, management contracts, turnkey arrangements, franchising, leasing, licensing and production sharing. Information on a franchise (a firm to which a business is subcontracted) or a company which sells most of its production to a foreign firm through means other than an equity stake are not usually reported under FDI, even though some countries have begun to contemplate doing so. For example, the OECD treats financial leases between direct investors and their branches, subsidiaries or associates as if they were conventional loans, and they are therefore included in the definition of FDI. Thus, the most important characteristic of FDI (which distinguishes it from foreign portfolio investment) is that it is undertaken with the intention of exercising control over an enterprise.[10]

Global FDI flows have reached unprecedented levels in the last few decades. From 1970 to 1990, average annual global FDI amounted to US$58 billion or less than 0.5 per cent of global GDP. In 2000, global FDI reached a total of US$1.5 trillion at 4 per cent of global GDP. However, only some 30 per cent of all global FDI between 1990 and 2001 went to developing countries; indeed, the developing countries' share fell off sharply between 1997 and 2000, from 39 to 16 per cent, after the foreign exchange crisis in Southeast Asia. In more recent years FDI has been on the rise again.[11] FDI is highly concentrated in ten mostly large developing countries, led by China, Brazil and Mexico. Between 1990 and 2000, the top ten garnered 76 per cent of the total FDI flowing into developing countries and the trend towards concentration seems to be intensifying. In 2006, developing countries attracted US$380 billion in FDI – more than ever before. While two-thirds of these flows went to rapidly growing markets in Asia, virtually all developing regions participated in the increase. Investments rose particularly fast in many countries that are richly endowed with natural resources.[12]

Among the developing regions, Asia – and in particular China – remained the main magnet for FDI after 2001, followed by Latin America. Africa's share in global FDI was small but its FDI growth rate has increased in the last few years, and a growing part of the FDI derives from China and other East and South Asian countries.[13] Within the UN system, the United Nations Conference on Trade and Development is mandated to monitor the movement of global capital (FDI) and the activities of TNCs. Thus the UNCTAD *World Investment Report* is the most reliable source of information on the flow of capital of TNCs through FDI.[14] The Country Fact Sheet on China (2006) reports for 2005 a total of US$72,406 million of inward FDI and US$11,306 million of outward FDI. This amounts to 9.2 per cent of gross fixed capital formation for China's economy in 2005. China's total FDI stock amounted to US$317,873 million, or 14.3 per cent of gross fixed capital formation (Box 4.1). Perhaps more revealing is cross-border merger and acquisition activity among Chinese and US corporations, which jumped from an annual average of US$36.118 million for 1990–2000 to US$147.551 million in 2005, to US 171.288 in 2006.[15]

The neoliberal tradition of development economics has consistently viewed the impact of FDI on developing countries as benign, a view that derives from prevailing neoliberal assumptions about the conditions of the market economy, as discussed in the previous chapter.[16] In this view, foreign investors contribute new or scarce resources – capital, technology, management and marketing skill – for the benefit of the host country. Their investment increases competition and efficiency while bidding up wages. From this perspective it is difficult not to arrive at the conclusion that FDI is good for economic development in developing countries. Increasingly, however, the outcome has been different, as we saw in the previous chapter, and the assessment of how TNCs affect the development process is much more complex than is traditionally assumed by Western economists.[17] While in theory the relationship between foreign investors and host countries is a bilateral one where the foreign investor has control over capital, technology, management and marketing skills needed to launch a project, and the host country has control over access before the investment is made and over the conditions for operation afterwards and distribution of benefits and profits, in fact the actual relationship is a rather uneven and unequal one, whereby the investor usually has a much stronger bargaining position and can threaten to invest elsewhere if negotiations do not lead to the desired outcome.[18]

As we saw, the central players in FDI are TNCs, which by the very nature of their organizational structure can shift investment easily from one country to another. The TNC is a multinational enterprise comprising affiliates in more than one country which operate under a system of decision-making where the parent company rules. The parent enterprise is linked to its affiliates by ownership, which determines that it exercises a significant influence over them.[19] TNCs locate production in a particular developing country either by purchasing an existing company, through merger or acquisition, or by building new plants and equipment in the form of 'greenfield' investment. For the most part, TNCs invest in other countries in order to gain access to new or larger markets, cheap labour or natural resources. Macroeconomic stability is often considered an important factor in FDI, while countries with volatile exchange rates and high and growing trade deficits tend to be avoided by FDI investors.

As indicated earlier, FDI is increasingly directed towards emerging or developing countries (South and East Asia in particular) and economies in transition (in East and Central Europe). Mexico and some other countries in Latin America are also attracting substantial FDI, and, as we have seen, more recently FDI from some of the emerging economies in South and East Asia is now occurring in other parts of the world. A growing number of TNCs from these economies are becoming major regional – sometimes even global – players.[20] The new links and networks these South and East Asian TNCs are forging with the rest of the world will have repercussions in the shaping of the global economic landscape and environmental climate-change negotiations in the coming decades.[21]

In analysing the geographical contours of the developing global economy, it is evident that TNCs are the drivers in the economic globalization process. Aided by increasingly sophisticated transportation and communications systems, complicated production networks have been developed covering several countries in several continents in ever shifting organizational structures. It is now common to conceive of the production of any good or service as a 'production chain': a linked sequence of functions in production of a good or service that involves a series of transactions between different producers and consumers worldwide. In a chain of production, 'production networks' of inter- and intra-firm relationships are important. In the global context it is the TNC that coordinates these production networks. TNC production networks can be internalized (performing functions 'in-house') or externalized (outsourced to other firms), and operate through a series of internal or external transactions. In fact, many global business firms contain a spectrum of different forms of coordination consisting of networks of interrelationships within and between firms. These networks are in a continuous state of flux, and the boundaries between internalized and externalized operations are constantly changing. The national state continues to be one of the most important bounded territorial forms in which production networks operate, but supranational institutions such as the IMF, the World Bank and the WTO, or regional free-trade areas like the EU or NAFTA, are becoming increasingly important actors in the regulatory regimes affecting TNCs.[22]

Intra-firm trade, transfer pricing and production chains

Products that are traded internationally but that stay within the organizational unit of a multinational enterprise or TNC represent a significant and growing portion of foreign trade for a growing number of countries, developed as well as developing. This type of trade is called 'intra-firm trade', as opposed to international trade among unrelated parties. Intra-firm trade is an important part of the process of globalization and is the essence of the establishment of production networks through foreign branches and subsidiaries or affiliates. The phenomenon of intra-firm trade is of interest to trade and environmental policymakers, including those working on climate-change policy. It is often assumed that intra-firm trade reflects the foreign production activities of TNCs as they transfer factors of production from one country to another. A growing literature is emerging on the phenomenon of intra-firm trade and we now begin to understand more about the production network structures that have been built up by TNCs in the past few decades.

In order to understand intra-firm trade patterns, we need to know about the relationship between the parent companies, their affiliates, and other firms involved in the transactions.[23] Data on intra-firm trade is hard to obtain and usually involves surveying the companies involved in FDI. In order to assess their overseas activities, the US Department of Commerce has begun to publish data on 'related-party', or intra-firm, trade between US affiliates and their foreign parent companies and between foreign affiliates and US parent companies.[24] It is estimated that in 2000 trade among related parties of TNCs represented approximately half of all US imports and one-third of all US exports, and perhaps one-third of worldwide merchandise trade flows (see Box 4.1).[25] Data on the trade of foreign affiliates with Japanese parent companies is available from Japan's Ministry of International Trade and Industry. The European Union does not provide consolidated figures that measure intra-firm trade, but patchy evidence suggests that FDI and intra-firm trade of European-headquartered TNCs is not dissimilar to US FDI and intra-firm trade.[26] Trade between TNC firms and (non-equity) subcontractors in countries where the assembly production is conducted is generally referred to as 'intra-industry trade'.[27] There is now a growing body of literature available on intra-firm and intra-industry trade in manufactured goods between several Asian and Latin American countries and US, EU and Japanese firms, and more recently other Asian firms. The activity often involves assembly-line production based on imported parts and components in different countries, and between different firms and subcontractors within and between different developing countries.[28]

Intra-firm and intra-industry trade between countries sometimes reflects the impact of regional trading blocs like NAFTA (between Mexico, Canada and the USA) or the EU (between Western Europe and economies in transition in eastern and central Europe). The elimination of tariff barriers and Mexico's relatively low labour costs have led to the setting up of a large number of maquiladora plants, which are under foreign control and located in the border region with the United States and devoted to the assembly and re-export of goods. Among the countries in eastern and central Europe intra-firm trade during the 1990s was the highest in the Czech Republic, Hungary, Poland and Slovakia. These countries are characterized by high and increasing flows of FDI, especially from Germany.[29] The correlation with high FDI inflows is consistent with the increasing extent to which TNCs have located parts of their production operations in these countries.[30] The growing complexity of these production networks involves outsourcing through vertical trading systems often spanning several countries. Although there is considerable anecdotal evidence concerning this phenomenon, there is surprisingly little in the way of data at the aggregate level by which to gauge its overall importance.[31] Input–output analysis can sometimes be used to measure the input of imported parts in the production of export goods, but these data are not consistently available. From some research in this area, vertical specialization is estimated at around 20 per cent of exports of the major emerging market economies in 1990 and accounts for about 30 per cent of the growth in these exports between 1970 and 1990.[32] Unfortunately, more recent information is not available and therefore only by extension can we guess what the importance of vertical specialization may be today.

BOX 4.2 **Summary on intra-firm trade and transfer pricing**

- Much intra-firm trade between high-income countries is of nearly finished goods destined for affiliate companies that are involved in marketing and distribution with little additional manufacturing processing taking place. About two-thirds of US intra-firm imports by TNCs with a foreign-based parent company is directed to an affiliate involved in marketing and distribution. This suggests that FDI usually occurs for reason of gaining market access.

- Some middle-income countries have intra-firm trade with highly developed countries. The foreign affiliate located in middle-income countries is likely to be manufacturing to produce goods that are destined for other markets, including the country of the parent company. In 2000, two-thirds of US imports from Mexico were intra-firm due to extensive maquiladora operations. In the case of Japan, most intra-firm trade was with Southeast Asian countries.

- Evidence suggests that the importance of intra-firm trade between emerging middle-income economies and highly developed economies has been increasing substantially during the 1990s and early 2000s. In the case of the United States intra-firm trade with China, Korea and Mexico has increased substantially while intra-firm trade with the rest of the world has remained stable or declined. In the case of Japan, intra-firm import trade from the rest of Asia increased much more than from other parts of the world during the 1990s.

- Based on the above findings it appears that international intra-firm trade has different characteristics than international trade between unrelated parties. An important question then emerges with respect to measures of traditional economic variables such as import/export, national income, balance of payments and balance of trade, and measurements and accounting for CO_2 emissions in climate-change policy.

- Various tariff provisions encourage intra-firm trade within TNCs by allowing low-duty or duty-free importation of goods set abroad for processing or final assembly. In the United States, two tariff schedules exist under the Offshore Assembly Provision (OAP), which encourages US companies to assemble goods for domestic consumption in countries with low labour costs.

Tariffs are collected only on the foreign value-added of the re-entering goods. If cheap labour represents the bulk of the value-added, the tariffs are correspondingly low.

• A significant portion of TNC intra-firm trade is conducted with tax avoidance in mind. Most countries collect income taxes but apply variable rates and types of deductions and credits so as to attract foreign investment. A TNC can play off one country's tax system against another through the exercise of transfer pricing. Transfer pricing allows a TNC to shift taxable income from a high-tax country to a low-cost country, or to hide taxable income altogether.

Source: Summarized from 'Intra-industry and Intra-firm Trade and the Internationalization of Production,' OECD *Economic Outlook* 71, 2002.

Intra-firm trade flows can obscure the true exchange of goods as TNCs use under-invoice or over-invoice intra-firm transactions through 'transfer pricing'. Transfer pricing is a system of preferential pricing of intra-firm transfers. It allows a TNC to shift taxable income from a high-tax country to a low-tax country or to hide taxable income altogether. In some instances, 'tax havens' are used to eliminate tax liability.[33] In other instances, transfer pricing occurs because of attempts at avoiding tariffs. In addition, a firm may not report any transactions due to confidentiality as firm-specific data are not usually or always disclosed.[34] Transfer pricing has taken on an increasingly important part in TNC activities and reflects their growing role in the global economy. It is estimated that intra-firm trade accounts for around one-third of goods exports from Japan and the United States, and half of all US goods imports and a quarter of all Japanese goods imports. In the case of the United States these shares have been broadly stable over the last decade, but in the case of Japan they have increased substantially. Moreover, given the increasing importance of FDI relative to both world trade and output (GDP), it is likely that the importance of intra-firm trade has increased at the global level as well. The manufacturing products subject to a high degree of intra-firm trade are also those with a high degree of intra-industry trade. Intra-firm trade is particularly heavily concentrated in transportation equipment, computer and electronic products, machinery and chemicals.[35]

These patterns in intra-industry and intra-firm trade reflect the increasing importance of the internationalization of production or the development of production networks. Thus, to the extent that a country's trade is dominated by goods that are part of a vertically integrated production chain or network spread across more than one country (and increasingly between developing countries and developed countries), the question has to be asked, how do we account for emissions created at one end of the production chain, and the consumption of or profit made at the other end of the production chain?

Managing the global commons in the era of globalization

The above analysis demonstrates that global climate change debates are being conducted within narrow conceptual parameters and fail to address fully the realities of the current global economy. Transnational corporations, not nations, are the primary economic actors. Moreover, while free-trade apologists point to the benefits of the growing liberalization of markets in increasing product choice and economic opportunity, they fail to address the growing centralized integration of global production networks. Although production may be taking place in more areas of the world and more goods are crossing national borders, the nexus of global economic governance is consolidating in the hands of TNCs, and as a result economic planning and decision-making are becoming further and further removed from those for whom it matters most – the workers and consumers of both the developed and the developing worlds.[36] As corporate power increases and cooperative networks between TNCs expand, hosting governments cede strategic economic and political decision-making and planning to corporations and markets; as a result citizen participation and environmental affairs are severely marginalized. Correspondingly, the ability of TNCs to externalize environmental costs within less developed and less democratic economic markets has increased. Given these macroeconomic dynamics, economic policy can no longer exist in a vacuum, disconnected from environmental and social policy. The failure to integrate these policy realms will serve to preclude effective and equitable global environmental management (see Figure 1.1).

As we have seen, much international trade actually represents the movement of goods within the integrated global production apparatus of TNCs, and thus the term 'trade' is a misnomer.[37] Yet economic analysts constantly invoke the trade mantra when speaking of the benefits of globalization. As economic production in developing countries is often foreign-based – or, more specifically, stateless through FDI on the part of transnational corporations – so are the environmental problems engendered through such TNC activities. So, even though the global economy – that is, the transnational activity of increasingly stateless corporations – is commonly characterized in terms of activity between nation-states, such a conceptualization masks the economic and managerial dynamics at work, as well as the responsibility for the environmental results of corporate production and development patterns. Any production chain is in essence a production system of materials flows, which place demands on the natural environment in two ways: (1) in terms of inputs to the process of production as resources; and (2) in terms of outputs to the natural environment in the form of pollution or emissions. With regard to these environmental concerns, the various aspects of global production, distribution and consumption raise issues about the regulatory governance dynamics linked to the current economic globalization process. The first observation we can make is that the divergent process of economic globalization and global governance has been highly uneven and has left many countries outside the global realm. Second, the degree to which integration in the international arena is developing points to a rapid pace of economic integration, as compared to a slow pace of progress on the part of the international institutional infrastructure addressing global governance challenges in the fields of environmental control, health and safety concerns, security, immigration and labour.

Clearly the failure of the Doha Round of negotiations at the WTO is an example of this, as discussed in the previous chapter. The Doha Declaration presented significant opportunities to build environmental concerns into the WTO, but so far has paid only lip service to these concerns, with little attempt being made to integrate environmental protection and trade expansion. The Declaration outlines a broad range of negotiating issues, including the relationship between existing WTO rules and specific trade obligations set out in various multilateral environmental agreements and the Kyoto Protocol, and the it directs the Committee on Trade and Environment (CTE) to act as a forum to identify and debate environmental aspects of the negotiations in order to help achieve the objective of sustainable development.[38] Yet, beyond its directive to the CTE, the Doha Declaration contains few specific mechanisms for the elaboration of policies that address the environmental issues it outlines. Moreover, its language is overly vague and sometimes contradictory. For example, while the Declaration states that no country should be prevented from taking measures to protect the environment and health at levels it deems appropriate, it also states that this should be in accord with existing WTO provisions. The Declaration commits to negotiations on multilateral environmental agreements but only on the narrow issue of same-party membership, and even then it says that the outcome of the negotiations cannot change existing rights and obligations under WTO rules. Furthermore, while the Declaration gives new instructions to the CTE, which could lead to negotiations on WTO rules, it says the existing rights and obligations of governments cannot be added to or diminished – so it may not be possible for the anticipated negotiations to accomplish much. And, finally, the Declaration makes no effort to reform the CTE, which has shown over the years that it is too narrowly based and lacks the resources to implement any policy changes. Indeed, the CTE has failed to make any policy recommendations of consequence with respect to environmental concerns and is only now starting the debate on climate-change mitigation. Director-General Pascal Lamy in a speech to a European Parliament Panel in May 2008 stated that an international accord on climate change is badly needed but that the WTO is still waiting for a global consensus on the issue.[39]

While in a few cases the emergence of an innovative international institutional framework has allowed worldwide concerted actions to prevent the deterioration of global environmental public goods, or 'global commons' – the most effective example of which is the ban on CFCs to prevent the depletion of the ozone layer – in many other areas the lack of such a framework has been manifest, as for instance in the area of climate change. Actions and tasks for the global governance of environmental issues are currently scattered in different institutions, with, on the whole, significantly lower budgets and political influence than similar bodies dealing with economic issues. While some analysts think that this gap should be filled through the creation of a 'world environmental organization' in charge of coordinating global environmental governance, others argue that a new agency will simply add another layer of bureaucracy to an already difficult-to-handle network of treaties and organizations.

If the global economic landscape were a more equal playing field and if the economic and socio-political benefits of globalization were more evenly distributed, issues like these would not matter so much. However, under the current conditions in the global economy, social and political impacts do matter as the perceived and actual benefits of globalization vary a great deal between different parts of the world and between different groups of people. Whereas in some parts of South and East Asia economic integration has led to rapid economic growth and in some cases reduced poverty levels and contributed to more equal income distribution, in parts of Latin America the opposite is the case.[40] For example, the annual average rate of GDP per capita growth of Mexico – one of the most open economies of the world – has been about 1 per cent per year during the 1990s. Many other countries in the region show similar or much worse performances. Concomitantly, inequality and poverty levels have increased in almost all the countries of the region.[41] The performance of many African countries – with few exceptions – has been most disappointing, in particular in the case of the least-developed countries in the sub-Saharan region. Even though many African countries have adopted structural adjustment programmes and have introduced policies liberalizing trade and capital flows, both the share of African exports as a proportion of global exports and the share of FDI targeting African countries as a proportion of total FDI in developing countries have fallen during the last decade, which indicates a 'marginalization' of the continent from the globalization process even though FDI inflows (in particular from South and East Asian countries) have been on the rise in recent years.[42]

These examples reveal that there is not a universal pattern in the relationship between global economic integration and economic and socio-political development. Whereas SAPs were set up to streamline free trade and create more open markets, many Latin American and African countries have low rates of FDI and TNC investment, in contrast to China, for instance, where economic policies were guided to a large extent by central (communist) government dictates, but in which case FDI and TNC investment has been a great deal more pronounced. Thus, the Latin American and African countries do not support what is commonly assumed to be the direct positive relationship between more open markets, trade expansion or increased FDI and economic growth and development. In the case of countries with low trade barriers, it is not clear which is the direction of the causal relationship: does growth lead to trade or is trade driving growth?[43] It seems, therefore, reasonable to conclude that there is no clear-cut relationship between economic globalization, economic growth and levels of poverty and inequality.[44] Ensuring sustained economic growth and maintaining export trade through FDI have become major challenges to many developing countries in the last decade. Competition for market share has become fierce as China and India, in particular, have become leading exporters of manufactured products. As South and East Asia have expanded production in the global economy, Latin America has seen a retrenchment. The political instability in many countries in Central and South America can be viewed as evidence of this.

The corporate threat to the global atmospheric commons[45]

As has been shown, much international trade actually represents the movement of goods within the integrated global production apparatus of TNCs, which poses a particular challenge for accounting of greenhouse-gas emissions.[46] It can be concluded that the failure to incorporate these dynamics of global production into climate-change negotiations would preclude effective and equitable solutions. The declining role of the state in the global economy and the increasing reach of transnational corporations throughout the world pose a serious challenge to the environmental integrity and success of international environmental treaties. This raises questions about the efficacy and equity of emissions trading under the Kyoto Protocol, as we will see in the following chapters. Patterns of FDI in the developing world support continued carbon-intensive development patterns, which will make the long-term goals of the Kyoto Protocol more difficult to achieve. Meanwhile, responsibility for, or ownership of, the pool of carbon emissions generated in developing countries through FDI raises questions about the justifiability of giving emissions rights and emissions credits to Annex I countries through emissions trading and CDM projects undertaken by transnational corporations.[47] Given the dynamics of the global economy, the climate-change treaty as it exists today will have little impact on greenhouse-gas reduction, and the failure of the Kyoto Protocol and the EU Emissions Trading Scheme may preclude effective and equitable solutions to global climate change for generations to come.[48]

The simultaneous efforts to institutionalize global trade policy through the WTO, the World Bank and the IMF, and the so-called free-trade model pursued in most parts of the world today, have opened up new locations for manufacturing production and new markets in developing countries and countries in transition in eastern and central Europe and Asia through privatization, FDI, and carbon-intensive development, seriously challenging the Kyoto Protocol. Considering that relocation of production considerations always plays a role in TNC decision-making, in the carbon-constraint economy of the EU, production relocation decisions on the part of transnational corporations are taking on an increasingly important role.[49] It is obvious that goods that contain more carbon or were produced in an energy-intensive way will be relatively more expensive under the ETS regime than goods that contain less carbon and were produced in a more energy-efficient way. Since the production cost of goods that have high carbon content and/or require high energy input will be priced higher in Europe than elsewhere, expansion or relocation of production to non-carbon-constraint countries would seem very likely (Figure 1.1).

Although various considerations play a role in location decisions, a factor of increasing importance noted by corporate investors and policymakers is differential environmental costs and regulatory burdens across national boundaries. Until recently, environmental costs of production were external to the cost of production, but under the conditions of the Kyoto Protocol and the EU ETS this is no longer the case. It is estimated that the cost of electricity derived from coal or oil may double and that the cost of energy production derived from gas may increase by 30 per cent in the EU, if all external costs in the form of damage to the environment and health are taken into account. This would make the cost of production, including energy costs for energy-intensive industries, substantially higher in Europe than is the case today. In addition, increasing environmental regulation within the developed economies is already forcing a partial internalization of regulatory costs; and, with the establishment of institutionalized international free-trade regimes, energy- or carbon-intensive industries may be induced to relocate to countries where environmental regulations are less stringent and where no carbon constraints apply. Simultaneously, host economies may encourage the export of manufactured products to nearby developed or home markets. Some developing countries have set up free-trade zones or 'export platforms', explicitly in order to serve the needs of trans-national corporations and developed-country home markets. Lower environmental and energy costs, along with lower labour costs, are among the corporate strategic considerations to locate in third-country 'free-trade zones'. The maquiladora system in Mexico is a good example of this. Free-trade zones or 'export platforms', typically, were set up to attract foreign investors and to facilitate the re-export of assembled products.

Over half of the largest 100 US corporations operated assembly plants in Mexico during the late 1990s after implementation of trade rules introduced by NAFTA, and many took advantage of less stringent environmental regulatory enforcement or access to subsidized or cheaper available energy sources.[50] It is now realized that the introduction of trading blocs like NAFTA or the EU, and of structural adjustment programmes implemented by the IMF and the World Bank during the 1980s and 1990s, have had serious adverse environmental impacts. Under the conditions of the reforms imposed upon developing countries and economies in transition, competitiveness was emphasized and sustainability was downplayed.[51] As a result, tighter environmental standards in the developed nations can lead to the decision to relocate energy- or carbon-intensive industry to the developing world if other market conditions justify the move. According to a report issued by the American Iron and Steel Institute (AISI), worldwide production of steel has increased by about 470 million tonnes during the last decade with most of the expansion occurring in countries that use less energy-efficient production methods and impose weaker environmental regulation or enforcement.[52] China's share of world production of steel, for instance, has almost tripled from 13 per cent in 1996 to 35 per cent in 2006, a 316 per cent increase (see Table 4.1). China's steel export also tripled, increasing 309 per cent between 1995 and 2005, and China is now the largest steel-exporting country in the world. India, similarly, is rapidly expanding its steel production capacity and export. The AISI report concludes that if measures to control greenhouse-gas concentrations do not take international trade and environmental costs into account, then GHG emissions will increase globally as producers in carbon-constraint countries move production to countries where environmental and GHG emissions standards and controls are less stringent and where environmental compliance costs are much lower.

A study conducted by researchers from the US National Center for Atmospheric Research (NCAR) confirmed this, and calculated that between 1997 and 2005 higher levels of Chinese exports to the United States increased total carbon dioxide emissions by some 720 million tonnes.[53] AISI supports a voluntary approach to climate-change policy and voices support for President Bush's proposal to develop a new post-2012 framework on climate change that would be global in scope, sector-specific, and foster development and deployment of clean energy technologies around the world through technology transfer and public–private partnerships.[54] In such a scheme, according to AISI, China, India, Brazil and other large emitting countries would have to become active partners in a programme that merely shifted manufacturing-related greenhouse-gas emissions to other parts

TABLE 4.1A **Changes in world steel production, 1996–2006**

Producer	Change (million tonnes)	Change (%)
China	320.9	316.9
Russia/Ukraine	40.0	55.9
EU	28.5	16.9
Japan/Korea	26.9	19.5
Other	16.6	22.4
India	14.3	60.4
Other OECD	9.9	41.3
NAFTA	7.0	5.7
Brazil	5.7	22.4

TABLE 4.1B **Changes in world steel exports, 1995–2005**

Producer	1995 (million tonnes)	2005 (million tonnes)	Change (%)
CIS	42.5	63.3	48.9
Other	32.3	50.3	55.7
Japan/Korea	29.4	48.1	63.6
China	6.7	27.4	309.0
EU	27.6	22.4	−18.8
NAFTA	15.0	20.9	39.3
South America	13.9	17.2	23.7
Other OECD	11.9	15.6	31.1
India	1.4	6.0	328.6

Source: American Iron and Steel Institute (AISI), 'Environmental Aspects of Global Trade in Steel: The North American Steel Industry Perspective, 2006: 4–5; http://www.steel.org/AM/Template. cfm?Section=Articles8&contentid=20532&TEMPLATE=/CM/ContentDisplay.cfm.

of the world, and thereby failed to address global climate-change concerns. Of course, such a scheme would greatly benefit better capitalized TNCs and be likely to undermine the competitive position of host-country domestic producers, but it might also actively encourage transfer in energy-efficient and low-emitting production technology.

Environmental costs in the form of pollution abatement and compliance and prevention are usually considered less important in comparison with other costs of production.[55] But, whereas this may be the case with many kinds of environmental problems, greenhouse-gas emissions-reduction costs are a different matter. Here, carbon constraints on production translate into higher energy costs and thus higher production costs. For example, in aluminium production approximately 35 per cent of the cost is energy. Furthermore, many developing countries have actively recruited energy-intensive industries with promises of cheap energy and suitable infrastructure. Therefore, even if labour costs, political stability and the size of the internal market are more important factors of location than environmental restraints, the fact that some countries have greater abundance of energy sources available and fewer carbon constraints may become a more determining factor in the future.

For as long as the contradictions and tensions between economic globalization and climate-change policy remain unresolved, there will be a greater likelihood that global warming threats will persist and get worse. Therefore, if we consider the atmosphere as the 'global commons', we will inevitably have to face up to the question of who is to blame, and who is to pay. As national economic and environmental regulation loses its primacy with the advent of multilateral trade agreements that institutionalize the legal rights of transnational corporations to export profits – as is the case under the WTO rules – no countervailing environmental rule of law has emerged to regulate their activities. As economic globalization makes it more difficult to track the operations of these firms, regulated oversight becomes increasingly necessary. To the extent that global economic dynamics have been considered, the policy measures devised have lacked the complexity and subtlety needed to address the environmental impacts of the globalization of the world economy.

As the Washington establishment points to the increasing environmental responsibility of the developing world, they simultaneously advocate policies that seek to institutionalize the strategic penetration of developing countries' economies by industrialized countries' global corporations. The possibility that the activities of transnational companies may be promoting unjust and unsustainable development patterns in the developing world is rarely considered.[56] Moreover, the central question of who stands to profit from certain development patterns within the globalizing world and whether the financial imperatives of transnational corporations are engendering the development of unsustainable economic and environmental systems is not raised. If it were, the developed countries would be forced to accept a substantial degree of responsibility for the economic and environmental consequences of the development pattern in the developing world. These key questions are conveniently hidden by the focus on global trade between nations rather than on the global economic integration of transnational corporate production and the extraction of national economic and environmental policy concessions to achieve the goals of transnational capital and to satisfy the legitimate aspirations for economic development on the part of developing countries. Thus, although international trade has often been emphasized by those speaking of globalization, it is actually the geographical expansion of investment and productive capabilities of transnational corporations that represents the true architecture of economic globalization.

5

The EU Emissions Trading Scheme
in the corporate greenhouse

The EU cap-and-trade system

In this chapter we will discuss the likely impact of the EU cap-and-trade or Emissions Trading Scheme on corporate investment strategies with respect to shifts in the global production of energy- or carbon-intensive manufacturing alluded to in the previous chapters. The EU ETS is the cornerstone of the EU climate-change policy, covering about 45 per cent of total EU CO_2 emissions. It is the showcase of the EU's commitment to reduce GHG emissions according to the Kyoto Protocol. Since the EU ETS is linked to the Kyoto Protocol's Flexible Mechanisms it also has a global reach and is possibly the model for climate-change policy worldwide. It offers the EU a platform from which to influence an eventual global trading scheme, and for that reason is watched closely by all potential participants in a post-Kyoto global emissions-reduction scheme. The ETS has been studied and analysed by business groups and environmental groups as they try to influence policymakers by showing how effective or ineffective or damaging the ETS is on global emissions and industrial competitiveness. Many considered the first phase of the EU ETS (2005–07) as an experiment or test case, and it certainly had an element of 'learning by doing'. We are now in the second phase of the EU ETS, which covers the period 2008–12. A number of changes were implemented in order to correct the shortcomings the ETS Phase I.

Emissions trading was chosen by the EU Commission as it promised to meet the EU GHG emissions reduction goal in the most cost-effective way.[1] The EU ETS, for now, covers only CO_2 emissions from large industrial and energy installations in a limited number of energy-intensive sectors such as refining, coke ovens, cement, pulp and paper, glass, steel and metal, and power generation. By establishing a market price for carbon, EU policymakers envisioned that industrial firms in these sectors would make investment decisions based in part on reducing emissions and improving energy efficiency. Combined with a robust compliance system, emissions trading would ensure that emissions-reduction targets would be met and as such the ETS would comply with the implementation of the Kyoto Protocol targets. As with any emissions-reduction scheme, the EU ETS has distributional impacts and there are winners and losers. Among the losers are some energy- or carbon-intensive industries in some EU countries, and, as we will see, the effect of implementation of the ETS is not always straightforward and predictable and the distributive impacts vary from country to country and sector to sector. In general, in balancing effectiveness and competitiveness, inefficiencies, unnecessary complexities, and sometimes perverse incentives have entered into the scheme, which has produced scepticism in the public's mind about the impact of the EU ETS.

The EU ETS introduced the national allocation of GHG allowances, which permits particular segments of industry to emit certain amounts of carbon dioxide, and each member state of the EU had first to submit a National Allocation Plan (NAP). Based on the agreed-to Kyoto reduction of CO_2 emissions, each EU member had established its own reduction target. In the NAP, member states could specify which industrial sectors would be covered and which would be excluded. Furthermore, each country could specify how new entrants, closures and transfers would be treated, and what kind of allocation methodologies would be used. In the decision-making process, industrial representatives, environmental groups and other interested stakeholders had a good deal of influence, and the ultimate reason why some sectors were included and others excluded was not always clear. Many believe that harmonization of NAPs and greater transparency are urgently needed for the EU ETS to gain credibility and for it to become the model for global CO_2 emissions trading. During the first phase of the ETS, support from EU member states required a high degree of decentralization and overallocation of CO_2 permits for reasons of competitiveness and distributive impacts. In other words, government help to struggling companies and regions affected by the impact of the EU ETS was a dominant but debatable feature of the trading scheme. Member states have been reluctant to impose stricter targets if they perceive that other countries are helping their industries and as the uncertainty about the survival of the ETS past the end of the Kyoto Protocol in 2012 remains.

Even though the EU ETS will ultimately be judged on the basis of its effectiveness as a tool to reduce GHG emissions, the underlying rationale for choosing emissions trading was based on economic considerations. By implementing the EU ETS an attempt was made to account for a market externality (CO_2 emissions) with a minimal impact on competitiveness. In theory, the market price of carbon is driven by the marginal abatement costs of CO_2 emissions reduction, ensuring that the target reduction is achieved at the least cost. By creating a market price for carbon, investment would be made in energy efficiency and better process technology, it was argued. The ETS offered business flexibility to achieve the objective by low-cost abatement or by allowing credits from the Kyoto Protocol's Flexible Mechanisms to be used for compliance. The EU established a special 'Linking Directive' in 2004 to achieve this objective. The principal drivers for using the Flexible Mechanism would be the price of carbon and the cost of abatement within the EU or in other parts of the world through investments in energy efficiency or improved process technology in developing countries that were not subjected to emissions-reductions commitments under the Kyoto Protocol. An important condition upon which the whole scheme rested was the proper balance between supply and demand for carbon permits and credits. Thus, allocation of the number of carbon permits per industry and installation became critical. Theoretically, the number of permits should be fewer than the CO_2 emissions reported in 1990; however, during the first round of allocation (2005–07), most member countries have allowed emissions from the covered sectors to rise and have allotted a far greater number of permits than would serve the carbon market despite the fact that many must reduce their emissions to achieve their Kyoto Protocol targets. Furthermore, all the allowances were allotted for free, which meant that there was hardly a price for carbon and therefore no incentive to invest in energy efficiency or improved process technology. At the end of Phase I of the ETS (2005–07), parties realized that Kyoto Protocol CO_2 emissions reduction was not on target, which led to an intensive debate within the EU about the effectiveness of issuing free allowances and the desirability of auctioning carbon credits in the second phase (2008–12).[2]

Under the regulations of the EU ETS, an industrial installation that surpasses the allotted amount of CO_2 permits has to buy extra allowances. Even though in practice few industries had to buy permits since they were all given for free and many industries received more than they needed, under the conditions of 'carbon constraints' energy-intensive industries in the EU began a public debate about the wisdom of the EU 'going it alone', as they anticipated that higher energy costs would eventually affect their global competitiveness and slow down investment in Europe with the subsequent expansion of production in non-Annex I countries or the USA. The overall effect of such a corporate response suggests that an increase rather than a reduction in global GHG emissions would be the result. It is this aspect in particular that we will discuss in this chapter. The outcome known as 'carbon leakage' has received a good deal of attention in the academic literature. We will discuss this with respect to investment in energy-intensive industries in China and India and other developing countries that are not legally committed to CO_2 emissions reduction under the Kyoto Protocol.

The EU Emissions Trading Scheme under the Kyoto Protocol

An emissions trading scheme is an economic instrument that enables parties to reach their agreed-to emissions targets in a cost-effective manner by taking advantage of the different marginal abatement costs of participating entities. In theory, this presents an economic incentive to trade. With the Kyoto Protocol signed in 1997, the European Union committed itself to reducing its GHG emissions by 8 per cent in 2012 compared to the level of 1990, and in order to address the reduction challenge cost-effectively the European Commission established the European Climate Policy Programme (ECPP). In March 2000, the Green Paper on Greenhouse Gas Emissions Trading in the EU was published. In this document, emissions trading was presented as the best instrument to deliver the proposed emissions-reduction target at lowest possible costs since large emitters could be easily identified. Several opinion papers, draft directives and compromise statements on emissions trading followed, and in September 2003 Directive 2003/87/EC was agreed to. The Directive began to take effect as the EU Emissions Trading Scheme on 1 January 2005.[3]

Under the EU ETS, of the six main greenhouse gases, only carbon dioxide is targeted. As part of the quantified emission limitations every country was assigned a number of Assigned Amount Units (AAUs), which are calculated in metric tons (tonnes) of CO_2 equivalent (MT CO_2e).[4] The scheme initially specified two periods: the first 2005–07; the second 2008–12 (corresponding to the first commitment period of the Kyoto Protocol). Compliance is required on an annual basis within these periods, but allocation is decided separately for the two periods. The three flexible mechanisms made up under the Kyoto Protocol also apply to the EU ETS.[5] The mechanisms were established in order to give Annex I countries substantial flexibility to reduce emissions. The Kyoto Protocol demands that the use of the mechanisms is supplemental to domestic action and that this should constitute a significant element of the effort made by each party included in Annex I to meet its quantified emissions limitation and reduction.

As discussed earlier, a provision negotiated in the Kyoto Protocol is the so-called 'bubble' arrangement which permits a group of Annex I countries to meet their commitments jointly. The EU subsequently decided to form the 'EU Bubble', which allows EU member states to meet their Kyoto target commitment as a group.[6] The overall commitment of the EU is a reduction of 8 per cent from 1990 levels, but under the burden sharing within the EU Bubble, Portugal

---

BOX 5.1   **Flexible mechanisms of the Kyoto Protocol**

- *Joint Implementation*, as defined in Article 6 of the Kyoto Protocol. The Annex I Parties can contribute to their emissions targets by investing in emissions-reduction projects in other Annex I countries. These investments eventually result in Emission Reduction Units which can be used for compliance under the Kyoto Protocol.
- *Clean Development Mechanism*, as defined in Article 12 of the Kyoto Protoco. Annex I Parties can undertake emissions-reduction projects in developing countries (non-Annex I), which lead to Certified Emission Reduction credits. These credits can be used for compliance in the industrialized countries.
- *Emissions trading*, as defined in Article 17 of the Kyoto Protocol. Annex I Parties can acquire emissions credits, Assigned Amount Units, from other Annex I Parties and use them for compliance under the Kyoto Protocol.

Source: UNFCCC: http://unfccc.int/kyoto_protocol/items/2830.php.

---

is allowed to emit 27 per cent more and Luxemburg has to reduce emission by 28 per cent from the base year. The European Union Emissions Trading Scheme is the largest multi-country, multi-sector greenhouse-gas emission-trading scheme worldwide.[7]

Emissions allowances, or AAUs, can in principle be used in international emissions trading worldwide and there are currently discussions under way between different emissions trading entities to streamline and harmonize the different systems. EU emissions allowances are called European Union Allowance (EUA), which is the 'currency' unit in European emissions trading. In the first-phase allocation of the EU ETS (2005–07), all allowances were given out free of charge to more than 12,000 manufacturing and power-generation installations. As indicated, in most member countries, allocations exceeded historic emissions and inflated baselines resulting in substantial overallocation for industries in some countries.

This caused a classic free rider situation, which benefited, as we will see, in particular the electric power sector.[8] For the second phase, which coincides with the Kyoto Protocol commitment period (2008–12), many member states are granted far fewer allocations and decided to auction part of their allocations in order to meet their targets.[9] In total, EU ETS governments will auction up to 411 million allowances in Phase II, of which Germany alone will auction 40 million every year during the period 2008–12, making a total of 160 million allowances.[10] By the end of the first commitment period of the Kyoto Protocol (2008–12) each country has to reach its CO_2 emissions-reduction target, buy allowances from other EU countries, or purchase credits from projects under the Clean Development Mechanism or Joint Implementation.

Certified Emissions Reductions are earned through CDM. CDM rewards emissions-reduction projects in developing countries with CERs, which can be used by national governments to meet their Kyoto target as well as by the private sector for compliance under regional emissions trading schemes like the EU ETS. JI projects function basically in the same way except the partner is another Annex I country with a Kyoto target.[11] In the case of JI, Emission Reduction Units are awarded. For both mechanisms specific requirements have to be met in order to prove that the emissions reductions are real. The main supply of extra credits or allowances was expected to come from Joint Implementation projects in eastern Europe – Russia and the Ukraine in particular, as these countries have emissions far below their Kyoto targets and thus have surplus to sell to countries that need the allowances to achieve compliance. In fact, this has not been the case so far for two reasons: (1) JI project credits can only be rewarded during the second EU ETS phase (2008–12); (2) because of procedural uncertainties (in Russia) and lack of regulatory infrastructure (in Ukraine), as we will discuss a little later. The CDM market, instead, has become the more important vehicle through which to earn extra credits.

As dictated by the Kyoto Protocol, CDM projects should only be granted credits for compliance if the projects contribute to sustainable development in the communities or countries where they are granted, and if the outcome of the CDM projects is an actual reduction in GHG emissions. Current use of CDM projects for credits has given rise to doubts about both the environmental and climate-change benefits of the credits granted and the impact of the projects on local communities in developing countries. So, for instance, sustainable development concerns have often been sidelined.[12] At a minimum, member states should set installation-level caps on CDM/JI credits low enough to ensure that domestic action continues to be the main means by which reductions are achieved. The trend today is for companies that fail to meet their emissions-reduction targets to buy up large volumes of external credits, and bank their own allowances for later use, or sell allowances at a profit at a later date. Many argue that in order to be effective and to guarantee that domestic abatement efforts are met, a cap on CDM and JI credits should be set at the installation level as specified by the 'Linking Directive' and be monitored for each installation and not at the sector level or for all ETS sectors combined, as is presently the practice. The EU Commission guidance document for the Phase II (2008–12) period stipulates that member states can apply the limit collectively to all installations or projects approved and for the whole trading period. Clearly, pressure from business has been to grant an almost unlimited amount of CDM/JI credits, which has led to rather skewed allocations, as in the case of Spain, which negotiated in its NAP that up to 50 per cent of the country's allowances can be covered by credit imports during the second phase of the ETS. Both governments and private companies can participate, but in the case of Spain it is not specified how much each party will be purchasing.[13] This, environmental and activist groups believe, could provide perverse incentives in which companies sell their (free) allowances at the higher market price and purchase project credits at the lower price to meet their emissions-reduction needs.

Several national governments – for instance Spain, Japan, the Netherlands and Italy – have recently been buying CERs and ERUs in order to meet their Kyoto targets. For this purpose some national governments have set up carbon procurement plans. Intermediaries like banks, funds and other private businesses speculate on prices for CERs and ERUs, and various exchanges have begun to launch futures and options contracts for emissions credits to facilitate the emissions trade. For as long as the costs of project investments in CDM/JI remain relatively low and the price of CERs and ERUs are not too high, we can expect an active market in carbon credits. However, if EU ETS demand for CERs and ERUs is strong and the purchasing power of governments becomes restrained, then we may see interest in this part of the carbon market decline. Eastern and central European EU members may become reluctant to sell large shares of their allowances because they may reserve the surplus allowances they now have for future use, and in addition they may find that there are more lucrative trading opportunities under ETS as most are now members of the EU. Russia and Ukraine (not within the EU), each had surpluses due to sharp declines in economic activity following the transition from Communism, and they are now in a position to sell credits under the JI umbrella.[14] In the meantime, 'hot air' trading is occurring whereby excess permits arising from the decline in production after the fall of Communism, rather than purposeful efforts to curb emissions, are traded with parties required to reduce their GHG emissions under the Kyoto Protocol.[15]

The Czech Republic in its National Allocation Plan for 2008–12 proposed a sharp increase in allowances to permit carbon dioxide emissions increases from the country's coal-powered plants as it anticipates 'making up' in emissions it did not produce early on in the Kyoto commitment period due to the transition to a market economy. With 12 tonnes of emissions per capita, the Czech Republic is one of the worst CO_2 polluters in the EU, yet the country is presently 25 per cent below its Kyoto target (see Appendix). The government justifies the proposed increased allotment on the basis of a promise that Czech industry leaders have made that the profits from excess allowances will be invested in energy efficiency and renewable-energy projects. As it is estimated that Czech businesses do not need that many allowances to cover their emissions, it is therefore reasonable to suspect that windfall profits will be made. Similar situations occur in other eastern and central European countries that have recently become members of the EU and that have seen a slowdown in their economy since the fall of Communism but expect to begin to benefit from integration in the EU market and attract foreign investment, thereby needing more allowances. Poland proposed in its National Allocation Plan an increase of 17 per cent in CO_2 emissions from the first phase, which would provide enough free allowances to high-emitting power plants using coal and lignite to forestall the commission of low-emitting plants using natural gas. This absurd situation removes any incentive to encourage the changeover from high-emitting fuels to fuels that emit less CO_2.[16]

The EU cap-and-trade system is closely observed by other countries, including the USA, which is currently not complying with binding emissions-reduction targets under the Kyoto Protocol but where various regional trading schemes are now being implemented. From surveys conducted, it appears that most Americans would rather see government-imposed energy standards or mandates as a means to reduce national greenhouse-gas emissions instead of a cap-and-trade system, whereas several states and private businesses have pressured the federal government to adopt a cap-and-trade system.[17] To this end, a number of US senators have introduced a mandatory cap-and-trade bill in Congress, following recommendations from their state governments and businesses, that would introduce a federal poliy in line with these states.[18] A very active participant in the discussions is California's governor Arnold Schwarzenegger, under whose guidance the State of California embarked on an emissions trading scheme. Among the recommendations are provisions to allow offsets, reward early movers, and allocate a significant portion of allowances for free at the beginning, with full auctioning later on. This approach was proposed by the Democratic senator from Delaware, Tom Carper, who called for an initial free allocation of 82 per cent of allowances to the electric power sector and the remaining 18 per cent to be auctioned. Carper's proposal includes a gradual transition to a full auction over a twenty-five-year period. The proposal received mixed reactions among large utilities, who like to see free distribution of all allowances, and a great deal of scepticism from environmental groups such as Clean Air Watch, which considers the plan a financial give-away to the major power companies.[19]

The Regional Greenhouse Gas Initiative (RGGI), a consortium of ten northeastern states, requires member states to auction at least

25 per cent of credits; and California's Market Advisory Committee (MAC) proposes either to auction 100 per cent of the state's emissions allowances or to use a mix of auctioning and free allowances that gradually transitions to a full auction over the years.[20]

The EU ETS reached record levels in transacted allowances in both volume and value in 2006 and greatly exceeded 2005 levels of transactions. Over 60 per cent of physical volume (measured in MT CO_2e) and 80 per cent of financial value derived from emissions trading within the EU 25. In total, 817 MT CO_2 changed hands, corresponding to €14.6 billion in 2006. Almost 35 per cent of volume and 17.5 per cent of value derived from CDM, and only a very small share derived from JI. *Point Carbon* (2007) reports that the disappointing results of JI are due to procedural uncertainties (in Russia), lack of regulatory infrastructure (in Ukraine), and issues related to 'double-counting' when some east–central European JI host countries recently joined the EU.[21] The JI market is mostly managed by governments in the public sector, while the CDM is mostly a private equity activity. Buyers in the JI market include Denmark (36 per cent), Austria (29 per cent), and the Netherlands (13 per cent). The World Bank participates in the JI market at 12 per cent. Sellers include the Czech Republic (21 per cent), Bulgaria (17 per cent), Romania, Russia, and Ukraine (each 15 per cent), with Poland (6 per cent) and other east and central European countries making up the rest.[22] The most significant project types among JI contracts in 2006 in terms of volume were renewable energy projects including biomass, wind and hydro projects (37 per cent), industrial processes (22 per cent), waste and landfill gas capture (16 per cent) and energy efficiency projects (15 per cent).

The CDM market covers more than 90 per cent of the entire project market and has shown a dynamic increase in Phase I of the EU ETS (2005–07). As the first phase has ended and the second phase has started, many participants are trying to accumulate CERs for compliance during the first commitment period of the Kyoto Protocol (2008–12). A large number of private companies participate in the CDM market, for which new financial vehicles have been established, contributing to very speculative investments. Italy and the UK together make up 60 per cent of the buyers' market, while

China is by far the largest CDM selling country, holding 70 per cent of the sellers' market, with India in second place with 12 per cent. Purchases of greenhouse-gas HFC-23 capture were the largest project allocations, with NO_2 removal projects, renewable alternatives, waste and landfill gas capture, and energy efficiency making up most of the remaining options.[23]

The impact of the EU ETS on energy- and carbon-intensive industries

As noted, the EU ETS introduced a cap-and-trade system which grants specific energy-intensive industrial installations the right to emit certain amounts of carbon dioxide, which accounts for 80 per cent of greenhouse gases. If a plant emits less than its allocation then it is allowed to sell the surplus. If it exceeds its allocation then the company has to buy credits or allowances from other companies, purchase ERUs or CERs, or face a fine. The EU ETS covers a total of more than 12,000 installations in the EU27 (including the original 15 EU members and the 10 new east and central European members which have joined since 1 May 2004). Bulgaria and Romania (admitted to the EU in 2007) entered in 2008 to participate in the second ETS phase (2008–12). Energy costs represent an important part of the total cost of production in energy-intensive industries and consequently it is expected that these industries will apply energy efficiency measures in order to comply with the EU ETS and to remain competitive. However, many of the industries face competition in the global marketplace and are therefore exposed to competitors that are not subjected to the binding commitments, or so-called carbon constraints, of the Kyoto Protocol. Generally, the industries are not or would not be able to pass on the extra costs linked to meeting their ETS target in the case that they had to purchase their allowances or make investments in energy-efficient processing equipment. On the other hand, their energy suppliers (i.e. power producers) are able to charge the value of their CO_2 allowances – which they largely received for free – as an 'opportunity cost' within the power price. In fact, the electricity sector has been accused of taking windfall profits during the first phase of the EU ETS (2005–07), as they can pass on the cost of carbon permits even when carbon-neutral electricity is produced. The situation is enhanced by the fact that European power markets are not truly competitive, and that, especially in the continental European market, monopoly positions persist.[24] This has resulted in some energy-intensive sectors like primary aluminium production slowing down investments in Europe, with production expanding in non-carbon-constraint or non-abatement countries. Consequently, there is now a lively debate going on in Europe about the wisdom of the EU 'going it alone'.

Energy-intensive industries have four choices in dealing with cost increases due to carbon trading. First, they can invest in more energy-efficient plants. This option is not always available as many EU energy-intensive industries have over the years maintained a high level of investment and achieved a high degree of energy efficiency. Further investment is therefore limited and new technologies are not always available. The second option is to buy allowances, provided these are available at a reasonable or financially attractive price. If they are not available at a reasonable price, a company may buy CERs or ERUs. The third option is to reduce production, which has a negative impact on business prospects and market share of the company. The fourth and final option is to relocate production outside the EU at a higher global environmental cost. The latter, obviously, is the least desirable, as well as the most contradictory and controversial, option considering that the EU ETS is part of the Kyoto Protocol effort at climate change mitigation through global greenhouse-gas emissions reduction. Ironically, whereas the EU ETS aims for EU reduction of CO_2 emissions, global emissions would increase as EU industries relocate to those countries where carbon constraints do not apply and where low-technology, energy-intensive, fossil-fuel, often coal-based energy systems supply the industry with cheap power, which results in higher emissions per unit produced. It would also generate cheaper imports of energy-intensive goods into the EU from countries with no carbon constraints. The combined impact would greatly undermine the efforts to reduce global CO_2 emissions – the main objective of the Kyoto Protocol. In this scenario, EU energy-intensive industries would cease to be competitive in the global marketplace. In addition to a defeat of the Kyoto Protocol, it would also be a defeat of the

Lisbon Agreements aimed at stimulating a competitive manufacturing industry through increased efficiency and new technologies within the EU.[25] Until recently – prior to the implementation of the EU ETS – energy-intensive industries in Europe had maintained global competitiveness and were considered highly energy-efficient in their production processes relative to other parts of the world. They could play a key role in innovation and technology development throughout the production chain and are considered the key players in dealing with the challenges of climate change and energy security, as well as being the potential carriers of technological change to developing countries. Policymakers consider the industries as potentially key players in the success of the EU ETS and argue that to undermine their position would be a great loss to global climate-change policy efforts. They thus respect the industries' concerns about complying with the EU ETS and work closely with leaders in order to solve problems that emerge with respect to their position in the global marketplace.[26]

Energy-intensive industries began a public debate about the wisdom of the EU 'go it alone' policy at the very beginning, when the EU proposal to target them was made. Anticipating that the EU economy under the Kyoto regime would become a carbon-constraint economy, industry leaders lobbied hard to give specific direction to the implementation of an emissions trading scheme. Carbon constraints would give value to allowances and would lead to changes in relative cost and price increases in the EU economy, industry representatives argued. It was anticipated that goods that contained more carbon or had been produced with greater energy intensity would be relatively more expensive than goods that contained less carbon or used less energy. Therefore, in a partly carbon-constraint global economy, carbon-constraint countries would import goods from non-abatement countries where no carbon constraints applied.[27] The Alliance of Energy Intensive Industries in Europe has been the main lobbying group for the industry in the EU. Representatives argued that higher energy cost would affect EU competitiveness in the global economy and slow down investment in Europe with the subsequent expansion of production in non-Annex I countries or the USA.[28] The net effect of such a corporate response would result in an increase in global GHG emissions rather than a decrease. Their prediction about cost

FIGURE 5.1 **The impact of the EU ETS on power prices, 2005**

Source: Alliance of Energy Intensive Industries, 'The Impact of EU Emission Trading Scheme (ETS) on Power Prices: Remedial Action Urgently Needed 10 Months after Start of ETS, November 2005, www.cembureau.be/Cem_warehouse/alliance%20ets%20and%20power%20prices.pdf.

increases related to the implementation of the ETS – in particular regarding increase in the price of electricity – is clear when we note the correlation between the costs of ETS allowances and power prices (Figure 5.1). The reports issued by the group following the implementation of the first phase of the ETS and in anticipation of Phase II alert us to the fact that urgent action is needed.[29] The metal industries report that the cost of energy generally represents more than 10 per cent, and can be up to 37 per cent, of the cost of production for aluminium and certain other metals. Due to a large-scale capital investment in the industries, big companies dominate the market and most are TNCs, which means that they can and do make choices as to where to expand and locate production.[30]

In November 2005, the Alliance issued a call for action on the part of the EU to resolve the fundamental problems associated with the rise in energy prices as the position of EU energy-intensive industries in the global market was seriously undermined.[31] As the EU manufacturing industry was paying the price for a hastily designed ETS, they argued, policymakers should take responsibility for the failure of the scheme and solve the problem by reforming the ETS. The Alliance recommended that CO_2 prices should be separated from power prices, and that windfall profits on the part of power providers should not come at the expense of energy-intensive manufacturers. Subsequently, the Alliance became adviser to and a strong supporter of a new energy strategy for Europe set out in the 2006 EU Green Paper, *A European Strategy for Sustainable, Competitive and Secure Energy*.[32]

There are currently no properly functioning electricity markets in the EU, and in recent years electricity prices have risen significantly above pre-liberalization levels and are still increasing. In Germany, the pass-through of CO_2 allowance prices in the power price is estimated at 60–80 per cent, leading to competitive disadvantages for the energy-intensive industry. Representatives of the industry report that they no longer engage in price negotiations with power providers or commit to long-term contracts as manufacturers in other parts of the world do. The EU has a relatively favourable energy mix and a power generation structure composed of wind, hydropower, nuclear power, oil, gas and coal. However, most of the power markets are still controlled by national power interests, and countries have differing energy mixes, which can severely distort internal EU competition. Most electricity producers pass on the cost of carbon credits regardless of whether they are carbon producers or not. This impacts on energy-intensive manufacturers immediately. In addition, gas providers often hold monopoly positions, especially in the LNG markets, which are highly concentrated and offer usually no choice of suppliers in specific regions, and the logistic or physical infrastructure, managed by only a few operators, has generated tight markets. Gas prices are linked to oil prices, which have been highly volatile. Because of uncertainty in the energy markets and over the future of the EU ETS, the EU has become a high-risk area for new industrial investments in the energy-intensive sector, while existing manufacturers have begun to slow or shut down production. Instead, countries like China and India have been expanding their market share in energy-intensive manufacturing, in particular in the iron and steel and aluminium industries. India and China offer growing markets for building and construction materials and have ample and secure supplies of energy in the form of coal. Within the EU, Poland and the Czech Republic have been gaining market share as expanding markets and excellent growth prospects as well as 'hot air' trading have made their products more competitive.[33] As a consequence and in order to preserve strategically important basic manufacturing within different European countries, policymakers are urged by company CEOs to regulate better and protect the interests of energy-intensive manufacturers. The Green Paper emphasizes that industrial competition requires a well-designed, stable and pre-dictable regulatory framework and functioning market mechanisms. One recommendation is ownership unbundling of production and delivery or distribution entities in the power industry and further liberalization of electricity markets.[34]

The Alliance for a Competitive European Industry, which, ironically, represents many of the same industries as the Alliance for Energy Intensive Industries referred to above, called on the European Union legislative institutions and member states to ensure swift implemen-tation of concrete measures to strengthen the competitiveness of industry in the EU and thereby the prosperity of members' econo-mies.[35] Besides concerns related to innovation and new technologies, energy and CO_2 emissions reduction figured high on the agenda. Their research showed that potential losses in market share depend on the extent to which EU producers can pass on the extra energy costs or CO_2 abatement costs to consumers and suppliers. Another aspect is how quickly non-EU producers can increase their productive capacity. This being the case, it is likely that the impact of the EU ETS may not be felt immediately as investors assume that, in due course, other countries will also become subject to carbon constraints as they may participate in a post-Kyoto climate-change policy scheme. In the transition period, competitive impacts of the EU ETS are closely monitored and are analysed on a sector-specifc level.

Sector-specific impacts of the EU ETS

From analysing reports and assessments on the impact of the EU ETS on competitiveness, it becomes clear that a sector-specific approach would be more effective than an industry-wide approach.[36] The impact on different sectors of the industry has to be taken

BOX 5.2 **Sector-specific impacts of the EU ETS**

- The Confederation of European Paper Industries,[37] representing 830 pulp, paper, and board-producing companies across Europe, employing 270,000 workers and accounting for €75 billion turnover in 2005, states that global competition is not of immediate concern. The European paper and pulp industry recycles a substantial amount of used paper and cardboard, and has been very successful at generating its own biomass electricity. The recycling rate of paper and board reached 56 per cent in 2005, making the EU the global leader in the recycling effort. Paper and pulp manufacturers are among the largest producers and users of biomass electricity, and biomass represents 50 per cent of the industry's total primary energy consumption. The industry leaders suggest that specific consideration be given to stimulate biomass for energy use and request tax exemptions on the use of biomass based electricity and guaranteed prices for Renewable Energy Sources (RES) electricity.[38]

- The European Cement Association,[39] representing the cement industry, one of the most energy-intensive industrial sectors in the Alliance, sees security of energy supplies as one of the most critical issues confronting the industry in the EU. Addressing global climate change is a challenge requires all major emitters of CO_2 worldwide to participate in emissions-reduction efforts, industry experts maintain. Whereas the European cement industry is committed to contributing to CO_2 reduction, the EU ETS will only be a valid policy option if adopted globally in a fair and more effective way. The European Cement Association also urges EU member states not to resort to auctioning off allowances. This would seriously compromise the future of the cement industry. The industries' competitiveness is already impaired by high energy prices and the uncertainty resulting from the present EU ETS, which already affects investments.[40] The cement industry is the basis for every construction project. Regarding its location, production usually takes place where the basic material is available. Transport costs are high relative to the end price of cement, which results in low levels of international trade. Marine transport has recently become more common and international trade has increased.[41] Cement production costs will increase by approximately 36 per cent due to emissions trading assuming an average price of €20/tonne CO_2 emissions.[42] Most of this will be due to direct emissions, as indirect impacts from higher electricity prices make up only a small share of overall cost increases. Thus, depending on the ability to pass on costs to customers, the European cement industry will face a moderate to significant cut in profit margins. The impact will probably be noticed in proximity to seaports where imported lower-priced cement (from non-abatement countries) would compete with domestic production. Some producers have applied new technology and now process cement with less clinker. Also, some manufacturers are using more non-fossil fuel and producing fewer emissions that way.[43]

• The European Association of Metals,[44] which represents the European non-ferrous metals industry – the mining, smelting, refining, semi-manufacturing and recycling of metals such as aluminium, copper, lead, nickel, zinc, as well as high-tech and precious metals – expresses concern about industrial security. Prices for metals are global and set on international commodity exchanges. Energy costs, competitively priced raw materials, and compliance with strict environmental regulation are direct components of the industry's cost structure. The extent to which these metal industries feed downstream industrial activities means that they have a significant role to play in the European economy. Non-ferrous metal industries employ more than 400,000 workers directly and another 800,000 indirectly, generating annual added value of €91,000 per employee. The largest non-ferrous metal industry is the aluminium industry, which lists carbon constraints as its number one concern. Although excluded from the EU ETS during the first phase, the aluminium industry is severely exposed to higher energy costs under the EU ETS because the price of aluminium is set at a global exchange. Half of the EU's aluminium in produced by primary smelting, half by secondary smelting/recycling. The process of smelting consumes over 15 MWh of electricity per tonne of aluminium. Many aluminium companies have long-term contracts with electricity companies, but when these contracts end they will have to buy their electricity from the grid or purchase power under less favourable (more costly) conditions. The importance of international trade has exposed the aluminium industry to much more severe competition than other metal industries whose markets are more European based and for which the competition is with other companies subject to the EU ETS. Thus, the risk factor in the metals industry is determined by the ability to pass on the costs of abatement or higher energy prices to the customer.[45] As the EU is losing its share of world metals production, particularly in aluminium production, which was 21 per cent in 1982 and was down to 9 per cent in 2005, the proprtion of European consumption supplied by European production in the last two decades has declined rapidly.[46] Many studies suggest that primary aluminium smelters will end production in Europe in the next twenty years.[47] Reports issued by industry specialists state that they are particularly vulnerable as the average price for power paid is expected to increase at a greater rate in the EU than in the key competitive regions of the USA and China. The slow progress made towards full energy deregulation along with the implementation of the emissions trading scheme in Europe are blamed for this situation.

- The European Confederation of Iron and Steel Industries,[48] representing the EU steel industry, has studied the impact of emissions trading on the sector, taking into account that steel is made in one of two ways: basic oxygen furnace (BOF) primary production, and electric arc furnace (EAF) production involving recycling of scrap metal.[49] Nearly 100 per cent of emissions in the EAF process are indirect electricity-related emissions, whereas 90 per cent of BOF production is direct – process-related – emission and only 10 per cent is indirect energy-related emissions. Products produced by the EAF process (recycling scrap metal) compete mostly in regional markets and are therefore able to pass on their production costs. On the other hand, the production of cold rolled flat steel using the BOF process is competing in global markets.[50] Assuming a €20/tonne carbon price, BOF flat products could experience a cost increase of 16 per cent, which could lead to a shift or relocation of production to countries without carbon costs. In the EAF sector – using scrap metal – the price of the product is determined by the price of scrap metal and the price of electricity. China is currently the fastest growing producer of EAF steel products as a result of increased domestic demand and scarcity of scrap metal.

into account in addressing concerns related to emissions trading. Clearly, some sectors are more competitive than others and exposure to international trade in the global marketplace is one significant differentiating factor.

Whereas energy costs are among the highest in the cement industry, since the industry's market is country- or EU-based, price increases in the sector are generally passed on in full to consumers in the building industry (except in some coastal regions where imports may have an effect). Similarly, price increases due to higher energy costs and carbon constraints in the steel sector are passed on for 65 per cent as the market is for 80 per cent EU based. Most of the growth opportunities in the iron and steel industry are in east and central Europe, where the industry has recently been expanding. A report presented by the European Confederation of Iron and Steel Industries states that the market and competition conditions are more favourable in eastern Europe than in western Europe, where the EU ETS has had a greater impact on carbon prices. In addition, the industry showed a significant increase in imports, primarily from China. Imports into the EU were projected to increase by almost 16 per cent for 2007 and have doubled since 2004 to contribute almost 20 per cent of the market share of iron and steel in the EU market. Meanwhile, exports were projected to decline by almost 10 per cent for 2007.[51]

The EU ETS impact on emissions reduction in the energy-intensive industries results from greater energy efficiency applied in the industry and, in some instances, from output reduction. In the case of primary aluminium production, significant reductions occur as companies cease production in the EU.[52] In the paper industry, a sector with medium energy intensity and opportunities to recycle and apply alternative energy inputs like biomass, the impact of the EU ETS on output is small and on profits is positive, as the industry has the benefit of opportunities to abate carbon emissions and to trade free allowances. In the cement industry, most of the increased costs are passed on to consumers in the building industries; and in the metal and the iron and steel industries, depending on the production process and the competitive nature of the market, firms will either slow down production or close the factory, sell the business or relocate production. Thus, overall, three factors determine the potential impact of the implementation of the EU ETS on a sector: (a) energy costs, (b) the ability to pass cost increases on to the customer, and (c) opportunities to abate carbon emission at low costs.[53]

Extensive research has been and is being conducted on the impact of the EU ETS on European competitiveness in the global marketplace.[54] The research network Climate Strategies, comprising economists and political scientists at Cambridge University and other European universities, has focused on the implementation and results of the current EU ETS and on Phase II allocation and policy changes.[55] Findings are published in the form of working papers on the network's website and in their journal *Climate Policy*. Their studies, which support the views presented by business groups, conclude that major challenges remain and that full implementation of the EU ETS remains uncertain. The loss of industrial competitiveness is a dominant theme in their research, which points out that short-term loss of profitability and long-term loss of market share due to the ETS are among the industries' main concern when making investment decisions. The research supports the industry's view that power utilities have an unfair advantage as they pass through costs and make windfall profits – in the case of Germany and the Netherlands, for instance, pass-through rates vary between 60 and 100 per cent of CO_2 costs.[56] This has an important impact on investment decision-making. Most energy-intensive industries are capital-intensive and production plants tend to be large and are often vertically integrated into companies that provide inputs for their own products. The sector contains many multinational or transnational corporation. New firms are relatively few, but instead, mergers and acquisitions are frequent and international competition is fierce.

In essence, under the EU ETS, CO_2 emissions become a factor of production that has to be paid for in the same way as labour or raw materials. CO_2 costs include direct costs in terms of the amount of CO_2 emitted in the production of a unit of output multiplied by the market price of allowances for EU ETS participants, and indirect costs in terms of the price of electricity – that is, the amount of electricity consumed in producing an additional unit of output multiplied by the price of electricity. The latter will affect all industries within the

EU but more so in the case of energy-intensive industries. For the sectors targeted by the EU ETS (i.e. the energy-intensive industries), marginal cost increases result both from the price of EUAs and from increases in the price of electricity due to pass-through of allowance costs. An increase in marginal costs has an impact on a firm's competitive position, depending on the nature of the market. In the local or national market, where other firms experience the same cost increases, the competitive impact is minimal and cost increases are passed on to the consumer. In the EU market, competition depends on marginal cost increases, which depend on the member state's allocation scheme and corrective measures, including support subsidies for threatened industries. At the global scale, EU firms are clearly exposed to increased competition as other countries like China and the USA are not imposing carbon constraints and are thus able to produce at lower marginal costs. Since the EU ETS changes the production costs of EU firms relative to global firms, market share is gained by non-EU firms for those sectors where international global trade is common or where prices are set at global commodity markets.[57]

Research on the cost effects of the EU ETS on the competitive position of firms in the energy-intensive sector shows some interesting trend predictions.[58] In most cost simulation studies in the paper and pulp, cement, and metal and steel industries, increased costs would be passed on to the consumer and profit margins would be preserved or increased. In some instances, as in the case of the aluminium industry where global market conditions prevail, pass-through to consumers would not occur and aluminium smelters would close, their place taken by companies operating exclusively outside the EU. The aluminium industry cannot pass on price increases as product prices are set by international commodity markets. In the paper and pulp industries, where markets are more local and where costs can be passed on to consumers or abatement costs are low, little or no effect of the EU ETS is predicted; in the cement and steel industries, location appears to be a factor. In those cases where coastal locations prevail, international trade opportunities may affect the profitability of the industry, whereas in the case of more land-inward locations, the effect of international trade may be less as transportation costs are higher.[59] In the aluminium industry, it is predicted that smelting, which is most exposed to international competition, will experience the greatest loss of market share under the EU ETS.[60] Electricity costs for aluminium smelting are on average a quarter of operating costs, with 95 per cent of the electricity used for smelting, which is equivalent to 80 per cent of emissions of all primary production of aluminium. With the pass-through of costs of CO_2 by utility companies, it is expected that the aluminium smelters in Europe will not survive international competition. In that case, substantial carbon leakage will occur under the global free-trade regime, which will have a significant negative impact on the efforts to reduce GHG emissions worldwide.

Trade liberalization, the EU ETS and carbon leakage

Carbon leakage refers to the increase in carbon emissions as a result of emissions reductions in Annex I countries that are committing to CO_2 emissions reductions and is considered a negative spillover of the implementation of the Kyoto Protocol.[61] The more positive effect of the Kyoto Protocol is the opportunity for energy efficiency and carbon-saving technological innovations and the diffusion of these innovations abroad through, for instance, the implementation of the CDM and JI. The implementation of climate-change policies in Annex I countries of the Kyoto Protocol such as the EU Emissions Trading Scheme, can thus have positive and/or negative impacts as the various flexible mechanisms are applied. As the objective of the UNFCCC is to reduce global GHG emissions in order to limit the impact of climate change, any negative or positive impacts from the implementation of the Kyoto Protocol are therefore of great importance.

Carbon leakage occurs mainly between Annex I and non-Annex I countries, including developing countries, and between those Annex I countries that have committed to CO_2 emissions reductions under the Kyoto Protocol and Annex I countries that did not ratify the Protocol and therefore did not commit to binding emissions-reduction targets (like the USA and, until recently, Australia). Carbon leakage can also occur among committed Annex I countries with high reduction targets, and economies in transition such as Russia, the Ukraine and some east European countries, because their agreed-to emission limits are above their actual or expected emissions due to greatly improved energy efficiency since the fall of Communism.[62] Carbon leakage is usually expressed as a percentage of the CO_2 emissions increase that results from emissions increase in a non-abating country divided by the reduction of emissions by a country subject to the emissions-reduction target under the Kyoto Protocol or CO_2 reduction policies in abating countries. Thus a 20 per cent carbon leakage rate means that 20 per cent of reductions in emissions in an abatement country are reversed as a result of increased emissions elsewhere. Direct measurement of carbon leakage is rather difficult as the increase in CO_2 emissions in any one country as the result of CO_2 abatement policies is difficult to separate from other factors that may determine CO_2 emissions. For instance, as developing countries develop and as the standard of living and cost of labour increases, a country's mix of industry and global market share of consumption and production may change, resulting in a different CO_2 emissions output. Still, by understanding the mechanisms through which carbon leakage can occur, it is possible to identify the channels of carbon leakage and to assess the impact of climate-change policies.[63]

The various simulation models give different emphasis to the four factors of importance (Box 5.3) and the estimated carbon leakage rates vary accordingly. The two most prominent factors determining carbon leakage are (1) and (2), with (3) international trade varying between countries but generally estimated to increase over time due to further trade liberalization. Most model estimates are derived from Computable General Equilibrium (CGE) models, which are considered to underestimate the impact of industry reallocation of investment (see factor 3) and carbon leakage rates are therefore estimated to be much lower than some expect will ultimately be the case.[64] CGE models are static models which only calculate differences between one state and another. The model cannot calculate the transition from one to another and cannot forecast the future. To account more fully for the effects of the anticipated market changes and geographical distribution of energy-intensive production, trade and leakage, models incorporating strategic interaction among firms producing energy-intensive products have been developed using hybrid

---

BOX 5.3 **Four factors of importance in simulation models for carbon leakage**

1. *International trade in energy goods* CO_2 emissions reduction plans in some parts of the world may have an effect on the demand for fossil fuels with lower demand in abatement countries and possibly higher demand in non-abatement countries.

2. *International trade in goods and services* CO_2 reduction policies may increase production costs of energy-intensive industries in abating countries and increase the prices of their goods. Market share for these goods may then shift to non-abatement countries.

3. *International trade in factors of production* CO_2 reduction policies can reduce the productivity of factors of production and can affect the distribution of the production of fossil fuels or energy-intensive commodities. International capital reallocation would be the result.

4. *International interaction among government policies* Carbon-reduction policies may affect income levels and cost–benefit balances of climate-change policies among different countries. This may either positively or negatively impact global climate-change policy.

Source: J.P.M. Sijms et al., *Spillovers of Climate Policy: An Assessment of the Incidence of Carbon Leakage and Induced Technological Change due to CO_2 Abatement Measures*, Netherlands Research Programme on Climate Change, December 2004: 13.

---

datasets based on the Global Trade Analysis Project (GTAP) data with the International Energy Agency (IEA) accounts on energy balances, prices and taxes.[65] Results from these different models and estimates vary greatly and have been the source of much controversy regarding the economic impact of the implementation of the Kyoto Protocol.[66] Typical CGE model estimated values of carbon leakage due to the implementation of the Kyoto Protocol are between 5 and 25 per cent worldwide, but some GTAP/IEA dataset-based models or GTAP-E models predict carbon leakage rates as high as 130 per cent.[67] In the latter case, the Kyoto Protocol would lead to a huge increase in global carbon dioxide emissions.

Needless to say, such variance in estimated carbon leakage rates derived from simulation models leads to a great deal of scepticism and speculation on the part of business groups and policymakers who hope to influence climate-change policy one way or another. Some observers and interest groups expect a lower rate of carbon leakage due to the implementation of cost-saving measures, the application of innovative technologies, and technology transfer by Annex I countries to non-Annex I countries to prevent industrial relocation, while others predict significantly higher rates of carbon leakage due to the non-participation of major Annex I countries such as the USA in addition to other major non-abatement and developing countries like China, India and Brazil. Some studies estimate that carbon leakage will be higher in some specific energy-intensive sectors that are vulnerable to global competition (such as the aluminium industry or some chemical or iron and steel industries), and that the supply of fossil fuels, especially coal, may explain the amount of carbon leakage that may occur. In all estimates, it is expected that the long-term impact depends on other factors as well, including the post-Kyoto mitigation commitments, the number of abating versus non-abating countries, and the sectors subjected to stringent abatement policies. In one study, it is estimated that the USA will be the largest contributor to carbon leakage in 2020 if the country decides not to sign up to a Kyoto-type agreement after 2012, but that China and other Asian countries will gradually increase their share as their economies continue to grow and as their energy consumption increases.[68] Without the participation of the USA, China and India, Kyoto-type GHG emissions-reduction schemes – unfortunately – are likely to have little effect on overall global carbon emissions reduction.

From the simulation model estimates presented, the impact of trade liberalization is generally viewed as a major contributing factor to carbon leakage and the two policies under the Protocol – climate-change policy and trade liberalization under the WTO – interact in many ways in opposite directions with respect to CO_2 emissions reduction (Figure 1.1). Regulation of emissions reductions in Annex I countries under conditions of liberalized trade will change production and consumption patterns and will affect the economies of non-Annex I developing countries through enhanced international trade and global investment flows. Concern about the impact of the Kyoto Protocol on the US economy was clearly expressed in the Byrd–Hagel resolution in the Senate in 1997, which opposed the ratification of the Kyoto Protocol. Free trade would weaken the effectiveness of the Kyoto Protocol and emissions-reductions schemes, according to US legislators, and would bring harm to the US economy and to the global atmosphere.[69] A fairly extensive literature focuses on the impact of trade liberalization on the relocation of production of energy-intensive industries, and there is a good deal of debate over how important the impact may ultimately be in the longer term.[70] While capital flight from abating to non-abating countries may not be of major significance during the first commitment period (2008–12) of the Kyoto Protocol as many investors take a wait-and-see position, data from FDI suggests that in a more fully developed post-Kyoto or second commitment period this may change. Supporters of the so-called 'pollution haven' hypothesis claim that trade liberalization will encourage a shift of energy-intensive industries to countries without carbon-abatement targets, implying that the rate of carbon leakage will increase due to trade liberalization and foreign investment. On the other hand, supporters of the so-called 'factor endowment' hypothesis assert that when emissions are concentrated in capital-intensive industries – as most energy-intensive industries are – then trade liberalization will lead to further concentration of these industries in relatively capital-abundant countries (i.e. Annex I countries), implying that the rate of carbon leakage may decrease due to trade liberalization.[71] This scenario recommends that the USA participate with binding emissions-reduction targets in place in the post-Kyoto commitment period. Therefore it would be very important to persuade the USA to come on board during the second commitment period, even if India and China are not ready to do so.

Spillover effects of the EU ETS

Worldwide, energy-intensive industries are responsible for about 50 per cent of GHG emissions. About three-quarters of these emissions are caused by industries that produce iron and steel, aluminium, chemicals, fertilizers, cement, and pulp and paper. The emissions intensity makes these industries important targets for climate-change policy, as is the case in the EU ETS. At the same time, particularly under the free-trade regime of the WTO, some of these industries are particularly vulnerable to global competition. If higher production costs resulting from climate change abatement policy prevail, then it is likely that shifts in market share or relocation of production will occur. Industrialized countries have already been losing global market share in the production of energy-intensive goods over the past three decades, and even though most of this was demand-driven – that is, caused by the development of new markets and by increased demand in developing countries for building and construction materials, chemical fertilizers, pharmaceuticals, plastics and other synthetic materials – some of the shift in production output may have been related to carbon constraints and increased cost of production in the EU. In fact, studies focused on trade liberalization and carbon leakage in energy-intensive industries, as discussed above, suggest a significant increase in the rate of leakage when abatement policies are more fully implemented by the EU, as we expect would be the case during a second commitment period of the Kyoto Protocol when the auctioning of carbon credits will take effect. It is therefore likely that long-term commitments towards CO_2 emissions reduction in parts of the world where abatement strategies are implemented will lead to the relocation of production of energy-intensive industries to non-abatement parts of the world, as the uncertainty factor will be reduced and the wait-and-see position of businesses will likely cease to exist if Europe continues 'going it alone'. Furthermore, continued trade liberalization under the WTO regime is expected, which will likely expand international trade and investment opportunities. Under this scenario, which many now believe will be the future, international trade in energy-intensive or high-carbon-content goods will continue, and relocation of factors of production will most likely follow.

First, in terms of international trade in energy-intensive goods, it is likely that fuel switching will occur as abating countries lower their demand for high carbon-content fossil fuels like coal and switch to natural gas, biomass and possibly nuclear energy.[72] In other words, the demand for coal would fall while the demand for oil and natural gas would likely continue to be relatively high. On the other hand, the demand for coal will increase in the non-abating countries as more manufacturing production occurs in non-abating developing countries, inducing an increase in carbon leakage. Second, carbon-reduction policies will increase the production costs of carbon-intensive goods production in abating countries, as we saw in the previous section, and therefore increase the prices of these goods. Developing non-abating countries are likely to see opportunities to expand production of these goods as they apply relatively cheaper energy sources and are not subject to carbon prices. Hence, comparative advantage will shift to industries in non-abating countries and affect production levels and trade. Factors that may influence the magnitude of increased production and trade in high-carbon-content goods from non-abatement countries to abatement countries would be opportunities to substitute between domestic and imported goods and the degree of international capital mobility. In many energy-intensive industries a small number of firms compete directly with each other in an oligopolistic market. If a firm in an oligopolistic international market reduces its supply because of the cost-increasing effects of CO_2 reduction policies in one country, competitors in other countries have a direct strategic incentive to expand their production (and emissions) and export their surplus. In a monopolistic market structure each firm produces a specific variety of a particular good. In this situation, in an abating country, production costs of individual firms increase and the number of domestic firms that can operate profitably decreases. This leads to a decrease of variety in the domestic market, which reduces substitution possibilities and is likely to result in mark-ups by foreign producers in excess of marginal cost increases. Consequently, foreign investments in production in non-abatement countries will likely increase. Third, international capital mobility may influence international trade of high energy- or carbon-content goods and may lead to trade in factors of production. If trade in goods and trade in factors of production are substitutes, an increase in one will reduce the other. Liberalization of the international capital market, as has occurred in the past few decades, can thus reduce the international trade in goods. A car company, for example, may start a foreign subsidiary to produce for a foreign market instead of shipping the cars abroad from its home production plant.

The location choice of firms is the subject of economic geography in which the potential impact of environmental regulation on international capital movements and international trade has recently been recognized.[73] Location factors in FDI decisions of multinational companies may include tax concessions, government policies, labour cost differentials and environmental factors, but the direct relationship between these location factors and capital mobility are generally rather weak. Environmental policies are only one determinant of plant and production location decisions. Some studies have determined that agglomeration economies, instead, continue to be more important in location choice.[74] Agglomeration effects may reduce or increase relocation effects and carbon leakage due to environmental policies, as various studies have demonstrated.[75] Overall, the empirical literature on the effect of environmental regulation on firm relocation is ambiguous and few general conclusions can be drawn.[76] It may well be that it is simply too early to tell or that the absorptive capacity of developing countries for foreign capital is still rather limited. Another factor may be that carbon leakage among domestic producers in non-abating countries due to higher output prices of energy-intensive industries will see their profits rise and can therefore easily finance the expansion of their own production out of extra profits, as may be true for China.[77] In this case, relocation of production would not really require additional capital flows and most of the carbon leakage would result from expanding production of non-abatement-country domestic firms. In the next section we'll explore these patterns as we analyse the expansion of energy-intensive industries in China.

The expansion of energy-intensive production in China

China's rise to economic power was accomplished through a good deal of state manipulation in the market with a one-party political system based on Communist or socialist principles.[78] Unlike the shock therapy prescribed by the IMF, the World Bank and the Washington Consensus for Latin America in the 1980s, or east and central European countries in the 1990s, China set its own terms under the guidance of Deng Xiaoping and to a large extent averted the exchange crisis that beset Russia and Southeast Asia in 1997–98. The country experienced spectacular economic growth, averaging close to 10 per cent a year, and rising standards of living for a growing segment of the population for more than twenty years. However, China's path of development has also led to social inequality and environmental degradation. Its economic policies were geared up (and still are) to pursue rapid economic growth in order to amass wealth and upgrade its technical (and likely military) capacities and capabilities and to secure its power base in its immediate geopolitical sphere of interest in Southeast Asia. It accomplished this, initially, with heavy reliance on FDI in which state control could be exercised, while at the same time permitting the Chinese business diaspora (Hong Kong in particular) to play an important role in setting up businesses in China. Then, when China joined the WTO in 2001, it was prepared to deal with the rules of international trade on its own terms.[79]

Low-wage advantages determined that China could compete with just about any other low-cost location in Southeast Asia or Latin America. During the 1990s, most of the investment in low-wage production occurred via the Chinese merchant community in Hong Kong and Taiwan and was channelled through state-owned enterprises in urban areas or through the township and village enterprise system in rural areas.

Subsequently, the Chinese government designated several 'open coastal cities' as well as 'open economic regions' for foreign investment. These so-called Special Economic Zones (SEZs) offered a range of inducements to foreign companies to invest, including tax abatement schemes, remittances of profits and improved infrastructure facilities. During the financial crisis of 1997–98, several state-owned and township/village enterprises went bankrupt, which convinced the government to make huge investments in the physical infrastructure of Special Economic Zones to clear the way for further investment in the manufacturing sector.[80] Meanwhile, road construction facilitated rapid urbanization, which served to absorb the growing rural immigrant stream. Five international airports were built in the late 1990s and more new ports, bridges, airports, highways and railroads are being constructed to accommodate foreign trade and export-led development.[81] Whereas foreign trade accounted for only 7 per cent of China's GDP in 1978, by the early 1990s this had soared to 40 per cent. China's share of world trade quadrupled during the same period. By 2002, over 40 per cent of China's GDP was accounted for by FDI, half of which was accounted for by manufacturing. By then, China had become the largest recipient of FDI in the developing world and TNCs from Japan, South Korea, the USA and the EU had all begun to invest in the country. By 2003, China had surpassed the United States in terms of total amount of FDI and measured in relative amount – FDI/capital formation ratio – China had become the major destination of FDI (see Chapter 4). Joint ventures between Chinese and foreign firms or wholly owned foreign subsidiaries took on a sizeable presence in the Chinese economy and in some industries have come to command a dominant position. By 2004 consumer production, ranging from automobiles, mobile phones, DVDs, televisions and washing machines, had received a large amount of FDI and a flood of foreign investment by Wal-Mart, McDonald's and other chain stores and restaurants followed. It now appears that China's FDI is levelling off, and it seems likely that the rate of investment in China will in the future depend more on the rate of domestic savings.

Meanwhile, the state still controls almost 40 per cent of investment in fixed assets, while approximately 46 per cent is held by private parties.[82] Much of the state's investment goes into developing infrastructure, while much of the private funding goes into developing the resource base and into export-based manufacturing production. Chinese exports exceeded US$100 billion for the first time in 1994, but had reached almost US$600 billion in 2004. In the meantime, China's need for more building and construction materials increased the market demand for cement, iron and steel, aluminium products and other materials, and offers therefore great opportunities for investment in energy-intensive industries. The coinciding circumstances of the impact of EU ETS on the competitive position of the industries in the EU and the increased demand for these products, clearly dictates a comparative advantage for production in China. Meanwhile, China's accession to the WTO has had a tremendous influence on FDI and TNC investment.[83] The WTO accession agreement built on earlier reforms that had first reduced and then eliminated non-tariff barriers and offered duty-free intermediate inputs in China's export-based industries. The dramatic growth of China's exports in the three years following accession in 2001 has made China the world's third largest exporter. China's heavy reliance on the export-processing trade and the very specific set of reforms undertaken in association with the WTO accession have set China on a course of FDI development that emphasizes TNC manufacturing.

China's emergence as an industrial nation is expressed in its growing importance as an assembly platform for exports of textiles, electronic equipment and automobiles, and as an importer of technology, raw materials, energy and intermediary components, and capital. As a labour-abundant economy China has specialized in the production of labour-intensive manufactures for export in foreign markets, but it is now focusing on attracting energy-intensive industries as it has an abundance of coal to use for processing – and as a non-abatement country is not subject to carbon constraints. Also, China has become an attractive place to invest as it has developed a key role in the regional supply chain that includes South Korea and various other countries in Southeast Asia and the United States.[84] By 2000, countries in Southeast Asia had become the largest trading partners for China, accounting for over twice the share of exports sold to the United States and over five times that sold to Western Europe. At the same time, China was importing more from every neighbour (except Hong Kong and Singapore) than it was exporting to them, most of which trade was part of an Asian-centred TNC supply and production network chain.[85] In 2003, China imported 30 per cent of the world's coal, 36 per cent of the world's steel and 55 per cent of the world's cement, and it went from relative self-sufficiency in oil in 1990 to being the second largest importer after the USA in 2003.[86] On the other hand, China has become a major exporter of aluminium products as it took advantage of comparative advantage in the global market. The projected relatively higher energy prices and the implementation of emissions trading in the EU were likely debit to this. Some of the increase in production and export of aluminium products is from 'home grown' domestic firms, as shown in the two examples presented in Box 5.4.

BOX 5.4 **Aluminium production in China**[87]

Kam Kiu Aluminum Products Brandname: KAP. 80 per cent of products are exported, mostly to European countries. Current (2005) capacity: 150,000 tonnes of aluminium extrusion productions/year. Sales offices in Beijing, Shenzhen, Vancouver, Chicago, Florida, Atlanta, New Jersey, Tokyo, Melbourne, Sydney, and London. First Chinese member in the American Aluminum Association in 2004.

- 1983 on: casting plant in Taishanis: city in Guangdong Province
- 1984: start of production of aluminium billets
- 1989: establishes regional headquarters in Hong Kong
- 1991: build its own aluminium plants
- 1992: first overseas office in Australia
- 1993: new plants for manufacture of aluminium doors and windows
- 1993: opens new office in Singapore
- 1995: awarded ISO-9002 quality certificate
- 1999: awarded Det Norske Veritas award
- 1999: new offices in Beijing, Shanghai and Shenzhen, and in Canada
- 2000–2002: new equipment installed to meet needs of growing markets; seamless tubes, drawn tubes, etc. under brand name KAP enter the EU, US and Japanese markets
- 2003: introduces electronic customer online order-tracking system
- 2004–05: rapid expansion; import of new machinery, technology and management skills, resulting in quality improvements and diversification of product line
- 2005 and beyond: applies for quality management certification (TS.16949) for automobile and aerospace products

Peng Cheng Aluminum, Zhong Wang Group[88] One of the largest and leading sources of aluminium and vinyl extrusions. Business locations in Los Angeles, Dallas, Atlanta, and upcoming facilities in other locations. Headquarters in Liaoyang City, Liaoning province, close to Anshan.

- Top 500 company in China
- Largest China foreign joint venture in northeast China

- Total assets over US$1 billion
- Employing over 10,000 people worldwide
- Offers aluminium and vinyl products/doors and windows
- Six fully owned subsidiary companies operating more than 40 branches in major cities and regional markets in China
- Committed technology, economies of scale and global development
- International standards in addition to Chinese national standards
- ISO 9001–2000 quality management system
- ISO 14001–1996 environmental management system

Sources: Kam Kiu Newsletter, www.kamkiu.com/english/news.asp; Peng Cheng Aluminum Zhong Wang Group: http://w3.pcaus.com/.

In other instances, competitive aluminium producers are TNCs – for example, Alcan or Alcoa – which have invested heavily in China through joint ventures.[89] Multinational producers are mostly involved in primary aluminium production, but semi-fabricated product capacity has also increased and many TNCs now have several other subsidiaries in neighbouring countries in Southeast Asia. The production networks have taken many different forms, but a common feature is that firms are allowed to import intermediate inputs from neighbouring countries through duty-free arrangements favourable for export processing and intra-firm trade. In fact, trade-related impacts of China's WTO accession on neighbouring countries and on the EU and United States are felt throughout the production chain. Exports from China in several product areas have increased competition in more mature markets and have clearly caused a shift in production, particularly in commodities that are traded on the global market, like aluminium products. Trade reports confirm this in the form of significant relative increase in primary aluminium production in Southeast Asia.[90]

Recently, China has come under increasing pressure to take action on climate change as the country has overtaken the USA as the world's leading emitter of carbon dioxide. In international negotiations, Beijing has resisted calls for global caps on greenhouse-gas emissions, but at home it has set ambitious goals for saving energy and reducing emissions. According to its 11th Five-year Plan of National Economic Development, for the period from 2006 to 2010, China's energy consumption per unit of GDP is predicted to decrease by 20 per cent.[91] Besides setting targets for improving energy efficiency, a package of supportive policies was also introduced. For example, in order to achieve structural energy savings through reducing energy use in industry, China has announced that it will reduce the emphasis on developing energy-intensive industries. It also plans to achieve energy savings through developing and marketing energy efficiency technology and to achieve better energy consumption management through strengthening the monitoring system of energy production, transportation and consumption.[92] Given an economy that has been growing at more than 9 per cent annually over the past twenty-five years, the plan's overall effect, if implemented, would be to slow the increase in GHG emissions but not reduce the absolute amount emitted.

China is the largest energy user in Asia and the second largest in the world after the USA. Coal is still by far the country's largest energy resource – accounting for 70 per cent of the mix – but oil and natural gas are gaining in importance, as we saw in Chapter 1. Oil is important particularly for transportation and natural gas plays a growing role in home heating. Coal continues to dominate China's energy use for manufacturing production and is the source of most of its air pollution problems and high CO_2 emissions rates. Energy intensity of coal use – the amount of coal consumed per unit of economic growth – has shot up over the last five years after falling consistently over the previous twenty-five years. What caused this rise was the shift from less energy-intensive light industries towards more energy-intensive heavy industries, as the country became a large producer of commodities such as steel, aluminium, glass, cement and paper. The shift was not the result of an economic policy planned by the central government but rather an outcome of international competition, FDI, and competition among provinces, counties and cities to expand the economy, capital stock, tax revenue and corporate profits.

China's continued rapid growth in industrial production has led to a significant increase in energy consumption, in particular in the production of crude steel, electrolytic aluminium, alumina, ferroalloy, coke and cement, according to the National Development and Reform Commission (NDRC).[93] The rapid growth came about due to strong domestic and international demand as well as supportive external factors, including improvements in coal and power supplies and transportation in response to increased demand. Investment in the rapidly growing aluminium smelting industry increased 49.3 per cent, and investment in the cement sector increased 39.4 per cent in 2006–07, the NDRC reported. Such growth has put enormous pressure on the country's power supplies. According to figures from the NDRC, China's steel, non-ferrous, chemical, power, oil processing, coking and construction material industries accounted for approximately 64 per cent of the country's total industrial power consumption in the first quarter of 2007. Total power consumption for the six industries rose by 18.2 per cent. Power shortfalls are now common. In some regions, such as Sichuan, inadequate river flows have limited hydropower output, putting additional pressure on power supplies, but NDRC statistics suggest that the country's generation capacity has continued to grow. Over 100,000 megawatts of generation capacity was installed in 2006 across the country, with a further 90,000 megawatts added during 2007. Whereas the promise of increased production capacity means that the country's power demands will be met in the future, the NDRC nevertheless believes that the rampant growth in the large energy-intensive industries needs to be reined in.

According to the NDRC, certain power or energy-intensive industries in China need to be restructured and made more efficient, while the rapid industrial expansion in some regions needs to be constrained. The NDRC believes that this could be achieved through stronger industry regulations and an increased effort to quickly phase out inefficient production capacities. Preferential policies that encourage investment in energy-intensive projects should also be avoided, while local land, tax and electricity price subsidies that deal with such industries should be removed. In order to draw in investment, local governments often seek to establish attractive local regulatory regimes that sometimes contradict national policies or fail to enforce the national differential electricity price policy established to restrain investment in energy-intensive industries. The NDRC pledged to continue its work to strictly enforce the policy. It singled out the alumina, electrolytic aluminium and copper smelting sectors in particular, arguing that future projects within these sectors that fail to comply with energy regulations should be prevented from operating. Indirect means of slowing down the sectors and their consumption have had a limited effect so far. While China's export tax rebate for certain steel and copper products was lowered in 2006, exports have continued to grow due to strong international demand. The country's export tax rebate will be lowered even further in the future and the NDRC has pledged to develop and enforce policies that discourage the production and export of highly polluting, energy- and resource-intensive industries.

From 'going it alone' to 'all on board'

The EU ETS has been a disappointment in more ways than one. First of all, it has failed to keep CO_2 emissions reductions on target during the first phase (2005–07), and it has yet to be seen if the second phase (2008–12) remains on target to meet the Kyoto Protocol commitment of 8 per cent reduction overall. Second, carbon leakage is a potentially serious problem, representing a substantial global CO_2 GHG emissions increase. Furthermore, the EU ETS is likely contributing to increased production in energy-intensive industries in non-abatement countries through TNC investments, which contribute greatly to increased CO_2 emissions. Under the current international trade regime guided by WTO principles, this process is set to continue unless more countries sign on to a Kyoto-type agreement after the first commitment period, or unless the international trade organizations correct for the negative spillover effects of the shift in production from abatement to non-abatement countries or relocation of production of energy-intensive industries. In this context one option would be import taxes imposed on high-carbon goods and services derived from non-abatement countries, or some other 'polluter pays' principle imposed on TNCs that relocate production to non-carbon-constraint parts of the world. Various proposals circulate through the climate change think-tanks, most of which recognize that go-it-alone emissions trading will benefit neither the global climate nor the EU economy.

One way to overcome at least some of the problems associated with the EU ETS is to apply a sectoral approach to emissions trading. Such a perspective derives from a concern about competition in a partially carbon-constraint global marketplace. As we have seen, different industries in different locations experience different cost structures and wherever energy-intensive industries are exposed to competition in a context of carbon constraints, trade exposure leaves them vulnerable if they cannot pass on the increased cost of production. Instead of accepting the status quo business-as-usual approach to competition, a particular sector or industry could take action at the international level, by agreement within its global trade associations, to commit to a sector-wide goal of reducing GHG emissions through increased energy efficiency. Naturally, this would involve large-scale technology transfer and cooperation to prevent carbon leakage – which under present circumstances is somewhat difficult to imagine. Such initiatives could seek endorsement from national governments or from regional economic entities like the EU or NAFTA. At the international level they would involve intergovernmental agreement on particular goals for specific industrial sectors, as proposed by the Bush administration through the Asia Pacific Partnership on Clean Development and Climate Change. A number of industrial sectors are presently exploring various sector-specific measures; the problem, however, is that 'industry' is not a party to the UNFCCC, and parties without specific GHG targets are therefore unlikely to participate in a 'voluntary' scheme as the Asia Pacific Partnership proposes. It is unlikely that countries like China, India, Brazil or South Africa would surrender their authority over energy-intensive sectors and at the same time not participate in a scheme to set emissions-reduction targets agreed to under the UNFCCC. For any kind of sector-specific approach to work, there would need to be binding sector-wide emissions-reduction targets on a global scale.

As suggested in the Stern Review, a sector-specific approach could be used as a transition to introducing carbon markets throughout the global economy, and to this end the report cites the Cement Sustainability Initiative (CSI).[94] The World Business Council for Sustainable Development took the initiative to gather the support of seventeen cement companies with manufacturing facilities in Europe, the United States, India, Southeast Asia and Latin America. Together they are responsible for more than 50 per cent of cement manufacturing outside of China. Through the CSI, the companies developed common standards for monitoring and reporting CO_2 emissions and pledged to set their own targets for reducing emissions per unit of output and report on progress made on a regular basis. They also developed guidelines to share best practice standards throughout the industry. The development of baselines and benchmarks could also be used. Whereas this initiative is laudable and increases transparency, the cement industry in most locations is not particularly vulnerable to global competition and in most instances carbon leakage through a shift in production or relocation is not the issue. A sector-specific approach could have a more pronounced effect if introduced in the iron and steel or the aluminium industry and if applied to multi-national or transnational corporations.

The levying of import taxes on high-carbon-content goods and services has also been considered as a way to curtail carbon leakage and some economists have suggested that the international trade regime (WTO) be used to channel such a measure. This could reduce the incentive to relocate energy-intensive production. However, there is an ongoing debate as to whether carbon content taxation would be legal under WTO rules. Several cases have been brought to the WTO, but most have been dismissed on the grounds that the measure could be interpreted as protectionism. In today's free-for-all global economy, it seems that there are few possibilities of dealing with carbon leakage under the Kyoto Protocol until everyone gets on board and supports a just and equitable climate-change policy regime.

The Clean Development Mechanism
in the corporate greenhouse

CDM and JI under the Kyoto Protocol and EU ETS

As part of the climate change and GHG reduction agreement, the Kyoto Protocol implemented several mechanisms by which countries and companies can reduce their GHG emissions. These Kyoto mechanisms include the Clean Development Mechanism, Joint Implementation and International Emissions Trading (IET). In this chapter we will address the issue whether or not carbon trading by means of the Kyoto mechanisms, in particular the CDM, has been or could be beneficial. First, we should ask ourselves the question, beneficial for whom or what? All things considered, the way to avert climate change is simple enough: what is needed is less use of fossil fuels for energy generation and more use of renewable energy sources. Nothing else will do if we are to succeed in diminishing the build-up of GHG (CO_2) in the atmosphere and hope to avert climate change. Thus, all efforts should be geared towards that end, and when we evaluate the impact of carbon trading on climate change we should keep this in mind.

In the real world of carbon trading, the criteria are very different. As we will see, carbon trading schemes are evaluated on the basis of return on investment rather than on the basis of the criteria for which they were designed. In fact, most political and business leaders are trying to have it both ways: more fossil fuels and less climate change.[1] Political and business group discussions emphasize energy security – by which is meant assuring greater supplies of fossil fuels – and at the same time urgent calls for action on climate change are made. For instance, oil companies such as BP and Shell continually boast of increased efforts to find and exploit new sources of fossil fuels and at the same time claim to be 'beyond petroleum'. In the same vein, the International Energy Agency, comprising mainly oil-consuming nations, recommends that the global oil industry invest over US$20 trillion in new facilities by 2030 to avoid higher oil prices. At the same time, the IEA warns that unless the world takes action to reduce energy consumption, global greenhouse-gas emissions will increase by over 50 per cent by 2030. From 1992 to 2004, the World Bank approved $11 billion worth of financing for 128 fossil-fuel extraction projects that will ultimately lead to more than 43 billion tonnes of carbon dioxide emissions, which is one hundred times more than the emissions reductions that signatories to the Kyoto Protocol are required to make between 1990 and 2012. The Bank's contribution to other fossil-fuel-related projects included $7.6 billion in spending in fuel-intensive sectors in 2004–05. This was 37 per cent of its total lending portfolio for the year.[2] These examples illustrate the contradictory aspects of climate-change policy and serve as reminders that what is being said and what is being done are not the same. In this chapter we will first discuss how CDM and JI are supposed to function under the Kyoto Protocol and then we'll examine what the actual business/corporate practices are with respect to the use of the flexible mechanisms under the Kyoto Protocol and EU ETS.[3]

The CDM and JI are based on the premiss that the impact of GHGs in the atmosphere is the same wherever on the planet they are released, and that it is cheaper to slow down emissions growth in developing countries or countries in transition in eastern and central Europe than in industrialized countries. CDM projects are also supposed to serve the interest of developing countries by helping them achieve sustainable development. The general rules and regulations for the CDM and JI were finalized in the Marrakesh Accords (COP7) in October 2001 and are summarized and reviewed in Chapters 1 and 2.

Both CDM and JI projects can be of different kinds: tree plantations ('carbon sinks'), renewable energy projects, or improvements to existing energy generation all fall under the category 'flexible projects'. Furthermore, greenhouse gases can be CO_2, methane or HFCs, and a CO_2 polluter can claim credits for any of the GHGs listed in the Kyoto Protocol, which means that whereas the concentration of GHGs in the atmosphere may be reduced, no reduction in use of fossil fuels is achieved as the result of credits obtained from planting trees in Honduras. CDM or JI projects often follow patterns of FDI in developing countries, and carbon-intensive development patterns are found side by side with flexible project investments. Since this is particularly the case with large-scale investment projects on the part of large multinational oil and electric power companies and their sponsors at the World Bank, it raises questions about the justifiability of giving credits to Annex I countries through flexible projects.[4]

As discussed earlier, the Clean Development Mechanism and Joint Implementation of the Kyoto Protocol allow industrialized countries with a greenhouse-gas reduction commitment – so-called Annex I countries – to invest in emissions-reduction projects in developing countries (CDM) or in other Annex I countries which have credits to spare (JI) and claim credits for the reductions achieved. In theory, this will help reduce Annex I compliance costs while providing new financing and new technology for developing countries and economies in transition. Power generation, industrial processes, and commercial and residential energy use are substantially less efficient in these countries. It thus stands to reason that expenditures on emissions reduction will have more effect in developing countries and in countries in transition than in highly developed industrialized countries, and the CDM and JI have often been touted as a win–win situation. Through the 'Linking Directive' of the Kyoto Protocol, the CDM was made available for use to the EU ETS. The EU Emissions Trading Scheme approved the use of CDM in emissions trading when the Kyoto Protocol took effect in February 2005. The most important criterion for a CDM project to qualify under the Kyoto Protocol is that it supports/contributes to sustainable development, and the most important critierion for a carbon project to be approved is that the project would not have gone forward without the additional incentive provided by emissions reduction credits (i.e. the 'additionality' crite-rion). For the EU, the JI is a way to integrate eastern and western European economies as higher energy efficiency in eastern Europe in particular is pursued. In fact, JI is seen as bilateral cooperation between participating Annex I countries' finance partners in western Europe and businesses in eastern and central Europe.[5]

The CDM is often presented as an effective and efficient way of transferring technology, capital and resources from developed to developing countries in order to improve energy efficiency and the use of renewable energy resources. Clearly, while principles of sus-tainable development and GHG reduction are the objective, business interests and carbon credits are very much the driving force behind emissions trading under the Kyoto Protocol and EU ETS. Both CDM and JI projects can be of at least three types : (1) monoculture tree plantations which absorb carbon from the atmosphere (called 'carbon sinks'); (2) renewable energy projects; and (3) improvement to existing energy generation and use. The financial arrangements between the contracting parties (i.e. governments, private companies, market intermediaries) to CDM projects can take a number of forms.[6] Often investments in CDM projects are equity investments via joint ventures or wholly owned subsidiaries, or indirect investments via purchase of securities that provide co-financing to projects that generate CER credits (e.g. Shell in India or other countries where it has subsidiaries and joint ventures). Here, investors receive the return/profit on investment and CERs. Another way to finance CDM projects is through developers who offer carbon purchase agreements or call options to purchase a specified amount of CERs generated by a CDM project upon delivery (called 'forward contracts'). And the third option to purchase CERs is on secondary markets in the form of spot or options transactions in existing CERs generated by equity investors or developers or by host-country sources through unilateral CDM projects.[7] The most common form of transaction is forward contracts to purchase CERs. The CDM is supervised by the CDM Executive Board and is under the guidance of the Conference of the Parties (COP) of the UNFCCC. The CDM arose out of the negotiations of the Kyoto Protocol in 1997. The United States government desired that there be as much flexibility as possible in

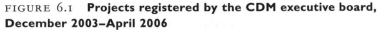

FIGURE 6.1   **Projects registered by the CDM executive board, December 2003–April 2006**

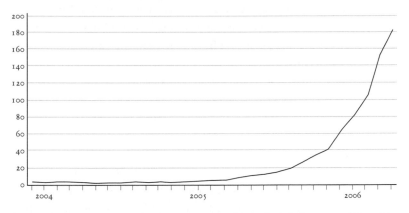

Source: Michael Wara, 'Measuring the Clean Development Mechanism's Performance and Potential', Program on Energy and Sustainable Development Working Paper 56, Figure 1, July 2006, Stanford University, http://iis-db.stanford.edu/pubs/21211/Wara_CDM.pdf.

emissions reductions, and proposed international emissions trading as a cost-effective way of achieving them. At the time it was considered a controversial element and was opposed by environmental NGOs and initially by developing countries, who felt that industrialized countries should put their own house in order first. Eventually – and largely upon US insistence – CDM and two other 'flexible mechanisms', JI and emissions trading (ET), were written into the Kyoto Protocol.[8] Most of the flexible project activity taking place now is in the CDM arena. Hence the rest of the discussion will focus on the Clean Development Mechanism.

The purpose of the CDM was defined under Article 12 of the Kyoto Protocol. As stated earlier, apart from helping Annex I countries comply with their emissions reduction commitments, it was also meant to assist developing countries in achieving sustainable development. In other words, it was to spur development of a low-carbon energy infrastructure in developing countries. To prevent industrialized countries from making unlimited use of the CDM, Article 6.1(d). has a provision that use of CDM be 'supplemental' to domestic actions to reduce emissions. This wording has led to a wide range of interpretations. The Netherlands, for example, aims to achieve half of its required emissions reductions from a business-as-usual (BAU) baseline by using CDM and JI. Before the Protocol entered into force in February 2005, investors considered it risky to invest in the CDM market because of the uncertainties of interpretation of 'supplemental use'. The initial years of operation yielded fewer CDM credits than supporters had hoped for, but in 2006 and 2007 a substantial amount of activity occurred as the end of the first commitment period (2008–12) of the Kyoto Protocol rapidly approached which enticed committed parties that were not able to keep on track in reaching their GHG emissions-reduction targets to buy extra credits (Figure 6.1).

To understand the increased activity of the CDM market, it is important to know what determines the price of CERs. First, there is the balance between demand and supply of all Kyoto carbon credits (AAUs or EUAs, ERUs and CERs) where the price signal for CERs is dominated by the EU ETS. Since the EUA or the EU Allowance price is broadly speaking determined by the Brent Oil Index, all other carbon instruments are priced in relation. So, the EUA price is fundamentally important to the price that buyers will pay for CERs. In addition, the strategy of Russia with respect to the management of its surplus emissions allowances (AAUs); the ability of non-Annex I countries to identify, develop and implement CDM projects; the efficacy of the CDM Executive Board regarding approval of methodologies and project registration; and the progress of Annex I countries in implementing domestic climate mitigation policies; and political decisions on the future of the UNFCCC/Kyoto regime beyond 2012 will all be important factors determining the price of CERs.[9] Based on these principles, Shell predicts that starting in 2008 the supply will be around 100 million CERs per year and the annual demand will be around 650 million Kyoto units (including, CERs, ERUs and AAUs/EUAs). So, demand is projected to exceed supply for the first commitment period of the Kyoto Protocol (2008–12) according to the Shell accountants.[10]

A government procurement office, a corporation, or a private party or developer that wishes to get credits from a CDM project must obtain the agreement of the developing country hosting the project that it will contribute to sustainable development according to the

Marrakesh Accords to the Kyoto Protocol.[11] Using methodologies approved by the CDM Executive Board, the applicant must then make the case that the project would not have happened without the CDM (the 'additionality principle'), and establish a baseline estimating future emissions in the absence of the project. The project is then evaluated and validated by a third-party agency, a so-called Designated Operational Entity (DOE), to ensure that the project results in real, measurable and long-term emissions reductions. The Executive Board decides subsequently whether or not to register (approve) the project. If a project is registered and implemented the Executive Board issues Certified Emission Reduction credits (one CER being equivalent to one tonne of CO_2 reduction) to project participants based on the monitored difference between the baseline and the actual emissions, verified by an external party. To avoid giving credits to projects that would have gone ahead anyway, rules have been specified to ensure 'additionality' of the project to make sure that a project reduces emissions more than would have occurred in the absence of the registered CDM project activity. The definition of 'additionality' is rather vague, suggesting that there is little agreement about its true meaning in use in CDM projects (Box 6.1).

The definitions in Box 6.1 are, in effect, definitions of 'financial additionality' or 'investment additionality' and were rejected by business groups in Annex I countries. These groups argued that it was not the intention of the Marrakesh Accords to define 'additionality' in financial or investment terms, and instead wanted to see a 'environmental' or 'emissions' additionality test included in the Executive Board's document on the CDM. The EU went so far as to claim that Paragraph 43 of the Accords, cited above, specifically refers to emissions additionality. In fact, the Marrakesh Accords contain no reference to either of the additionality tests and provides no legal basis for rejecting one in favour of the other. There is a significant difference, however, between the different definitions: namely, the 'financial' or 'investment' additionality test rules out business-as-usual, but instead would have stimulated investment in 'greenfield' carbon reduction projects, which would have caused the price of carbon credits to rise. In the end, the Executive Board dropped specific mention of what kind of additionality test it would apply, and the guidelines read:

BOX 6.1 **'Additionality' in CDM parlance**

There are currently three quite different 'additionality' definitions in use in CDM parlance, which causes substantial confusion and debate. The different definitions are:[12]

1. 'Environmental additionality' which means that a project is additional if the emissions from the project are lower than the baseline. It generally looks at what would have happened without the project.
2. 'Project additionality' which means that the project would not have happened without the CDM.
3. 'Financial additionality' or 'investment additionality' means that a particular investment would not have been made without the benefit of the CDM CERs.

Paragraph 43 of the Marrakesh Accords of the Kyoto Protocol (2002) gives the following explanation of 'additionality':

A CDM project activity is additional if anthropogenic emissions of greenhouse gases by sources are reduced below those that would have occurred in the absence of the registered CDM project activity.[13]

This means that if a project would have been implemented without CDM registration, then it is 'non-additional', which is also the definition that the EU's CDM programme on accounting and baselines states. It reads:

It is generally recognised that credits for GHG emissions reduction should only be granted for projects that are additional; that is, for projects which would not have taken place in the absence of the crediting procedure or trading scheme.[14]

When the CDM Executive board issued its first draft of the CDM Project Design Document (PDD) in July 2002, it included a definition of an 'additionality test', which reads:

Developers are asked to provide affirmation that the project activity does not occur in the absence of the CDM and ... the project itself could not occur in the absence of the CDM or the ability to register the proposed project activity as a CDM project activity.[15]

Sources: Ben Pearson and Yin Shao Loong, 'The CDM: Reducing Greenhouse Gas Emissions or Relabelling Business as Usual', Third World Network and CDM Watch, March 2003, www.cdmwatch.org, and www.twnside.org.sg. For details on the CDM Project Design Documents see: http://cdm.unfccc.int/Reference/index.html.

> Brief explanation of how the anthropogenic emissions of anthropogenic greenhouse gas by source are to be reduced by the proposed CDM project activity, including why the emissions reduction would not occur in the absence of the proposed project activity.[16]

Without further clarification, this rather vague and open-ended guideline has opened the door for many non-carbon-reduction business-as-usual projects. The additionality test is now usually interpreted as an 'environmental' additionality, which suggests that the CDM is considered a kind of subsidy. Given this potential of the CDM, developers of CDM projects often inflate estimates of 'environmental additionality' in order to maximize the potential for the generation of CERs. The amount of emissions reduction, obviously, depends on the emissions that would have occurred without the project. The construction of such a hypothetical scenario is known as the baseline of the project. The baseline may be estimated through reference to emissions from similar activities and technologies in the same country or other countries, or to actual emissions prior to project implementation. The partners involved in the project could have an interest in establishing a baseline with high emissions in order to acquire a large number of CERs, which carries the risk of awarding credits for little or no actual GHG emissions reduction. Independent third-party verification is meant to prevent this potential problem. However, the CDM community of financial advisers, accountants and consultants is a very tight network, with ties to investment bankers, which raises doubt about independent verification. Private parties that have been assigned emissions allowances by their governments may purchase CERs and use them as permits to emit in excess of their assigned allocations or as an alternative to purchasing allocations from other participants in their domestic market. If the CDM were used to subsidize new clean power capacity in the developing world in exchange for the premature retirement of old dirty power capacity, then it could substantially lower the cost of compliance with a potentially beneficial outcome in terms of reduced CO_2 emissions. However, the majority of CERs derive not from energy efficiency or alternative energy projects but from waste treatment and gas capture projects of non-CO_2 gases (including methane), and therefore the original intent of the CDM to spur development of a low-carbon energy infrastructure in the developing world is not being met. Indeed, we suspect that with the privatization in the energy and electricity markets in developing countries, foreign investors seek to expand production in energy-intensive production with the aid of the CDM subsidy. This strategic manipulation can lead to perverse misuse of the CDM as a mechanism to reduce GHG emissions, as we will see.

In terms of the number of credits generated, CDM project activities currently under development are concentrated in three sectors: (1) renewable electricity generation, (2) reduction of methane emissions (waste from landfill), and (3) decomposition of gases from industrial processes (particularly capture of HFC_{23} and N_2O).[17] Short- and long-term impacts of emissions reductions from these different project activities vary substantially, and whereas HFC_{23} and N_2O capture and reduction projects render quick carbon credits, the activities do not significantly change the business-as-usual fossil-fuel development pattern long term.[18] As mentioned, in the search for CDM projects, Annex I countries seek out projects that deliver large volumes of cheap credits in the short term. These are most often projects that capture or destroy gases with high global warming potential like methane, nitrous oxide (N_2O) and hydrofluorocarbons (such as HFC_{23}) at existing facilities. These projects do not usually deliver sustainable development benefits to the host countries and do not contribute to a fundamental shift in energy production and use. These typically involve investment in an already existing plant or landfill ('brownfield') in order to reduce emissions of a waste stream of GHG rather than a 'greenfield' renewable energy project, which would involve a great deal of investment, a long approval and implementation period, and a limited number of short-term carbon credits. From evidence presented, the search for short-term least-cost carbon credits is paramount in CDM, and energy efficiency and renewable energy projects that would help in the long-term transition of a country's energy system are sidetracked. The time frame for project approvals, construction and implementation is 2008–12 and the uncertainty of the carbon markets post-Kyoto means that project developers typically do not want to get involved in 'greenfield' or renewable energy projects. On the other hand, a 2004 OECD overview revealed that the scale of gas capture and decomposition projects is huge.[19] Of the

240 million credits being claimed up to 2012 by 111 projects at the time (2004), 40 million were from two HFC_{23} projects and another 70 million from one N_2O project – which amounts to about 46 per cent of all credits from these three projects alone. Two additional HFC_{23} projects in India and a twelve-plant $HCFC_{22}$ project in China that would yield 60 million credits a year from 2008 to 2012 were at the time awaiting approval.[20] Thus, while some developing countries like China, India and Brazil are actively pursuing CDM investment as a way to take part in technology transfer for energy-efficient and renewable energy systems, the number of projects that qualify are still very small.[21]

Although the cost of applying for and implementing a CDM project are considerable, the financial benefits for interested parties to invest in developing countries are substantial. With costs of emissions reduction typically much lower in developing countries than in industrialized countries, there are ample opportunities to benefit from CDM project investment and to accumulate CERs for as long as there is a market. Considering the fact that many participating countries (including the EU countries) may not meet their agreed-to binding reduction targets during the first commitment period of the Kyoto Protocol (2008–12), the market would seem guaranteed. An example will illustrate the case. The cost of switching from a coal to a gas power plant in the EU in 2006 could be in the order of €40–50 per tonne CO_2 equivalent, whereas CERs from CDM projects at the time traded for between €5 and €20 per tonne CO_2 equivalent. However, the risks of earning these credits could be substantial, depending on whether the CDM's Executive Board or the host countriy approves or rejects the project, or if the project for some reason produces fewer credits than expected and the buyer does not receive CERs in time to meet the reduction target for the first commitment period. These risks are usually only taken when the CDM project produces assured CERs in the short term, and therefore most CDM projects approved and guaranteed to deliver CERs for the first commitment period are waste-treatment and gas-capture projects rather than new energy-efficient power plants or alternative energy projects, which take longer to develop and only deliver the CERs when emissions reductions are proven.

This being the case, emissions trading is rife with controversy and double-dealing. Although it is presented as part of the solution to reduce GHGs in the atmosphere, in practice, emissions trading is part of the problem of business-as-usual and is prone to fraud, some argue.[22] If not fraudulent, many emissions reductions schemes under the CDM are nevertheless highly questionable. In early 2007 the CDM was accused of paying €4.6 billion for projects that would have cost only €100 million if funded by development agencies rather than with CDM CERs.[23] These involved refrigerant-producing factories in non-Annex I countries (particularly China) that generate the powerful GHG HFC_{23} as a byproduct. By destroying the HFCs, the factories can earn CER credits. To capture and destroy the HFCs requires a simple and relatively inexpensive piece of equipment called a scrubber, which probably costs no more than €100 million for factory owners to purchase and install.

There are also indications that traditional Official Development Assistance (ODA) given by developed countries is being used to fund CDM projects by those countries needing to supplement their carbon credit portfolios. These parties might promote tree-planting projects to offset their carbon footprint rather then drinking-water projects because they do not qualify for CDM credits. This perverse situation is occurring quite regularly as a reduction in the emission of one GHG (e.g. carbon dioxide) enables a polluter to claim reductions in another (e.g. methane). Thus, whereas progress in reducing GHG emissions in the atmosphere might appear to be moving forward, closer scrutiny reveals that no actual reduction of CO_2 emissions occurs.[24] Yet CDM and JI are often touted as the instruments ('Flexible Mechanisms') by which energy efficiency and renewable energy systems will be transferred from the developed countries to the developing world and by which induced technological change will occur.

Technology transfer, energy efficiency and renewable energy

Induced technological change through the use of CDM or JI is often presented as the opportunity for Annex I countries to engage developing countries in climate-change policy and at the same time

transfer energy-efficient and renewable-energy technology to participating non-Annex I countries. The prospect for such a transfer of
technology almost completely diverts attention from business-as-usual
in the developed world. For instance, the World Business Council
on Sustainable Development outlines key areas for future action
on climate change, including efficiency, nuclear energy, government
support for energy research and development, and technology transfer
to the South, but neglects to mention any measures for phasing out
fossil fuels in industrialized countries. The International Emissions
Trading Association – a corporate lobby group established through
the cooperation of UNCTAD and the World Business Council for
Sustainable Development – obviously has adopted this approach and
lists as its members BP and Shell, but also Chevron Texaco, Conoco
Philips, and Statoil.[25] The IETA in its review of the EU ETS reports
its position on the carbon market and promotes a global carbon
market in which opportunities for linking CDM and JI to emissions
trading are viewed as major trading components and beneficial in
technology transfer and engagement of developing countries.[26] The
report notes that the CDM has shown a tremendous growth over
the last few years and that CER transactions increased over 420 per
cent between 2004 and 2006.[27]

In the conclusion of the report there is no mention of any benefit
for reducing CO_2 emissions in the atmosphere or any intention of
replacing the fossil-fuel-based infrastructure with renewable energy.
Could it be that this is not considered an issue since most simulation models predict that induced technological change – including
innovation and diffusion of new technologies at home and abroad
– will occur with the implementation of emissions trading under the
Kyoto Protocol? In fact, most models suggest that carbon constraints
stimulate new technology as a side effect of internalizing the costs of
CO_2 abatement and that these technologies will be diffused through
the spillover of emissions trading to non-Annex I countries.[28] For
example, the wind power industry, which has grown rapidly, notably in
industrialized countries such as Denmark, Germany, the Netherlands
and Spain, has also been adopted by India and China and some other
non-Annex I countries that have experimented with new energy-
saving technology through CDM projects. Models suggest that the

costs of wind power will decline steadily due to the accumulation of knowledge and experience resulting in a diffusion of technology and adoption of new energy systems in various locations around the world. Governments can encourage this process by promoting R&D investments in new technologies and stimulating their deployment through subsidies and by implementing climate change policies that raise the costs of carbon permits. As a result, these technologies will become relatively cheap, which means that they may diffuse to other Annex I countries, and potentially to non-Annex I countries, through CDM or other emissions trading schemes or direct investment. Similarly, climate-change policy could also lead to technological innovation in the biomass and bio-energy industry and benefit non-Annex I countries, and thereby lead to a global reduction in CO_2 emissions.[29]

Since the mid-1990s, the energy and climate policy framework has been favourable for stimulating the development and transfer of biomass and bio-energy technologies, at least in some European countries (for example the Netherlands). Special programmes were developed to encourage R&D of biomass and bio-energy technologies, and fiscal instruments to lower the costs of renewable energy projects were implemented. In some cases (e.g. the Netherlands since mid-2003) production subsidies were in effect to stimulate electricity generation from renewable resources, and an energy tax on the use of electricity generated from fossil fuels was imposed in most European countries.

The same countries that attract CDM project developers are also major recipients of FDI and often receive funding from ODA.[30] It stands to reason that there is a mutual reinforcing relationship between these finance flows, and that FDI and ODA flows are attractive enabling conditions for CDM investment.[31] Funds available for CDM financing as of 2004 were approximately US$800 million.[32] One way to facilitate funding for energy efficiency and alternative energy projects is through the World Bank's Global Environmental Facility (GEF) for climate change investments. While the total budget is rather limited, it sometimes exercises significant leveraging power through co-financing with other private and public entities so that the implementation of climate change mitigation projects is feasible.[33] The relationship also works the other way round. CDM and GEF project

FIGURE 6.2   **ODA and FDI, 2002**

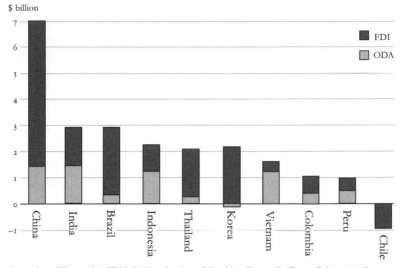

Source: Jane Ellis et al., 'CDM: Taking Stock and Looking Forward', *Energy Policy* 35(1), January 2007: 1, Figure 3, www.sciencedirect.com/science/journal/03014215.

financing may exercise sufficient leverage for other FDI investments to become attractive, and thus, whereas the objective is to transfer energy-efficient and renewable technology, CDM may also be the enabling mechanism by which FDI in energy-intensive manufacturing is facilitated. This perverse relationship is the concern of many environmental groups and activists who see in CDM a scheme for gaming and misuse.[34] The World Bank estimates that CDM financing used as leverage for other financing amounts to about 1:6 or 1:8 of total project costs. CDM-leveraged finance for the entire Kyoto period is estimated at just over 10 per cent of FDI and ODA funds going annually to developing countries. GEF funding for climate change investments totalled about US$1.4 billion from 1990 to 2002. Using the estimates developed by the IEA (2003) with respect to projected investment in the energy sector in developing countries for the period 2001–30, CDM-leveraged financing could become an important part of the energy investment portfolio, if we take US$1 billion as an estimate of the amount of financing available for CDM in the coming years.

FDI to developing countries has the potential to assist with critical technology transfer and could be a means of improving environmental performance provided the proper environmental regulatory frameworks are in place. But FDI is also selective and occurs most often in countries and locations where relatively strong enabling conditions for investment already exist and where market conditions promise profitable enterprise. Very important for successful FDI is the development of infrastructure (electricity, transportation, access to energy, etc.), and thus ODA investment and investment from public–private partnerships are crucial. During the 1990s, ODA funding for improvements of the economic infrastructure more than doubled worldwide, of which investment in energy, transportation and distribution/storage contributed over 90 per cent of the total ODA investment.[35] Figure 6.2 shows the flows of investment from FDI and ODA sources for ten developing countries where large numbers of CDM credits are expected to be generated.

Many developing countries see in CDM projects opportunities to build further investment capacity. CDM institutions have grown very rapidly since the Kyoto Protocol initiated opportunities to engage developing (non-Annex I) countries in project development, and by December 2004, 68 countries had Designated National Authorities (DNAs). DNAs can help formulate national CDM policy and develop criteria to judge proposed projects and reject projects deemed undesirable for sustainable development. For example, China has indicated that priority will be given to energy-sector and CH_4-capture project activities that will bring about GHG emissions reductions, financial investment and technology transfer.[36] As discussed in the previous chapter, the National 11th Five-Year Plan (2006–10)[37] aims to ensure that energy consumption per unit of GDP will decrease by 20 per cent within five years. China is interested in alternatives to coal production and to that end the country is pursuing an energy mix of gas supplies that includes domestic production, international pipelines and imported liquefied natural gas. In 2004 it completed the east–west pipeline to bring gas to coastal markets, and the first of several planned LNG terminals came online. In addition, the country actively pursues access to foreign oil and gas fields through equity investments. In all these cases, technology transfers through CDM investments in energy efficiency are helpful. To prompt these CDM activities, China issued a document 'Measures for the Operation and Management of CDM Projects'.[38] As of 2007, with thirty-seven registered projects and more than 40 million tonnes of CO_2 reduction per year, China has become the biggest CERs supplier in the world.[39] Many business groups and climate change institutes welcome China's move to improve its energy efficiency and express their support; these include Carbon Trust, Climate Strategies, the Netherlands Research Programme on Climate Change, and the Joint Implementation Network.[40] More critical are some environmental groups and NGOs like Climate Action Network Europe and Green Peace International, as well as various academic and research institutes.[41] Some see in emissions trading a scheme to put the atmosphere up for sale through climate shopping and view corporate activities in developing countries as exploitation.[42] Their position is that the EU ETS and the Kyoto Protocol are substantially weakened by loopholes that allow polluters to buy cheap 'offset' credits abroad.[43] A paper mill or power company lacking enough EU permits to cover its emissions can offset the shortfall by buying credits from a windfarm in India, a HFC_{23} extraction project in China or Korea, or a landfill gas-burning plant to generate electricity in Brazil.[44] While such projects achieve *in situ* reductions in GHG emissions, they should not replace a commitment to reduce CO_2 emissions from installations in Annex I countries, as some argue.[45]

Under the Kyoto Protocol, legal entities such as corporations are encouraged to participate in Clean Development and Joint Implementation projects even if they do not operate under shared emissions caps. This makes CDM projects particularly problematic in the context of globalization as the impact of a transnational corporation's total emissions portfolio is largely ignored, and by extension the climate impacts of investments by TNCs headquartered in Annex I countries in the developing world are essentially overlooked. This allows for the capture of transnational emissions-reduction credits while ignoring carbon emissions engendered through other transnational investment activities. Under the current Kyoto Protocol framework a corporation can invest in a HFC- or methane-capture project under CDM rules, while simultaneously making investments in other carbon-producing projects in other or the same parts of the world. Shell's investment in tar-sand oil extraction in Canada (Annex I) is a good example.[46]

Shell installations in different Annex I countries (Canada, EU and Japan) own about 65 million tonnes of CO_2 per year in total. At the same time, Shell generates CERs and ERUs at its installations around the world in various CDM and JI projects, including an energy-efficiency project (CO_2 removal in an ammonia plant) in India; three HFC decomposition projects in Ulsan, South Korea; two projects involving thermal oxidation of HFC_{23} at manufacturing facilities in India; a landfill gas-management project in Brazil, a biomass electricity generation plant in Rajasthan, India; and a small hydroelectric project in Honduras. The total number of CERs issued between October 2005 and March 2006 from these projects was around 2.5 million.[47] One of the projects in India was registered to a nylon plant (SRF, located in Jhiwana, Rajashtan), which emits a large amount of HFC_{23}. By investing in a special process applying thermal oxidation, Shell is entitled to 500,000 tonnes extra CO_2 emissions rights, which it needs in order to derive oil from tar-sand at its installation in Canada. Extracting oil from tar-sand is energy-intensive, and thus Shell predicts that it will not be able to reduce its CO_2 emissions in Canada sufficiently without the extra carbon credits to meet its agreed target.[48] Meanwhile, Shell is rapidly expanding its fossil-fuel infrastructure in developing countries, including India, where it is not subject to CO_2 emissions reductions.

Shell is in fact one of the largest foreign investors in the fossil-fuel industry in India. Its presence in India dates back to 1928, when it established an oil distribution company by the name of Burmah Shell. Shell has joint ventures with several other companies in India: Bharat Shell Ltd in the marketing of lubricants; Hazira LNG Terminal and Port Project in the liquefied natural gas (LNG) market; Shell India Marketing Private Limited (government licence granted in July 2004) to set up a network of up to 2,000 fuel retail stations in India; Shell Gas (LPG) India Private Limited for marketing and distributing of 'Shell Gas' (LPG), which is used in the chemical, food-processing, textile, metal, ceramics, plastics, glass, and automobile industries in India; Pennzoil–Quaker State India

Limited for marketing a range of lubricants; and Shell Technology India (STI), based in Bangalore as a Shell Centre for Technology, which will conduct technical services for Shell across the globe as well as supporting activities in India. The services will span upstream exploration and production activities as well as downstream refinery and chemical operations. Shell has made the largest foreign direct investment in India among all integrated oil companies (around US$1 billion) and is the only global oil company to have a retail licence in India similar to BP's interests in China.[49]

Thus, countries expected to generate the most credits from CDM projects are also the countries that are targeted by and major recipients of FDI. In fact, some of the first CDM projects were clearly linked to FDI investments, in which cases CDM investment was considered leverage or subsidy for new technology implementation.[50] In 2003, the private sector accounted for 45 per cent of the total volume of emissions reductions contracted for in developing countries. This was double the share in 2002. This suggests that international investors, including TNCs, see opportunities in investing in CDM projects.[51] At the same time, the financial services industry is also engaged in strategic asset-seeking FDI (i.e. merger and acquisition activity or joint ventures). Financial institutions like Carbon Trust and Price Waterhouse Coopers are the elite troops in carbon trading, which raises the question of conflict of interest.[52] Price Waterhouse Coopers has a network of more than 150 climate-change specialists around the world helping organizations and businesses with strategic development in emissions trading and carbon offsets and CDM projects. Carbon Trust is a UK government-funded independent company which helps businesses and the public sector to cut carbon emissions and to exploit the financial potential of emissions trading and flexible projects.[53] Financial advisers from these firms offer consulting and accounting services and at the same time function as verifiers on emissions-reduction projects, while all along representing the interests of large corporate investors. These conflicts of interest were among the scandals revealed during the court proceedings of Enron and Arthur Andersen, both pioneers in emissions trading.

Privatization of energy markets

To understand the dynamics of the emissions trading world we need to go back to the privatization and globalization of energy markets during the 1980s and 1990s, a process that began back in the early 1970s when the USA began to deregulate its domestic energy sector. At the same time Margaret Thatcher's government in the UK had begun to privatize various utility companies and other public institutions. In the 1980s, structural adjustment programmes in Latin America recommended the sale of public and state-owned companies in order to reduce government-accrued debt, and foreign investors were encouraged to buy them. In the 1990s, formerly Communist countries in central and eastern Europe privatized their state-owned energy and utilities companies. In the early 2000s, China and several Southeast Asian countries began to privatize and deregulate their energy markets.[54] For many countries, privatization was the only effective method of raising investment capital. High levels of public-sector borrowing had saddled them with large levels of debt. As a consequence, they had little recourse but to sell state assets to reduce debt, generate revenue and raise investment capital.

Privatization was closely connected with the development of the international energy company. Until a few decades ago, outside of the world's few major integrated oil companies, only a handful of energy companies were considered multinational. Most energy and utility companies were national or regional-based and operated under government regulations. Today, in addition to oil companies, many coal companies, petroleum pipeline companies, electricity utilities, and power-generation equipment and construction companies are multinationals. Through consolidations, mergers, acquisitions and strategic alliances, the world's energy companies have also become more integrated in other sectors. Oil and gas companies have become electricity companies; domestic regional electricity utilities have become multinational electricity companies; electricity distribution companies have become generation companies; and generation companies have become distribution and transmission companies.

Foreign investment has been an important factor in the privatization process, but the role of FDI varies from country to country. In countries like Chile and Argentina, in the forefront of the privatization process, almost unlimited foreign investment in the energy sectors has occurred. In other cases, restrictions on foreign investment have inhibited investors. Several of the former Communist regimes, for example, have undertaken relatively moderate and often vacillating steps towards opening up their energy markets to foreign investment. In most cases, even among still avowedly socialist regimes such as China, investment partners rely on joint ventures with state-controlled enterprises as the vehicle for foreign investment, but a move to free market-based reforms and privatization has been evident for several years. Virtually all of Latin America has adopted some form of privatization. In fact, Chile, Argentina, Peru and Colombia have all privatized their public utilities. Among developing Asian nations, electric-power privatization has been most prominent in Pakistan, the Philippines, Malaysia and Indonesia, and more recently in India and China. In some countries – for instance Venezuela and Russia – privatization has faltered, due, in part, to nationalistic attitudes towards energy resources and security. In more than one instance, privatization has been halted because the legal and institutional framework was absent.[55]

Privatization has opened up enormous opportunities for foreign investors, and independent power producers are among the most common foreign investors in the newly emerging energy markets. In several cases, US and European utilities have formed independent power-producing subsidiaries as a vehicle of entry into foreign markets. Oil companies and natural-gas transmission companies have also set up independent power-producing subsidiaries abroad. In several former Communist countries, and in some Latin American countries (e.g. Venezuela), most foreign investment commitments have been restricted to joint ventures with a domestic company (sometimes state-owned). In some cases, such as Russia, the government has also allowed foreign companies to purchase a limited stake in domestic petroleum companies, although here the investment climate has subsequently deteriorated.

Accompanying privatization of energy producers abroad, several US power companies – including Enron and El Paso (see Box 6.2) – participated in investing in joint implementation projects around

BOX 6.2 **The Enron Corporation and emissions trading**

The Enron Corporation was one of the best-known independent power producers. It became notorious for financial scandal and subsequent collapse in late 2001. Its roots were in Omaha, Nebraska, with Northern Natural Gas Company, formed in 1931 and reorganized under a holding company in 1979, InterNorth, which purchased the smaller Houston Natural Gas in 1985, changing its name to Enron in the process. After the new Enron named former Houston Natural Gas CEO Kenneth Lay as its head, it moved its headquarters to Houston, Texas. Enron was involved in the transmission and distribution of electricity and gas throughout the United States, and in the development, construction and operation of power plants, pipelines and other infrastructure abroad.

Enron was a pioneer in the marketing and promotion of power contracts and communications bandwidth and traded in over thirty different products including petrochemicals, plastics, power, pulp and paper, and steel, and was involved in oil and LNG transportation, broadband, risk management for commodities, shipping, water and waste management, and was also a futures trader in sugar, grain, hogs and other meat products. The company was involved in project development of energy infrastructure, financing and operation of power plants, global exploration and production of oil and natural-gasfield services, and in electricity utility services abroad, and it owned thousands of miles of natural-gas and oil pipelines in Argentina, Brazil, Bolivia and Colombia. The company was named 'America's Most Innovative Company' by *Fortune* magazine for six consecutive years, from 1996 to 2001, and was on the Fortune 100 list in 2000.

By the mid-1990s, Enron was the owner and operator of a US interstate network of natural-gas pipelines and had transformed itself into a billion-dollar-a-day commodity trader, buying and selling contracts to deliver natural gas, electricity and many other 'utilities'. By then, the company had become heavily involved in trading carbon offsets. Since 1990, the Clean Air Act Amendments had authorized the Environmental Protection Agency (EPA) to put a cap on how much pollutant the operator of a fossil-fuelled plant was allowed to emit. Enron mostly benefited from the Clean Air Act as it was a trader in natural gas and so the company rallied for and helped set up a cap-and-trade emissions scheme for SO_2 (and NO_2) emissions.

Then, when in the mid-1990s the discussions about the Kyoto Protocol began, Enron, along with other members in the so-called 'Clean Power Group' including El Paso, NiSource, Trigen Energy, and Calpine, became great supporters of a CO_2 emissions trading scheme and paid millions of dollars in campaign contributions to the Clinton Administration and the US Senate to support the Kyoto treaty. The Clean Power Group members hoped to cash in by masterminding a worldwide trading network in which major industries could buy and sell credits to emit CO_2. Enron appeared to be on the verge of success when then vice-president Al Gore signed the Kyoto Protocol in November 1997. Meanwhile, Enron and other companies – including El Paso, the company with which Enron held joint ventures in Latin America – had begun to explore opportunities for investing in CDM projects under the US Initiative on Joint Implementation.

Source: Loren Fox, *Enron: The Rise and Fall*, Wiley, Hoboken NJ, 2003.

the world in the 1990s.[56] In 1993, almost immediately upon taking office, the Clinton–Gore administration set up the US Initiative on Joint Implementation (USIJI) programme, run by an inter-agency group co-chaired by the EPA and the Energy Department. The USIJI solicited applications for projects sited around the world that could reduce CO_2 emissions. It would review each project proposal and then credit the project with so many tonnes of annual CO_2 emissions reduction. Earlier, in 1995, Enron had secured financing for the Dabhol power plant in India (in which it had an ownership stake of 80 per cent) with loans from the US Export–Import Bank totalling US$298 million to cover about 32 per cent of the project costs.[57] This way the company was able to secure another US$100 million in investment money from the US federal agency Overseas Private Investment Corporation (OPIC). In 1996, the investment corporation provided another US$200 million in 'political risk insurance' for the India project, according to OPIC documents. Later in that year, the Clinton administration helped Enron during the company's negotiations over a natural-gas project in Mozambique. The top negotiator on the gas project for Mozambique was Minister of Mineral Resources John Kachamila, who complained about outright threats to withhold development funds if Mozambique did not sign on with Enron. Mozambique was receiving over US$40 million during this time from the US Agency for International Development (USAID). In another case, involving China and India, a memo from a senior director for environmental policy and compliance at Enron (October 1996), it was noted that the Clinton administration sought the company's help in gaining support from China and India for proposed climate change regulations. The memo was sent to a number of Enron corporate officials and lobbyists, who noted that they had been asked how Enron could help set up joint implementation activities in China. The memo suggested that there was an opportunity to get administration support and maybe money, to identify natural-gas-related activities in China that link to climate change in general and joint implementation projects in particular.[58]

In Latin America, the US Initiative on Joint Implementation (USIJI) busied itself in particular in Argentina and Brazil. The largest project was the CAPEX Power Generation Project in Argentina,[59] a US$200 million project consisting of the conversion of a 354 MW single-cycle natural-gas-fired power plant to a 539 MW combined cycle plant. It was expected to result in GHG emissions reductions of 30 million tonnes of CO_2 over its thirty-year lifetime. Technically, this was considered an efficiency project since it involved increasing plant output without requiring additional fuel combustion. The project was submitted by El Paso Energy International, a partner of Enron headquartered in Houston, with significant investments throughout the developing world but particularly in Latin America. El Paso owned 45 per cent of the adjacent natural gas field that supplied the power plant and 13.8 per cent equity in the power plant itself. At the time, the CAPEX project was suspected of not meeting the 'additionality' test under the CDM. In fact, the project would likely have gone ahead without receipt of emissions-reduction credits. Many international corporations were developing combined-cycle natural-gas plants, which, due to their favourable economics and enhancement of the economic value of the natural gas reserves they controlled, had become the standard new technology. These plants were then among the most economical to build, with low capital costs and high operational efficiency. By improving the efficiency of an existing plant it partially owned, El Paso Energy International guaranteed that the plant's investment value would be maintained. As a result of the CDM investment, El Paso would increase the long-term revenue flow from the gas field and the power plant the company partly owned. In the grand scheme of investments that El Paso held in power installations and natural-gas projects, the CAPEX project was insignificant. El Paso Energy International held an interest in over 7,000 MW of generating capacity in the developing world. Annual CO_2 emissions were estimated at over 19 million tonnes and over 7 million tonnes on an equity basis. The annual emissions reduction of the CAPEX project was estimated at 1 million tonnes of which El Paso could lay claim to between 138 and 450 billion tonnes of annual emissions-reduction credits, depending on how equity interest was to be determined. Thus, even if emissions credits were based upon El Paso Energy International's 45 per cent equity in the natural-gas field, the emissions reduction from the CAPEX project only represented roughly 6 per cent of the company's estimated annual greenhouse-gas emissions from its full portfolio of electric power projects.[60]

It seems quite obvious that the CDM fits into the scheme of emissions trading of Enron, El Paso and the like. Once a cap-and-trade emissions scheme was implemented, natural-gas producers and CDM emission credit suppliers could make huge profits from the emissions trade. The Clinton administration's interest in obtaining an international agreement to fight global warming meshed with the Clean Power Group's dream of huge profits from new investments in natural-gas fields, utilities and pipelines. Ratification of the Kyoto Protocol would have played into their hands by forcing the USA to switch from coal-fired power plants to cleaner-burning natural-gas plants. The trading in emissions credits would have funnelled an ever-increasing flow of cash into more investment opportunities in the liberalizing natural-gas sector worldwide. Unfortunately for Enron, this turned out not to be the case. As primarily an energy broker, Enron began to worry when it became clear that the Clinton administration was not going to put the Kyoto Protocol to the test of ratification. As part of the strategy to make things go their way,

Enron and other members of the Clean Power Group then joined the Business Environmental Leadership Council of the Pew Center for Global Climate Change.[61] The Pew Center had waged an expensive propaganda campaign aimed at convincing journalists and the public that global warming was a real threat. Enron also began to cultivate new friends in the environmental community. From 1994 to 1996, the Enron Foundation had donated funds to the Nature Conservancy, Greenpeace, and other environmental groups that were advocating international controls to curb GHG emissions. Enron's CEO, Kenneth Lay – later convicted of fraud – also joined the Union of Concerned Scientists and the Natural Resources Defense Council, both major supporters of US ratification and implementation of the Kyoto Protocol. In 1998, Kenneth Lay wrote to President Clinton asking him to create a bipartisan blue-ribbon commission that would have shut off the scientific debate on global warming. A primary consultant to Enron was James Hansen, a well-known supporter of the UNFCCC/IPCC findings on global warming.[62] In the end all these efforts counted for nothing, as the company went bankrupt amidst scandals involving mismanagement and fraud.

But there is profit in saving the Earth!

Since 2005 – with the implementation of the EU ETS – Royal Dutch Shell and E.ON, a major UK-based power company, have been earning substantial profits from emissions trading and have positioned themselves for the second phase of the EU ETS (2008–12) and the post-Kyoto period. E.ON is an important EU power broker operating in the UK, western Europe, and central and eastern Europe, which, like Enron, has benefited from the privatization of energy markets abroad. Like Enron, E.ON bets on further implementation of emissions trading and stands to profit when that happens. Privatization in the European energy market was occurring alongside the demise of Communism and collapse of the Soviet Union. As a precondition of their entry into the EU, central and eastern European countries had to effect a transition into market economies and prepare for competition and integration with those of the western European countries. In response to EU directives and policies, the European energy markets liberalized and integrated at a breathtaking pace. One of the major objectives of the EU is to eliminate barriers to trade between member states and to harmonize different national energy markets by adopting European community-wide legislation (like the EU ETS). In Lisbon in 2002 EU leaders agreed to transform western Europe into the 'world's most competitive and dynamic economy'. Integration of European energy markets, transportation and communications networks were among the most important infrastructural conditions for accomplishing this objective. In March 2002, the European Parliament approved draft legislation that would allow cross-border energy competition and full deregulation of electricity and gas markets by 2005. Previously, since 1999, the Internal Market for Electricity Directive 96/92 for energy liberalization had been designed to harmonize different national legislations, though restrictions on trade and competition had still been allowed for environmental reasons, including the implementation of policies to stimulate power production from renewable sources. In 2000, the Directive for the Internal Market in Gas addressed the liberalization of natural-gas markets and specified rules on its storage, transmission, and supply. Energy providers have to operate on a commercial basis but states may impose public service obligations for reason of security of supply and services, quality and price of gas, and environmental protection. Primary requirements of the Directive are that member states open up at least 33 per cent of their gas market to competition by 2008 and that third parties have access to pipelines and other facilities on a non-discriminatory basis.[63]

As a result of the accession of central and eastern European countries to the EU, national economies must comply with the requirements of the European Union and open up their energy and power markets for private enterprise and competition. This had widespread consequences for foreign investment by mostly western European energy providers. Most new members to the EU are now part of the European internal energy market and participate along with foreign investors in the private market in generation and distribution of electric power and energy. For example, in Romania, where the privatization began in earnest in 2005 in preparation for entry into the EU, foreign investment played a very important role. As a net exporter of energy,

Romania would benefit from integration into the internal European energy market, but its electricity distribution system was in poor repair and in need of updating. Therefore several regional electricity utilities were privatized and sold to foreign energy producers including E.ON (UK) which purchased shares in or paid cash for outdated regional systems.[64] In addition, gas distribution networks have been acquired by foreign investors, including the Hungarian company MOL, Russia's Lukoil, E.ON and Gaz de France.[65]

E.ON Ruhrgas AG is E.ON's continental European operation, selling some 55 billion cubic metres (bcm) of gas with revenues of €10.5 billion in 2002. Ruhrgas is the market leader in Germany and one of the five leading gas companies in Europe. It procures gas cost-effectively and on a long-term basis from sources in Germany and abroad and delivers it to distribution companies, industrial consumers and power stations in Germany and, increasingly, other European countries. Ruhrgas has been a member of the E.ON Group since March 2003 and is responsible for the pan-European gas business. Together with E.ON, Ruhrgas is opening international markets through vertical integration – the gas supply chain from the wellhead to the consumer – not only in Germany but also in other markets where the E.ON Group has secured major positions. The company receives natural gas from Norway, the Netherlands, Denmark and the UK, as well as Russia. Regional and local gas companies, industrial enterprises and power plants in Germany and abroad are the customers of Ruhrgas. The company delivers natural gas to ten European countries, operates an 11,000 km gas pipeline system and has its own large underground storage facilities. More than 12,000 employees are working for the company. Ruhrgas also holds shares in twenty-three other gas companies in Germany and in twenty-one operating elsewhere in central and eastern Europe.[66] At present Ruhrgas AG holds a minority equity share of stocks in Gazprom. There is an agreement between Gazprom and Ruhrgas AG to coordinate privatization of gas industry facilities and transit gas pipelines in Slovakia, the Czech Republic and Hungary. In October 2000, Gazprom and several western European power companies including Ruhrgas AG and Gaz de France signed a memorandum of understanding on the construction of twin gas pipelines through

Belarus and Poland to diversify the export supply routes of Russian gas and to ensure reliability of delivery to enhance energy security. In March 2002, the consortium won the tender for privatization of the Slovak company SPP. The cooperation is set up to optimize gas transmission operations throughout central and eastern Europe. The cooperation between Gazprom, E.ON and Ruhrgas includes several Joint Implementation projects. Significant reductions in gas consumption through technical improvements of compressor station drive systems can be made, and thus E.ON Ruhrgas stands to benefit from ERUs or EUAs as these credits come due.[67] E.ON Ruhrgas AG's net sales increased from €17.9 billion in 2005 to €24.9 billion in 2006 with total assets valued at €30.7 billion in 2005 and €36.7 billion in 2006.[68]

CDM projects and energy companies in the global economy

Under the Kyoto Protocol, legal entities – such as corporations – are encouraged to participate in flexible projects. This is particularly true for CDM projects, which do not operate under shared emission caps. As a result, CDM projects are particularly problematic in the context of economic globalization as the impact of a transnational corporation's portfolio of global investments is basically ignored. By extension, the climate change impacts of investments by developed nations in the developing world or in countries in transition are mostly overlooked. This situation allows for capture of transnational emissions-reduction credits while ignoring carbon emissions engendered through other transnational investment activities. Under the current Kyoto Protocol framework, a transnational corporation can invest in a CDM or JI project while simultaneously investing in other carbon-producing projects in the same country or in other locations in the developing world. This allows the corporation to invest in international carbon reduction projects to earn CERs or ERUs in order to meet emissions-reduction obligations in other countries where it is investing in carbon- or energy-intensive production, as we saw in the case of Shell, Enron–El Paso and E.ON Ruhrgas. At the same time, the corporation is driving energy-intensive development. In addition, because of carbon leakage from the implementation of the

EU ETS, energy-intensive manufacturing is expanding in non-Annex I countries where available energy and the infrastructure developed by multinational energy and electricity utilities is facilitating energy- and carbon-intensive development. This situation is the reality of emissions trading, which makes it doubtful that the long-term goal of the Kyoto Protocol to reduce GHG emissions in the atmosphere will be accomplished. Many FDI investments engendered through globalization are locking developing countries and countries with economies in transition into development patterns and infrastructure stocks that promote business as usual. Whereas CDM/JI induced technological improvements may have some effect on CO_2 emissions reduction, the overall net effect of the impact of FDI engendered by multinational energy companies should be considered negatively since the main drivers in this global development are multinational energy and electrical power companies.

The privatization of formerly state-owned energy and utility companies in developing countries and in formerly Communist countries, promoted by the World Bank and the IMF through the Washington Consensus, are the basis of this process. Investments by US and EU utilities and independent energy and power producers increased rapidly during the 1990s when a steady process of energy and electricity sector restructuring in developing and developed nations hastened the momentum towards foreign investment that had begun slowly in the 1980s. This development occurred alongside the implementation of structural adjustment programmes in Latin America and South and East Asia, as well as in countries in transition in formerly centrally planned economies in eastern and central Europe. Presently, FDI by energy and utility companies is occurring at a rapid rate worldwide. The big oil and energy companies like BP and Shell, as well as major utility and gas companies like E.ON Ruhrgas and Enron–El Paso, are (or were) the main participants in this process. As illustrated by the example of Shell's FDI investment and CDM strategy, TNCs and developed Annex I countries are free to avail themselves of international investment opportunities in CDM, which help reduce their domestic emissions-reduction commitments without a corresponding assessment of the climate change impacts of their corporate investments portfolio in the rest of the world. This situation rewards so-called climate-friendly CDM investments without assessing the climate impacts of energy- and carbon-intensive investments and development patterns engendered through TNC FDI. The result is a regime which offers opportunity without corporate responsibility (regardless of the impression given by slogans such as 'Beyond Petroleum'). Under such a regime, transnational corporations can drive energy-intensive development in developing countries and economies in transition while simultaneously receiving emissions-reduction credits. Here it appears that there is a fundamental disconnect between the dynamics of the global economy and attempts at reducing CO_2 and GHG emissions under the Kyoto Protocol. The Kyoto flexible mechanisms are implemented within narrow conceptual parameters which fail to address fully the real conditions of the global economy. Transnational corporations, not nation-states, are the primary actors driving energy- and carbon-intensive development. Unless this is fully recognized, we will see limited progress in the reduction of GHG emissions.

One alternative to emissions trading is to focus to a greater degree on the primary global economic actors: the transnational corporations. This would, first of all, require greater transparency of corporate activities. Full disclosure of ownership as well as a full accounting of corporate activities would be imperative under such a framework. Moreover, it would also acknowledge that with increasing corporate power and legal rights (as promoted by the WTO) comes substantial responsibilities. As national economic and environmental regulation loses its primacy with the advent of multilateral trade agreements that institutionalize the legal rights of transnational corporations to export profits, no countervailing environmental rule of law has emerged to regulate their activities. As economic globalization makes it more difficult to track the operations of transnational firms, regulated oversight becomes increasingly necessary.

7

Towards a more equitable and sustainable climate-change regime

Politics and climate-change policy

With the 2007 Nobel Peace Prize being jointly awarded to Al Gore and the International Panel on Climate Change, climate-change policy in the USA and elsewhere belatedly assumed centre stage in public debates. Al Gore pledged to donate his share of the prize (half of approximately US$1.5 million) to the Alliance for Climate Protection, an organization he founded and presently chairs. The Alliance's stated mission is 'to persuade people of the importance, urgency and feasibility of adopting and implementing effective and comprehensive solutions for the climate crisis'.[1] Al Gore's objective and the Alliance's approach is not to be political but to be persuasive in convincing the American public that climate change is with us and needs to be addressed. But while the European Union moved ahead full force and is toughening the carbon constraints and regulations imposed on greenhouse-gas emissions, the United States sat on the sidelines in the climate-change debates leading up to the post-2012 Kyoto era. Congress has debated several proposals to impose emissions constraints in the USA but – given opposition in the White House – little was expected to happen until after President Bush's term in office has ended.

Many environmental, economic and social issues find common ground in climate change and individual and political action can take many forms, all of which have the ultimate goal of limiting and/or reducing the concentration of greenhouse gases in the atmosphere. Individual action is about making various personal choices in lifestyle and consumption. Political action is about changing laws and regulations that relate to climate change, such as tax incentives and greenhouse-gas emissions limits, or establishing a regulatory framework within which measures to combat climate change can be taken. Political action is often challenged by powerful vested interests within the business community, which has played an important role in climate-change policy since the Earth Summit in Rio de Janeiro in 1992 and continues to play a significant role in the politics of global warming, especially in the United States.[2]

From 1989 until 2002 the Global Climate Coalition (GCC), a group of mainly United States businesses opposing immediate action to reduce greenhouse-gas emissions, was active in opposition to the UNFCCC and the Kyoto Protocol. The GCC opposed the IPCC's findings until a major scientific report on the severity of global warming by the IPCC in 2001 led to large-scale membership loss. Since 2002 the GCC has been dormant – in its own words, 'de-activated'. Since 2005, the United States Climate Action Partnership (USCAP) – an alliance of major businesses and leading climate and environmental groups, including the Pew Center on Global Climate Change – has come together to call on the federal government to enact legislation requiring significant reductions of greenhouse-gas emissions.[3] Their view is that climate change challenges will create more economic opportunities than risks for the US economy. After intensive debate and dialogue, the coalition produced a set of principles and recommendations to guide the formulation of a regulated economy-wide, market-driven approach to climate protection. Clearly, business plays a key role in the mitigation of global warming through decisions to invest in research and implementation of new energy technologies and energy efficiency measures. And business plays a strategic role in decision-making about investments abroad and international trade. Ironically, it is in this latter arena that energy security and climate change issues come together and that the international debate may move forward.

There is now a growing awareness that the global energy future marks a distinct departure from past trends and patterns of energy production and use. The trend pattern that emerges has as much to do with energy security as with the challenge of climate change, which requires reduction in emissions of GHSs, particularly carbon dioxide. The 2007 annual report of the International Energy Agency presents a very bleak picture of the future, and projects that under both a business-as-usual scenario and an alternative energy scenario a pathway to long-term stabilization of the concentration of greenhouse gases in the atmosphere at around 450 parts per million will be almost impossible to achieve.[4] The IPCC's future scenarios of energy use, which focus on a range of alternative energy technologies that are expected to be implemented in the coming years and decades, provide some hope for mitigation of emissions of GHGs but a business-as-usual approach to climate change still mostly prevails.[5] As the scientific evidence on the need for urgent action on climate change has now become stronger and more convincing than ever, it is clear that future solutions lie in the use of renewable energy technologies, greater efforts at energy efficiency and the dissemination of decentralized energy technologies and options.[6] The IPCC report provides an analysis on the basis of well-researched materials to stimulate thinking on options that could be adopted in these areas, but like the IEA report it fails to offer realistic policy options. The Synthesis Report for Policy Makers of the *IPCC Fourth Assessment Report* issued in November 2007 called for urgent measures and the need for the USA, China and other developing countries to participate in a meaningful way in future climate-change policy.[7] Response from the White House was guarded.

Renewable energy combined with increased energy efficiency can deliver half of the world's energy needs by 2050, according to a recent Greenpeace study.[8] All that is missing – according to Greenpeace – is the right policy support. The report stresses that the future of renewable energy development will depend on political choices by both individual governments and the international community. Taking into account the principles of equity and sustainability, by choosing renewable energy and energy efficiency, developing countries can virtually stabilize their CO_2 emissions while at the same time increasing economic growth, according to the report. Research at the Center of Energy and Environmental Policy at the University of Delaware confirms such a reduction scenario if the right measures are taken now. OECD (or Annex I) countries would have to reduce their emissions by up to 80 per cent.[9] Unfortunately, time is running out and the overwhelming consensus of scientific opinion is that human-induced climate change will occur if action is not taken soon. If left unchecked, climate change will have disastrous consequences.

A business-as-usual scenario, based on the IEA's World Energy Outlook projection, is not an option for future generations. CO_2 emissions would almost double by 2050 and temperatures at the earth's surface would increase by more than 2°C. That would have catastrophic consequences for the environment, the economy and human society. In addition, it is worth remembering that the former chief economist of the World Bank, Sir Nicholas Stern, in his report *Stern Review on the Economics of Climate Change* (2007), pointed out that those who invest in energy-saving technologies and renewable energies today will be the economic winners of tomorrow.[10] Inaction will be much more expensive in the long run than taking action now. The political choices of the coming years will determine the environmental and economic outcome for many decades. Therefore, we cannot afford to stick to the 'conventional' energy development path relying mostly on fossil fuels. Renewable energy and energy efficiency will have to play a leading role in the world's energy future. But do we stand a reasonable chance of keeping the average increase in global temperatures to less than 2°C?

Worldwide energy demand is growing at a staggering rate and over-reliance on energy imports from a few, often politically unstable, countries, along with volatile oil and gas prices have pushed security of energy supply to the top of the political agenda as it threatens to inflict a massive drain on the global economy. While there is a broad consensus that we need to change the way we produce and consume energy, there is great indecisiveness and disagreement about how to do this. At the same time a growing concern about energy security has emerged. The International Energy Agency's *World Energy Outlook Report 2007: China and India Insights* details increased energy use and projected carbon emissions increases worldwide, with a special focus on India and China.[11] The *Report* predicts that in a business-as-usual scenario, energy consumption worldwide will continue to grow, potentially increasing by 57 per cent over 2005 levels by the year 2030. Almost half of that growth is expected to derive from the rapid increase in fossil-fuel demand in China and India. Coal is likely to account for the largest increase in demand, as production of other energy sources like oil and gas have peaked or will do so in the near future.[12] Using a 'stabilization' level of CO_2 emissions at 450 parts per million – a figure the IPCC has used to set the pathway for long-term stabilization of CO_2 in the atmosphere – global emissions should soon peak and not increase further after 2012, and then would have to fall sharply below 2005 levels by 2030. This pathway scenario, to become a reality, would require exceptionally quick and vigorous policy action by all countries and involve unprecedented technological advances and substantial costs (see Figure 2.1).

China and India have accounted for about 70 per cent of the increase in energy demand since 2005; their energy use is projected to double from 2005 to 2030, by which date the two countries will have accounted for nearly half the increase in global demand. China and India take the position that it is unfair to blame them for what has occurred, and they have resisted calls to limit carbon emissions for as long as they are catching up with the development levels of Annex I countries. Although China has overtaken the USA as the largest CO_2 emitter, on a per-country basis, China's per capita emissions are still only a fraction of their Western counterparts.[13] The IEA report recognizes the legitimate aspirations of China and India to improve the lives and living standards of their people, but the agency does not acknowledge any factors that may explain the rapid growth in fossil-fuel use or measures that should be taken to overcome the structural conditions underlying the rapid increase. The report only states that in the next five to ten years fossil-fuel use has to be drastically curtailed in order to reverse the unsustainable course of development, and refers to tougher efficiency standards in industry, buildings and appliances, and the transport sector, the need to switch to nuclear power and renewable energy sources as well as deployment of CO_2 capture and storage. But how and by which means this is to be accomplished is not clear.

The corporate greenhouse

In previous chapters I have tried to explain that economic globalization through FDI and international trade is the driving force behind the increase in consumption of fossil fuels and CO_2 emissions and the development of a fossil-fuel-based infrastructure in developing countries. Through FDI, corporations headquartered in industrialized countries have become increasingly integrated in the economies of the developing world as markets have opened up and as state-owned enterprises have been privatized. Global institutionalized trade policy, as promoted by the WTO, the World Bank and the IMF, has made so-called 'free trade' the model pursued in most parts of the world, and has thereby greatly stimulated FDI. At the same time, the current greenhouse-gas accounting and reduction regime based on emissions by nation-states ignores the fact that transnational corporations dominate the global economy and that their activities are not bound by national borders.[14] Considering the complex web of relationships between global energy and resource use, production and throughput, economic growth and trade activity, we must begin to conceptualize global environmental impacts in the same manner.

In this respect, three noteworthy aspects of the current economic globalization process are evident: (a) the increasing importance of transnational corporations and international investors as economic and political agents with worldwide leverage; (b) a generalized adoption by development agencies and governments of the proposition that export trade and foreign investment are major engines of economic growth; and (c) an enlarging connectivity and dependency between different world regions and production/consumption nodes, through rising flows of information, capital, goods and services at the global level.[15] Thus, critical questions need to be addressed when considering the environmental effects of global economic activity. These include questions like: Who is benefiting from specific economic activities and therefore bears primary responsibility for the attendant use of global resources and creation of environmental pollution or GHG emissions? Who controls the decision-making apparatus that determines development patterns, resource use and pollution control measures within nations, both ostensibly and in reality? To what degree can pollution or emissions within national borders be connected to the internal economic activity of individual nations within the context of the global economy? Who bears the primary responsibility for a nation's resource use and pollution/emissions: the domestic producing nation, the foreign countries that consume the products manufactured abroad, or the companies and investors who directly or indirectly benefit from the production occurring through TNCs?[16] Solutions that do not address these key questions stand to be incomplete and potentially inequitable, thereby ensuring that climate-change policy will continue to be contentious and may preclude widespread support when implemented.

Throughout the 1990s, world trade expanded at rates substantially faster than the growth of global GDP. Spurred by the Uruguay Round and the WTO, both foreign trade and FDI as well as the growth and reach of transnational companies have increased. The 1990s also saw the first major effort by the world community to deal with a global environment under stress from human activities (UNCED in Rio de Janeiro in 1992), and the initiation of several agreements to begin to address some of the most serious global environmental problems. More and more, the increased and enlarged complexity of global production and consumption networks has connected economic agents in very distant places. These global networks create a shift in relation to the traditional economic paradigm that conceives production and trade essentially as an endogenous and national process. As FDI between industrialized developed countries and from industrialized developed to developing countries has occurred at an ever faster pace, corporate or intra-firm trade relative to total trade at the global level has increased even more, which marks a significant departure from traditional trade flows between countries with associated problems and raises concerns about the lack of transparent behaviour in international exchange.[17] As market concentration due to mergers and fusions of large transnational corporations in several sectors and in several parts of the world has increased, the relative amount of foreign trade (in relation to GDP) has increased as well following a general dismantling of trade barriers in almost all regions of the world. While the financial and trade regimes became more and more interconnected, periodic economic crises in developing countries related to instability in financial markets and exchange rates resulted in interference by the World Bank, the IMF and other international financial institutions through so-called structural adjustment programmes, with the objective of streamlining the global trade regime and opening up markets for investment, as discussed in previous chapters.

While all this occurred in the global economic arena, national governments in their attempts at environmental protection and regulation often submitted to competitive deregulation, and the relative cost–benefit balance of economic development and environmental impact became problematic.[18] So, the question arises: are nation-states responsible for the pool of carbon emissions originating within their borders or do the foreign owners of carbon-emitting infrastructures and production, or indeed the consumers of goods manufactured by transnational corporations in developing countries, hold a share of the responsibility for the emissions created? Assigning primary responsibility to nation-states, as is the case under the UNFCCC and the Kyoto Protocol in managing global greenhouse-gas emissions, while simultaneously moving to usurp their power over economic and environmental decision-making within their borders, creates problems when attempting to address the global climate change crisis. Therefore, we must acknowledge the lack of equitable distribution of political and economic power and decision-making on the part of nation-states in the global economy today. A more equitable climate-change policy regime in the era of economic globalization must therefore account for trans-boundary economic activity and for the energy embodied within products produced throughout the world. Simply to monitor end-of-pipe pollution and emissions within national borders poses serious problems in the context of a highly integrated yet economically polarized global economy. Some kind of reallocation of access to natural resources and responsibility for pollution and emissions becomes paramount in the era of globalization. Questions such as who 'benefits' from pollution, environmental degradation or greenhouse-gas emissions and who 'pays' for the damage caused, both from a producer's and a consumer's perspective, become critical.[19]

To date, developing countries have taken the position in the international climate-change debates that action should first be undertaken by developed industrialized countries, and only after a more equitable distribution of the benefits of value-added from industrial production has been achieved would they themselves be held accountable. Therefore, as we concluded in Chapter 2, Annex I countries should indicate to non-Annex I countries that they are prepared to participate in a full debate on equity and sustainability and that future proposals will include more equitable allocations of 'rights to the atmospheric commons' based on some kind of 'emission rights' scheme. This would inevitably lead to discussion on the disjuncture between the current climate change regime and economic globalization. Without a serious debate about the disconnection between the realities of the global economy and the Kyoto Protocol, negotiations may not proceed. In order to implement principles of sustainability and equity within climate-change policy, we need convincing greenhouse-gas emissions-reduction schemes that will make a real difference. In the OECD (Annex I) countries, this would involve drastic emissions reductions.[20] Climate-change policy negotiations have mostly abandoned developing countries' interests and have moved from sustainability and equity concerns to economic cost and the marketplace.[21] For the long term, massive emissions reductions will be needed, which will be well beyond what technology transfer and financial transfer can accomplish. Without reconciliation and cooperation from the developing countries and a dramatic change in the global economic accounting order, however, it is doubtful if much can be accomplished.[22]

So far, the climate-change policy debate has focused on national targets. When quantitative targets are discussed, the recent history and allocation of emissions based on present fossil-fuel use become the guiding principles. However, developing countries – having forgone their share in economic development in the past but hoping to catch up soon – are clearly at a disadvantage when such allocation schemes are used, and it is for this reason that developing countries have been, and remain, unwilling to commit themselves to reduce greenhouse-gas emissions under UNFCCC agreements.[23] Allocation of emissions based on population size – that is, the per capita emissions criteria suggested by some developing countries – is a much more equitable form of allocation for developing countries; but this has not been received positively by the developed industrialized countries under the current political-economic regime. Therefore, the setting of (national) targets to which all countries of the world could agree is a real challenge and warrants the search for alternative approaches to the problem.[24] Developing countries have taken the position that global environmental problems are mainly the fault of the developed industrialized countries and that in all fairness developing countries should not be called upon to foot the bill. As a result, international negotiations for mitigating global warming have been painfully slow and complex. As we have seen, the US Senate has vowed that it will not pass a binding greenhouse-gas emissions-reduction plan if developing countries like China, India and Brazil (to name a few) do not also commit to binding reduction targets. Meanwhile, the EU Emissions Trading Scheme – effective under the Kyoto Protocol since early 2005 – may actually lead to a shift in production of energy-intensive and/or carbon-intensive goods from the EU to countries that have not committed to binding CO_2 emissions-reduction targets, thereby undermining the overall objective of reducing global GHG emissions. This possibility forces us to consider crucial aspects of the global economy, and in particular the role of the transnational corporations.

In the global economy power is shifting from national governments and politicians and being vested instead in transnational corporations and global institutions. We now live in a world where corporations and business appear more powerful than governments, and where commercial interests are paramount. The top 300 global corporations now account for 25 per cent of the world's assets and many individual companies possess more wealth than many countries in the developing world. Corporate sales account for two-thirds of world trade and one-third of world output, while as much as 40 per cent of world trade now occurs within multinational corporations. This economic dominance gives multinational corporations enormous power. Consequently, unless multinational corporations sign up to efforts to reduce fossil-fuel use and curb global CO_2 emissions – both in the West and in developing countries – business as usual and further growth will likely occur.

In *Green Alternatives to Globalisation* (2004), Michael Woodin and Caroline Lucas assert:

We are witnessing a 'slow motion coup d'état', a process of political osmosis by which power is seeping out of increasingly flaccid national governments to swell the already turgid TNCs and international trade and finance institutions. Any resistance to the coup from conventional politicians ceased long ago. They have become its willing accomplices and the distinction between government and big business is becoming increasingly blurred.[25]

One wishes that our governments would, without vested interest, consider objectively the fate of present and future generations – making wise and precautionary decisions to improve the long-term sustainability of our society. But such is clearly not the case when regulations and subsidies favour the very industries whose primary strategy is to gain greater profits in the global marketplace. Climate-change policy without recognition of this cannot therefore succeed. As we call on national governments and international organizations to help shape and implement climate-change policy, we need first to acknowledge the vested interest corporations have in business as usual and pro-growth government strategies. Assigning primary responsibility to nation-states for managing global environmental emissions while their power over political and economic decision-making is curtailed, creates a disconnect with the climate-change crisis. Moreover, with respect to managing a global greenhouse-gas emissions-reduction scheme, we must acknowledge the lack of equitable distribution of political and economic power and decision-making on the part of developing countries. As global production chains expand and a carbon-intensive fossil-fuel infrastructure is being developed, an effective global climate-change policy is in jeopardy unless we recognize these plain facts.

Equity, sustainability and burden-sharing

While the EU holds steady to its position that drastic emissions reductions targets and timetables are necessary, the USA, along with China and India (among others) are reluctant to commit to them. At the June 2007 meeting of the G8+5 this became all too clear when Angela Merkel's 'progressive Europe' squared-off with George Bush's 'self-interested America' position, which called into question the non-participation of China and India and other developing countries. For all its many attempts to move the climate-change policy agenda forward beyond the Kyoto Protocol, the EU has not been able to persuade the Americans, or the Chinese and Indians for that matter, to get on board. Thus, as the debates and negotiations for the post-Kyoto era begin, we have a stalemate.

One of the primary reasons for the reluctance of countries to get on board is the absence of concrete proposals for burden-sharing that supports rapid emissions reductions without short-changing developing countries in their development aspirations. In addition, non-Annex I countries maintain that as long as Annex I countries fail to live up to their commitments under the UNFCCC and the Kyoto Protocol, there is no justification for involving them in the post-Kyoto era. Whereas Annex I countries call for a new round of 'comprehensive' negotiations, non-Annex I countries point out that the promises of the UNFCCC and the Kyoto Protocol have not been kept.

At the UNFCCC COP13 climate-change negotiations in Bali, Indonesia, in December 2007, it was clear from the start that developing or non-Annex I countries were not prepared to consider binding emissions-reduction commitments while little progress was being made by Annex I countries. Under the UNFCCC (Articles 4.5 and 4.7) developed countries are committed to cutting their emissions and to assisting developing countries through financial assistance and technology transfer.[26] The clash over technology transfer almost derailed the Bali climate talks when a controversy erupted at the meeting of the UNFCCC Subsidiary Body for Implementation (SBI) between Annex I and non-Annex I countries over the implementation obligations under the UNFCCC and the Kyoto Protocol.[27]

Another issue that proved contentious at the Bali meeting was international trade. Recognizing that international trade, development, and climate change are related in a fundamental way, multilateral actions in the context of both climate change and international trade become essential. In the dialogue between Annex I and non-Annex I countries during the meeting, the role of international trade was recognized in as far as it has an impact on climate change and economic development. While the dialogue was generally positive on the important role of international trade in global economic development and welfare, there were divergent views on how trade can help to mitigate climate change while keeping development objectives in mind. The main topics for discussion centred on (a) reducing or eliminating barriers for environmental goods and services in order to mitigate climate change or facilitate adaptation, and (b) the critical role of technology transfer for developing countries.[28] In the discussions it was stressed that whatever policies or mechanisms were implemented to combat climate change, they had to minimize adverse social and economic impacts in such a manner that development objectives were not impaired. A variety of trade-related policy options were discussed, but the role of multinational corporate investment strategies on GHG emissions was not on the table for discussion. On the other hand, developing countries feared that trade sanctions might be imposed if they didn't get on board, and/or that efforts to cap emissions could result in stalled development momentum and trade competitiveness.[29]

Considering the geopolitical situation and the lessons from the past, it is perhaps no surprise that reluctance on the part of key developing countries to participate in the next round of climate-change negotiations prevails. Further inaction on the part of the United States will of course only make matters worse. The first and foremost priority for the developing countries is economic and social development, and measures to address climate change should assist, not impede, the goal of sustainable development. Unfortunately, the current situation, as described in *The Corporate Greenhouse*, is not conducive to further cooperation, and for as long as we are unable to comply with the principle that countries should be asked to meet different requirements – based upon their historical share or contribution to the problem and their relative ability to carry the burden of change – there is little chance that climate-change negotiations will render positive results.[30]

Burden-sharing or differentiation of future commitments to GHG emissions reduction has been an important part of the UNFCCC and is the key issue for non-Annex I parties in terms of future participation in emissions-reduction commitments. During the negotiations of the UNFCCC, developing countries always maintained that given their historical emissions, the industrialized countries should bear primary responsibility for the climate-change problem and should be the first to act. Models for differentiation of commitments often use formulas that relate to different equity principles and multiple criteria relating to both economic and environmental dimensions of climate change regimes. For example, the 'contraction and convergence' approach defines emission permits on the basis of a convergence of per capita emissions under a contracting global emissions profile, with commitments on the part of all parties participating in a climate-change regime and emissions allowances converging to equal per capita levels over time (see Figure 2.1).[31] From this perspective, the right to economic development is a key element. Other approaches to future commitments include a proposal made by Brazil to use differential contributions to the global-mean temperature increase under the 450 parts per million.[32] This proposal is based on the 'polluter pays' principle, with the greater share of the burden placed on those countries that have contributed in the past to global temperature increase, but with the early participation of middle-income developing nations like Brazil, Argentina, Mexico and South Korea and the somewhat later participation of India and China according to agreed-to participation thresholds.[33] The implementation of participation thresholds would reward both emissions reductions by industrialized countries as well as efforts by developing countries to control the growth in their emissions. This would encourage developing countries that receive investment from TNCs to put more stringent carbon emissions regulations into FDI. In other words, global GHG emissions control becomes a pollution control problem, in contrast to the 'contraction and convergence' approach which considers the atmosphere to be a 'global commons' to which each human being, in principle, is equally entitled. While deviation from the principles of equal per capita rights to the global atmospheric commons may not be the ideal or most principled solution, the present state of affairs dictates that extraordinarily rapid emissions reductions are necessary and that TNCs ought to pay for their share of the problem.

Unfortunately, there is a critical absence of concrete proposals for burden-sharing that puts TNCs' share of responsibility on the table and that is capable of supporting rapid emissions reductions without at the same time circumscribing the prospects and hopes for developing countries to keep their aspirations for economic development alive. This has led to a stubborn denial of the severity of the crisis on the part of some important political leaders from developing countries, some of whom have resisted official recognition of climate-change science – as, for instance, China did during the drafting of the IPCC's recent *Working Group I Report: Summary for Policymakers* (2007). In fact, some policymakers from developing countries have concluded that the politics of global climate emergency have as much to do with the developed world's fears about energy security than about climate change, and that emissions-reduction strategies may lock the South into long-term underdevelopment. A more productive climate-change policy may be to show developing (non-Annex I) countries that the developed (Annex I) countries are committed to a future in which development no longer depends on high fossil-fuel energy input and rising carbon emissions but rather on rapid global decarbonization. In this scenario, developmental justice is not a matter of equalizing per capita emissions but a matter of technical assistance from the North to the South, or Annex I to non-Annex I countries, to develop alternative energy technology and promote energy efficiency. Several private and government-sponsored projects are currently being implemented in a number of developing countries to achieve that goal, but in order for these projects to be perceived as fair and equal it is probably best not to align them with the Clean Development Mechanism under the Kyoto Protocol (see Chapter 6). A more convincing strategy might be for the South to propose an emergency architecture with their signature on it, so that other developing countries could agree to an emergency transfer strategy and Annex I countries could show their true commitment. Furthermore, commitments to reduce CO_2 emissions should probably no longer be on the basis of the two-division Annex I and non-Annex I countries but on the basis of historical responsibility with respect to global warming and capacity to pay, which could include middle-income countries. Agreed-to participation thresholds based on a Capability–Responsibility Index defined as the sum of the per capita GDP which relates to the capacity to act and of per capita CO_2-equivalent emissions reflecting the responsibility in climate change, could then be the guiding principle.[34]

The standoff between the US and the EU

For this to be an acceptable and effective scheme we would have to have clear recognition on the part of TNCs of their share of responsibility and the full participation of the United States. Given the dominant position of the USA in world affairs, it seems unlikely that a solution could come about without a shift in its policy. In order for this to happen, our political and business leaders must align themselves explicitly with principles of equity and sustainability. The scientific evidence of climate change is clear. If it is accepted that equity and sustainable development provide the only coherent basis upon which to transform the fossil-fuel-based global economy, then we must lift the Washington establishment out of its complacency. It means that our political leaders will have to convince constituents to see the world in a very different way and as in need of radical change. And it means that we confront corporate capitalism head-on. This is a big task and one that no US politician on the right or the left has so far been ready to undertake. To criticize capitalism is to stand exposed and be called a socialist or communist. Until the financial crisis of autumn 2008, even suggesting that a transformation of capitalism is necessary in order to pursue equity and sustainability was suspect in the USA.[35] US society holds a deep belief that corporate profit creates wealth and that prosperity for society means that economic growth is necessary even if it means a growing inequality between income groups and social classes or between developed and developing nations and great damage to the environment and the atmosphere. Furthermore, it tends to believe that change can come about through techno-fixes and therefore that no real behavioural and structural change is necessary.[36]

To illustrate, US corporations now make a serious effort to be supportive of climate-change policy, at least in the public relations department, and on record like to be 'beyond petroleum', to use BP's slogan. To convince the American public that corporate change is on the way and that climate-change policy would be served by active participation on the part of major corporations, the US Climate Action Partnership has sent out a call for action and a set of recommendations for climate-change legislation to Congress.[37]

Their stated position is that legislation should require actions to be implemented on a fast track while a cap-and-trade programme is put in place. Simultaneously, aggressive low-emitting energy technology and energy efficiency should be implemented and new investments in high-emitting facilities should be discouraged. The cap-and-trade emissions-reduction programme envisioned would be an 'upstream' programme which would put the burden on the consumer, adding the cost of emissions-reduction allowances to the price of fossil fuels. Furthermore, the partnership recommends that part of the obligation to reduce GHG emissions be met through the purchase of 'offsets' from carbon sinks, domestic sources of emissions that are not subject to the cap, and projects outside the USA. Allowances should initially be distributed free to cap-and-trade entities and to economic sectors particularly disadvantaged by the secondary price effects of a cap-and-trade system, including transition assistance to adversely affected workers and communities. Free allocations should be phased out over a reasonable period of time, and credit agreed to for early action – to reward those firms that have already acted to reduce GHG emissions. In addition, the Partnership recommends a set of technology-specific and sector-specific policies and measures and calls on Congress to strongly urge the administration to safeguard US interests by engaging in international negotiations aimed at establishing commitments by all major emitting countries, and that urges the post-2012 climate change framework to establish international GHG markets and boost support for climate-friendly technology in developing countries. No mention is made of the transnational nature of corporate production networks and no corporate responsibility in burden-sharing is referred to.

So, should we be hopeful or pessimistic based on the recent shift in corporate strategy in the United States? Based on the research for *The Corporate Greenhouse* I remain sceptical about corporate intentions. For as long as corporate interest means seeking profit for shareholders, and high salaries, bonuses and stock options for corporate CEOs and officers if they deliver such, public interest and climate-change policy remain secondary. In essence, corporate law casts ethical or moral and social concerns as irrelevant and as stumbling blocks to be overcome. In almost all countries of the world where TNCs operate, corporate law is designed to protect shareholder interest and to minimize the cost of production. Any attempt to scrutinize and question business interests is taboo in the USA and is met with the cry of 'protectionism' which is anathema to 'free trade' believers.

And how about in Europe, where a tradition of social democracy and common purpose has much deeper roots than in the USA and where climate-change policy is now being pursued very aggressively: is there any chance that such policy may prevail over corporate governance? The Third Way political philosophy of governance with its mix of market and interventionist approaches still has a significant following in the European Union. The Third Way emphasizes technological development, education and competitive mechanisms to achieve economic progress and governmental objectives. Third Way policies pursue welfare measures to counter laissez-faire capitalism. The recent move to the left on the part of the German Social Democrats (SPD) may be an indication that Third Way political thinking is still alive.[38] The SPD also signalled to the Green Party that it was ready to consider a political coalition in the future. The move was a grassroots realignment and not a move on the part of the party leadership. In the deliberations, grassroots delegates argued for social justice and equality whereas the party leadership expressed more concern about financing the social security system.

In this context we may also refer to the Netherlands where the 'Polder Model' has been the guiding principle in economic and environmental planning.[39] Jared Diamond, in *Collapse* (2005) refers to 'The World as a Polder', when discussing the world's most pressing environmental problems and how society deals with them.[40] In his concluding chapter, Diamond contrasts US policy with its strong interest in expanding its reach in the global economy with economic and environmental policy in the Netherlands.[41] Under circumstances of high vulnerability in a country where over time a good part of the land was reclaimed from the sea and where dykes were built to protect the land from flooding, one-third of the land area is below sea level, and common purpose in terms of protection and prosperity becomes paramount. In 1953, nearly 2,000 Dutch drowned in a heavy storm and tidal surge, following which the dike system and tidal barriers had to be rebuilt. This experience and the knowledge that global warming and polar ice melt will make the low-lying areas of the Netherlands extremely vulnerable to flooding in the future have made the Dutch determined to deal with global climate change. The Netherlands' economic and environmental policy reflects this, inasmuch as it has pursued a unified coordinated effort in the cause of future security. In Dutch economic and environmental policy, stakeholder involvement in the design and implementation of policy is encouraged, and cooperation between government, business and environmental groups is actively pursued. Emissions-reduction targets are established with respect to water and air pollution and CO_2 emissions, and financial incentives and legal enforcement measures are used to implement these policies. For the most part market-based tools using 'polluter pays' principles apply. These include gas taxes and user fees. But the government also uses subsidies to encourage behavioural change and technological developments that are environmentally friendly. For instance, fuel-efficient cars are subsidized through fuel tax revenue. Needless to say, such a plan requires support from all sectors of society – business, energy providers, trade unions, and consumers. What is interesting is that when President George W. Bush first appointed Christie Whitman as head of the Environmental Protection Agency (EPA), he did this with reference to the Netherlands, where consensus and cooperation on environmental policy prevailed, rather than confrontation and division, a style Whitman presumably aspired to follow. Of course, we know that Whitman did not last very long at the EPA.

The likelihood of the USA changing its strategy and playing a constructive role in the UNFCCC climate-change debate is greater now under the Obama administration than was the case under the Bush administration. Still, we expect that most of the initiatives for a fruitful climate-change policy will come from Europe. The EU has had a series of climate-change policies in place since 2000 and it considers itself the leader in emissions trading under the Kyoto Protocol. The EU appears fully committed to the Kyoto process and hopes to negotiate a follow-up to the Protocol to take effect after 2012. With Australia now on board under the new Labor leadership, the USA will hopefully follow suit. However, the USA has consistently expressed its opposition to binding CO_2 emissions cuts under a global climate change agreement and will likely put forward a separate proposal during the next few rounds of negotiations under the UNFCCC. Be that as it may, the EU has earned its stripes in the UNFCCC efforts to bring other parties on board, and with its status as a growing economic power may carry the day in upcoming climate-change negotiations. Experience of the implementation of the ETS suggests that the EU may become the 'hub of a global carbon market', in which case it is desirable that certain changes be made to the existing trading regime.

How to deal with CO_2 'embodiment' in global trade

Under the current climate-change policy regime, emissions trading is contributing to an expansion of production in the most energy-intensive sectors of the global economy in countries that are not committing to CO_2 emissions reduction (non-abatement countries). Under the current international trade regime, guided by the principles of the WTO, this is expected to continue to be the case unless international trade organizations correct for the negative spillover effects or the shift in production from abatement to non-abatement countries (relocation of production of energy-intensive industries). In this context, as suggested in Chapter 5, we might think of introducing import taxes (tariffs) on high-carbon-content goods and services or impose some other 'polluter pays' principle on TNCs that relocate production to non-carbon-constraint parts of the world. Under these circumstances it would seem reasonable that upon the entry of high-carbon-content goods, or goods produced with high energy input, some kind of tariff could be imposed at the border of the abatement country. Such a measure could reduce the incentive for relocation of energy-intensive production, but it might be interpreted as protectionism in disguise, which, under the political-economic conditions in the global economy and given the North–South division, would not be well received in the developing world.

Derived from the same concern about unfair competition in a partial carbon-constraint global economy, I also suggested that we might apply an energy-intensive sector-specific approach to emissions trading (Chapter 5). Such unfair competition leaves some industries in a highly disadvantaged position. As we saw in Chapter 5, different industries in different locations experience different cost structures, and wherever energy-intensive industries are exposed to competition when carbon constraints apply, trade exposure leaves them vulnerable if they cannot pass on the increased cost of production. I suggested that, instead of accepting the status quo business-as-usual approach to competition, a particular sector or industry could decide to take action at the international level by agreeing through their global trade associations to pledge to achieve a sector/industry-wide goal of reducing GHG emissions through sharing best practice standards throughout the industry wherever located, and stimulate increased energy efficiency and technology transfer. Sector- or industry-specific initiatives could seek endorsement from national governments, but since industry is not a 'party' to the UNFCCC and parties without specific GHG targets are therefore unlikely to participate in a 'voluntary' scheme as the Bush administration's Asia Pacific Partnership proposes, the scheme has little chance of success. At the April 2008 UNFCCC meeting in Bangkok, Japan presented its proposal for a sector-specific emissions-reduction approach. EU business representatives endorsed the proposal, stating that it would be less harmful for their competitive position in the global economy and that it would reward the best performers and stimulate financing for innovative technologies. The Japanese move was widely criticized by most developing countries and some NGOs – for instance the World Wildlife Fund – which warned that by pushing for a sector-specific approach, developed countries might alienate developing nations and undermine the cooperation needed to move negotiations forward.

One alternative to the problems associated with the current climate-change policy regime is to focus the frame of reference more specifically on the multinational corporations and their trade component. Some researchers have recognized the complexity of CO_2 'embodiment' in global trade, and it has been argued that national climate-change policies which are predicated on controlling domestic emissions may not be effective if imported goods from non-abatement countries result from offshore manufacturing and FDI.[42] Some have questioned whether under those circumstances the producer or the consumer should be responsible for the GHGs emitted.[43] In a paper published in 2006, Shui and Harris, try to estimate the scale of CO_2 emissions avoided in the USA by the importation of Chinese goods, how much of China's CO_2 emissions derived from production of goods for export to the USA, and what the impact of US–China trade is on global CO_2 emissions. They estimated that during 1997–2003, US CO_2 emissions would have increased from 3 to 6 per cent if the goods imported from China had been produced in the USA and that between 7 and 14 per cent of China's CO_2 emissions were the result of producing export goods for US consumers. US–China trade was estimated to have increased CO_2 emissions by 720 million tonnes. They concluded that improved international accounting standards for assigning responsibility for CO_2 emissions must be designed to account for the impact of international trade.[44]

Full disclosure of ownership and full accounting of corporate activities throughout the production chain would be imperative under such a framework. In other words, at every step in the production process we would need to know how much CO_2 is added to the national GHG pool; this amount would then be subtracted from the total amount of the country where TNC production occurs and be added to the TNC's headquarter or home country and/or the country to which the product is shipped for consumption. Hypothetically, we could also attribute CO_2 emissions on a profit-rate basis. If a refinery in China operated by a TNC generated 100 million tonnes of CO_2 per year, and if 50 per cent of the profits are returned to headquarters or to the TNCs' shareholders, then 50 million tonnes of CO_2 emissions should be accounted for and subtracted from the host-country national budget and added to the home country's GHG budget. All this would require far greater transparency than is presently the case, which will likely be resisted by the corporate establishment, but unless we come to realize that global climate-change policy requires global consensus and worldwide cooperation we will not make much progress in global GHG-reduction efforts. In the end, unless we manage to overcome the North–South divisions that exist, it is unlikely that we will succeed in solving climate change problems. As part of reaching global consensus and worldwide cooperation, global corporations will have to restructure the way they operate in developing countries, and their contributions to global GHG emissions will have to be accounted for.

As the UNFCCC in Bali ended without a firm commitment from the United States or China to reduce emissions of CO_2 and other greenhouse gases a bill is winding its way through the US Congress that might offer an opportunity to deal with carbon leakage and relocation of production of energy-intensive goods to non-abatement countries. The Lieberman–Warner Climate Security Act – as the bill is known – intends to cap American carbon consumption through a tradeable permit plan, thereby introducing a measure to deal with import of carbon-intensive and energy-intensive goods from countries not committed to binding emissions reduction. By focusing on carbon consumption, not emissions, a tradeable permit system could force consumer prices for goods to reflect the harm that the production of those goods causes the global atmosphere. For instance, a television made in a low-emission factory would require fewer permits, lowering its relative price to a television produced in a high-emission factory, but a television manufactured in a country with no emissions cap would likely still be cheaper and consumers would be inclined to buy the imported item. In this case, importers of goods from countries without carbon caps would have to obtain permits for the emissions resulting from the goods' production in a non-abatement country and then pass the increased costs on to the consumer.

Under this scenario, if the USA adopted a tradeable permit system that treated emissions from domestic producers identically to emissions associated with imported goods, then products that are more energy- and emission-intensive, whether domestic or imported, would require more permits and thus be more expensive; therefore producers in the USA and abroad would have an incentive to reduce greenhouse-gas emissions to make their goods more competitive. This measure would take away the incentive for TNCs to relocate energy-intensive production to non-abatement countries in order to expand market share. In the same way, the EU could take the same measures relative to US producers, which may entice the USA to commit to a binding global agreement on GHG emissions reduction and eventually persuade developing countries to take on binding measures of their own. A carbon-consumption provision would face scrutiny under the current WTO trade regime, but it might open the door for serious negotiations at the WTO to change its trade rules and for Climate to finally find a partner in Capital.

Change in greenhouse-gas emissions 1990–2005 (%)

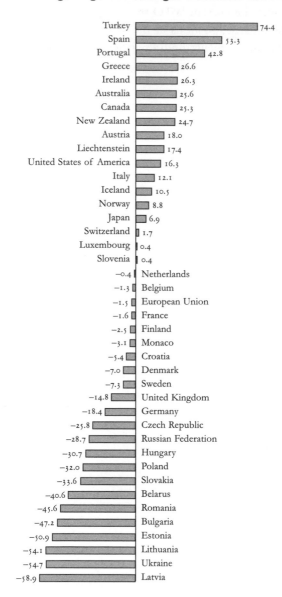

Turkey	74.4
Spain	53.3
Portugal	42.8
Greece	26.6
Ireland	26.3
Australia	25.6
Canada	25.3
New Zealand	24.7
Austria	18.0
Liechtenstein	17.4
United States of America	16.3
Italy	12.1
Iceland	10.5
Norway	8.8
Japan	6.9
Switzerland	1.7
Luxembourg	0.4
Slovenia	0.4
Netherlands	−0.4
Belgium	−1.3
European Union	−1.5
France	−1.6
Finland	−2.5
Monaco	−3.1
Croatia	−5.4
Denmark	−7.0
Sweden	−7.3
United Kingdom	−14.8
Germany	−18.4
Czech Republic	−25.8
Russian Federation	−28.7
Hungary	−30.7
Poland	−32.0
Slovakia	−33.6
Belarus	−40.6
Romania	−45.6
Bulgaria	−47.2
Estonia	−50.9
Lithuania	−54.1
Ukraine	−54.7
Latvia	−58.9

Source: United Nations Framework Convention on Climate Change (UNFCCC), www.unfccc.int/.
Note: Data are for changes excluding LULUCF. The parties that are allowed to use a base year other than 1990 have also provided data for their respective base year: Bulgaria (1988), Hungary (average, 1985–87), Poland (1988), Romania (1989) and Slovenia (1986). For Croatia, Greece and Turkey, data from 2006 submissions are used; for 2005, 2004 values are used as the latest available estimate.

Notes

Introduction

1. The series of papers, written between 1999 and 2005, are as follows: Yda Schreuder and Christopher Sherry, 'Global Corporations in the Greenhouse: Developing Equitable Accounting Measures', *Bulletin of Science, Technology and Society* 19(6), December 1999: 511–20; Yda Schreuder and Christopher Sherry, 'Flexible Mechanisms in the Corporate Greenhouse: Implementation of the Kyoto Protocol and the Globalization of the Electric Power Industry', *Energy and Environment* 12(5/6), 2001: 487–98. Yda Schreuder, 'EU Emissions Trading Scheme in the Corporate Greenhouse: A Predicament for Power Intensive Industries', *Forum on Public Policy: Special Issue: Trade and the Environment* 1(1), 2005: 190–204.

Chapter 1

1. Intergovernmental Panel on Climate, *Climate Change 2007: The Physical Science Basis. Summary for Policymakers*, February 2007: 10.
2. Ibid.: 13.
3. The Annex B countries are identical to the Annex 1 countries of the UNFCCC except for Turkey and Belarus, which are not included in the Annex B group, and Kazakhstan, which voluntarily joined Annex B. Under the 'Flexible Mechanisms' of the Kyoto Protocol, Annex B countries are allowed to purchase emission permits from other Annex B countries with GHG emissions rates that are below their Kyoto targets. Annex B countries may also receive credits towards target reductions through project-based emissions reductions or sink expansions in other Annex B countries, through

Joint Implementation, and Annex B countries can earn Certified Emission Reductions from project activities in developing countries through the Clean Development Mechanism.

4. Thomas C. Schelling, (2002) 'What Makes Greenhouse Sense? Time to Rethink the Kyoto Protocol', *Foreign Affairs*, May: 2–9.

5. For a history and discussion of the EU–ETS, see Hillebrand Bernhard et al., *CO₂ Emissions Trading Put to the Test: The Design Problems of the EU Proposal for an Emission Trading System in Europe*, LIT Verlag, Munster, Hamburg and London, 2003.

6. For clearly written general overviews of climate-change policy, see Catrinus J. Jepma and Mohan Munasinghe, *Climate Change Policy: Facts, Issues, and Analyses*, Cambridge University Press, Cambridge, 1998; Urs Luterbacher and Detlef F. Sprinz (eds), *International Relations and Global Climate Change*, MIT Press, Cambridge MA, 2001; and Eileen Claussen et al. (eds), *Climate Change: Science, Strategies, & Solutions*, Brill, Leiden and Boston, 2001.

7. IPCC Fourth Assessment Report 2007: Working Group I, www.ipcc.ch/ipc-creports/ar4–syr.htm-.

8. F. Yamin et al., 'Kyoto Mechanisms: Key Issues for Policy-Makers for COP6', *International Environmental Agreements: Politics, Law and Economics*, 1, 2001: 187–218.

9. It was agreed that if 55 signatory countries representing 55 per cent of Annex I countries' emissions of CO_2 in 1990 had certified the Protocol, then the Protocol would be implemented with legally binding commitments to reduce GHG emissions to the agreed to level.

10. The World Bank's Prototype Carbon Fund (PCF) represents a consortium of six governments and seventeen major utility and energy companies, on whose behalf it purchases credits. It became operational in 2000. As the first carbon fund, its mission was to pioneer the market for project-based greenhouse-gas emissions reductions while promoting sustainable development and offering a learning-by-doing opportunity to its stakeholders.

11. The International Emissions Trading Organization (IETA) is an independent, non-profit organization dedicated to the establishment of effective systems for trading in greenhouse-gas emissions by businesses. See www.ieta.org.

12. The online Climate Policy Map offers interactive information on international climate policy that allows comparisons of key statistics on energy and GHG emissions. See www.climate-policy-map.econsense.de/userguide.html.

13. 'National greenhouse-gas inventory data for the period 1990–2005: Change in GHG emissions excluding LULUCF', UNFCCC, www.UNFCCC.int.

14. The Global Carbon Project was established in 2001 in recognition of the enormous challenges facing the world community in dealing with the global carbon cycle in both its biophysical and human dimensions. See www.globalcarbonproject.org.

15. M.R. Raupach et al., 'Global and Regional Drivers of Accelerating CO_2 Emissions', Proceedings of the National Academy of Sciences of the United States of America, 22 May 2007, www.pnas.org.

16. The Global Carbon Project is responding to this challenge through a shared partnership between the International Geosphere–Biosphere Program (IGBP),

the International Human Dimensions on Global Environmental Change (IHDP), the World Climate Research Program (WCRP) and Diversitas. This partnership constitutes the Earth Systems Science Partnership (ESSP). See www.globalcarbonproject.org/about/index.htm.

17. See www.globalcarbonproject.org/misc/carbontrends.htm.

18. IPCC, *Climate Change 2007: The Physical Science Basis: Summary for Policymakers*, February 2007: www.ipcc.ch.

19. Preliminary estimate by the Netherlands Environmental Assessment Agency (MNP) using recently published BP energy data and cement production data. In the 1990–2006 period, global fossil-fuel-related CO_2 emissions increased over 35 per cent. See www.mnp.nl/en/dossiers/Climatechange/moreinfo/ChinanownoiinCO2emissionsUSAinsecondposition.html.

20. J. Byrne, Y.D. Wang, H. Lee and J. Kim, 'An Equity- and Sustainability-based Policy Response to Global Climate Change', *Energy Policy* 26, 1998: 335–43; J. Byrne, L. Kurdgelashvili and K. Hughes, 'Undoing Atmospheric Harm: Civil Action to Shrink the Carbon Footprint', in P. Droege (ed.), *Urban Energy Transition: From Fossil Fuels to Renewable Power*. Elsevier, Oxford, 2008: 27–54.

21. 'Contraction and Convergence' is a global framework for reducing GHG emissions to combat climate change. Conceived by the Global Commons Institute in the early 1990s, the Contraction and Convergence strategy consists of reducing overall emissions of greenhouse gases to a safe level while setting per capita emissions equity as the ultimate goal. See the Global Commons Institute, www.gci.org.uk/.

22. Bin Shui and Robert C. Harris, 'The Role of CO_2 Embodiment in US–China Trade', *Energy Policy* 34, 2006: 4063–8.

23. Raupach et al., 'Global and Regional Drivers of Accelerating CO_2 Emissions'.

24. OECD, *International Investment Perspectives: 2006 Edition*, OECD, Paris: 23, Table 1.3.

25. See US Department of Energy, Country Analysis Briefs, China 2006, August, www.eia.doe.gov.

26. See 'Choking on Growth', *New York Times*, 26 August 2007, www.nytimes.com/interactive/2007/08/26/world/asia/choking_on_growth.html.

27. British Petroleum, *BP Statistical Review of World Energy*, BP, London, 2005, www.bp.com.

28. See Energy Information Administration of the US Government, www.eia.doe.gov.

29. See Climate Policy Map Fact Sheet on Greenhouse Gas Emissions, www.climate-policy-map.econsense.de/userguide.html; *State of the World 2006: Special Focus: China and India*, World Watch Institute, W.W. Norton, New York and London, 2006: Table 8, Box 1.1, www.worldwatch.org/brain/images/pubs/sow/extra/2006-box-1–1.jpg.

30. Intergovernmental Panel on Climate Change, *Climate Change 2007: The Physical Science Basis: Summary for Policymakers*, IPCC, 2007: 2, www.ipcc.ch/pdf/assessment-report/ar4/wg1/ar4–wg1–spm.pdf. Ppm (parts per million) is the ratio of the number of greenhouse gas molecules to the total number of molecules of dry air.

31. Millennium Ecosystem Assessment, *Ecosystems and Human Well-Being: Synthesis*, Island Press, Washington DC, 2005. See also www. maweb.org.
32. Energy Information Administration, 'Carbon Dioxide Emissions from Energy Activities', EIA, Washington DC, 2004. See www.eia.doe.gov.
33. EIA, *International Energy Outlook 2006*, EIA, Washington DC, 2006: Table A-10.
34. China's landmark renewable energy law took effect on 1 January 2006, prompting the government to issue a number of pertinent new rules and technical criteria, in particular, financial subsidies and tax incentives for the development of renewable energy sources, including wind power, solar energy and biomass. See www.renewableenergyworld.com/assets/download/China_RE_Law_05.doc.
35. See www.bp.com.
36. See www.bp.com/sectiongenericarticle.do?categoryId=9015498&content Id=7028087.
37. For BP in China, see www.bp.com/sectiongenericarticle.do?categoryId= 9004963&contentId= 7010305.
38. Gary Dirks, 'Energy Security: China and the World', International Symposium on Energy Security: China and the World, Beijing, 24 May 2006. See www. bp.com/downloadlisting.do?categoryId=9004960&contentId=7009431.
39. Aaron Cosbey, 'Reconciling Trade and Sustainable Development', *State of the World 2006*, 2006: 134–15.
40. Hilary French, *Vanishing Borders: Protecting the Planet in the Age of Globalization* World Watch Institute, W.W. Norton, New York and London, 2000: 92.
41. See *International Energy Outlook 2006*: 103, Table A-10.

Chapter 2

1. Statement at the opening of the UN Conference on Environment and Development, Rio de Janeiro, Brazil, 3 June 1992.
2. M.A. Levy, P.M. Haas and R.O. Keohane, *Institutions for the Earth: Promoting International Environmental Protection*, MIT Press, Cambridge MA, 1992.
3. World Commission on Environment and Development, *Our Common Future*, Oxford University Press, Oxford, New York, 1987: 3. Also known as the Brundtland Report.
4. UN Resolution 44/228, New York, 22 December 1989, part 1.3.
5. UNCED, Rio de Janeiro, 3–14 June 1992, www.un.org/documents/ga.
6. The Ecologist, *Whose Common Future? Reclaiming the Commons*, New Society, Philadelphia, and Earthscan, London, 1993.
7. Wolfgang Sachs, *Planet Dialectics: Explorations in Environment and Development*, Zed Books, London, New York, 1999.
8. See also Wolfgang Sachs, 'Ecology, Justice and the End of Development', in John Byrne et al., *Environmental Justice: Discourses in International Political Economy*, Energy and Environmental Policy vol. 8, Transaction, New Brunswick and London, 2002.
9. WCED, *Our Common Future*.

10. That this is not the case with CO_2 emissions has been shown since. See Nicholas Stern, *The Economics of Climate Change: The Stern Review*, Cambridge University Press, Cambridge, 2006: 191–2, Annex 7A.

11. Sachs, 'Ecology, Justice and the End of Development'.

12. World Bank, *World Development Report: Development and Environment*, Oxford University Press, Oxford, 1992.

13. J.K. Holmberg et al., *Facing the Future: Beyond the Earth Summit*, International Institute for Environment and Development, Earthscan, London, 1993.

14. The Ecologist, *Whose Common Future?*

15. Richard Peet, *Global Capitalism: Theories of Societal Development*, Routledge, London and New York, 1991; D. Slater and P.J. Taylor (eds), *The American Century: Consensus and Coercion in the Projection of American Power*, Blackwell, Oxford, 1999; S.B. Cohen, *Geopolitics of the World System,* Rowman & Littlefield, Oxford, 2003.

16. World Bank, *World Development Report*: 67; quoted in The Ecologist, *Whose Common Future?*: 111.

17. Stephen Schlesinger, *Act of Creation: The Founding of the United Nations*, Westview Press, Boulder CO, 2003. See also Peter Gowan, 'US/UN', *New Left Review* 24, November–December 2003.

18. R. Nader et al., *The Case against Free Trade: GATT, NAFTA, and the Globalization of Corporate Power*, Earth Island Press, San Francisco, 1993; F.M. Edoho (ed.), *Globalization and the New World Order: Promises, Problems, and Prospects for Africa in the Twenty-First Century*, Praeger, Westport CT, 1997; Hilary French, *Vanishing Borders: Protecting the Planet in the Age of Globalization*, W.W. Norton, New York, 2000.

19. L.K. Caldwell, 'Political Aspects of Ecologically Sustainable Development', *Environmental Conservation* 11, 1984: 299–308.

20. R. Boardman, *International Organizations and the Conservation of Nature*, Indiana University Press, Bloomington IN, 1981.

21. M.T. Farvar and J.P. Milton (eds), *The Careless Technology: Ecology and International Development*, Stacey, London, 1973; R.F. Dasmann et al., *Ecological Principles for Economic Development*, Wiley, Chichester, 1973.

22. L. Anell and B. Nygren, *The Developing Countries and the World Economic Order*, Methuen, London and New York, 1980.

23. R.L. Rothstein, 'Foreign Policy and Development Policy: From Non-Alignment to International Class War', *International Affairs*, October 1976: 598–616; R.L. Rothstein, *The Weak in the World of the Strong: The Developing Countries in the International System*, Columbia University Press, New York, 1977; Robin Broad (ed.), *Global Backlash: Citizen Initiatives for a Just World Economy*, Rowman & Littlefield, New York, 2002.

24. Brandt Commission Report, *North–South: A Program for Survival*, Pan, London, 1980.

25. L. Anell and B. Nygren, *The Developing Countries and the World Economic Order*, Methuen, London and New York, 1980: 104–5.

26. W.M. Adams, *Green Development: Environment and Sustainability in the Third World*, Routledge, London, 1980; F. Schuurman (ed.), *Beyond the Impasse: New Directions in Development Theory*, Zed Books, London, 1993.

27. M.R. Biswas and A K. Biswas, 'Complementarity between Environment and Development Processes', *Environmental Conservation* 11, 1984: 35–43.
28. R. Clarke and L. Timberlake, *Stockholm Plus Ten: Promises Promises?*, Earthscan, London, 1982.
29. *Caring for the Earth: A Strategy for Sustainable Living*, IUCN–UNEP–WWP, Gland, 1991.
30. W. M. Adams 'Sustainable Development and the Greening of Development Theory', in Schuurman (ed.), *Beyond the Impasse*.
31. WCED, *Our Common Future*.
32. R. Gelbspan, *The Heat is On: The High Stakes Battle over Earth's Threatened Climate*, Addison-Wesley, New York, 1997; J. Leggett, *The Carbon War: Global Warming and the End of the Oil Era*, Penguin, New York, 1999.
33. Under the Kyoto Protocol, 'hot-air trading' can occur when the emissions ceiling agreed to exceeds the actual GHG emissions level and when the surplus thus created is sold to other countries that do not meet their agreed emissions reduction target. See E. Woerdman, 'Hot Air Trading under the Kyoto Protocol: An Environmental Problem or Not?', *European Environmental Law Review* 14(3), 2005: 71–7. Carbon sinks refer to the natural ability of trees and other plants and the soil to absorb carbon dioxide and temporarily store the carbon emitted in the atmosphere.
34. Leggett, *The Carbon War*. 290.
35. See Chapter 1 n3, above.
36. John Byrne et al., 'Reclaiming the Atmospheric Commons: Beyond Kyoto', in V. Grover (ed.), *Climate Change: Five Years After Kyoto*, Science, Enfield NH, 2004: 429–52.
37. For a breakdown by EU member states and the total EU target commitment of emissions reduction, see *Joint Implementation Quarterly*, June 1999: 5.
38. L. Ringius, 'Differentiation, Leaders and Fairness: Negotiating Climate Commitments in the European Community', *International Negotiation* 4, 1999: 133–66.
39. F. Wagner and A. Michaelowa, 'Burden Sharing Targets for the EU Bubble in the Second Commitment Period: CO_2 from the Energy Sector', in J. Klaus-Dieter and D. Rubbelke (eds), *Klimapolitik in einer erweiterten Europaischen Union*, Shakaer Verlag, Achen, 2005: 79–100.
40. John Byrne et al., *Climate Shopping: Putting the Atmosphere Up for Sale*, Environment, Economy and Society 5, TELA, Melbourne, 2000.
41. The UNDP's *Human Development Report* had already recognized this in 1998 by stating the 'poor countries have to accelerate their consumption growth, but they must not follow the road taken by the rich and rapidly growing economies in the past half century.'
42. Wolfgang Sachs et al., 'The Jo'burg Memo: Fairness in a Fragile World', World Summit Johannesburg Paper No. 18, Heinrich Böll Foundation, 2000.
43. Byrne et al., 'Reclaiming the Atmospheric Commons': 429–452.
44. Projections based on IPCC Climate Change 2001 Synthesis Report: A1B-Scenario, which describes a future with rapid economic growth and global population that peaks in the mid-twenty-first century and declines thereafter with a mix of fossil and non-fossil energy sources. See also J. Byrne et al.,

'Undoing Atmospheric Harm: Civil Action to Shrink the Carbon Footprint', in P. Droege (ed.), *Urban Transition: From Fossil Fuels to Renewable Power,* Elsevier, Oxford 2008: 27–53.

45. IPCC, *IPCC Second Assessment Synthesis of Scientific-Technical Information Relevant to Interpreting Article 2 of the UN Framework Convention on Climate Change,* World Meteorological Organization and United Nations Environment Programme, Geneva and New York, 1996.

46. J. Byrne et al., 'An Equity- and Sustainability-Based Policy Response to Global Climate Change', *Energy Policy* 26, 1998: 335–43.

47. IPCC, *IPCC Second Assessment Synthesis of Scientific–Technical Information.*

48. Stern, *The Economics of Climate Change.*

49. J. Byrne et al., 'Undoing Atmospheric Harm: Civil Action to Shrink the Carbon Footprint', in P. Droege (ed.), *Urban Transition: From Fossil Fuels to Renewable Power,* Elsevier, Oxford, 2008: 27–53.

50. J.K. Holmberg et al., *Facing the Future: Beyond the Earth Summit,* International Institute for Environment and Development and Earthscan, London, 1993; John Byrne and Leigh Glover, 'A Common Future or Towards a Future Commons: Globalization and Sustainable Development since UNCED', *International Review for Environmental Strategies* 3(1), 2002: 5–25; Sachs (ed.), 'The Jo'burg Memo'.

51. Byrne et al., *Climate Shopping.*

52. Thomas C. Shelling, 'Economic Response to Global Warming: Prospects for Cooperative Approaches', in Rudiger Dornbusch and James M. Poterba (eds), *Global Warming: Economic Policy Responses,* MIT Press, Cambridge MA, 1991: 197–221. William D. Nordhaus, 'To Slow or Not to Slow: The Economics of the Greenhouse Effect', *The Economic Journal* 101(6), July 1991: 920–37.

53. John Byrne et al., 'The Postmodern Greenhouse: Creating Virtual Carbon Reductions from Business-as-Usual Energy Politics', *Bulletin of Science, Technology & Society* 21(6), December 2001: 443–55.

54. Sachs, *Planet Dialectics;* Vandana Shiva, 'The World on the Edge', in A. Giddens, and W. Hutton (eds), *Global Capitalism,* W.W. Norton, New York, 2000; H. French, *Vanishing Borders: Protecting the Planet in the Age of Globalization,* W.W. Norton, New York, 2000.

55. World Bank, *World Development Report: The State in a Changing World,* World Bank, Oxford University Press, 1997.

56. Yda Schreuder and Christopher Sherry, 'Global Corporations in the Greenhouse: Developing Equitable Accounting Measures', *Bulletin of Science, Technology & Society* 19(6), December 1999: 511–520.

57. Peter Dicken, *Global Shifts: Mapping the Changing Contours of the World Economy,* Guilford Press, New York, 2007.

58. Christopher Flavin and Gary Gardner, 'China, India, and the New World Order', in World Watch Institute, *State of the World,* W.W. Norton, New York and London, 2006: 3–23.

59. Wolfgang Sachs, *For Love of the Automobile: Looking Back into the History of Our Desires,* University of California Press, Berkeley, 1992.

60. Sachs, *Planet Dialectics:* 142.

61. A. Adriaanse et al., *Resource Flows: The Material Basis of Industrial Economies*, World Resources Institute, Washington DC, 1997.

62. V. Shiva 'The World on the Edge', in A. Giddens and W. Hutton (eds), *Global Capitalism*, W.W. Norton, New York, 2000.

63. See for instance, Byrne et al., 'Reclaiming the Atmospheric Commons': 429–52; Paul Baer (et al.), *The Right to Development in a Climate Constrained World: Greenhouse Development Rights Framework*, Heinrich Böll Foundation, Berlin, 2007.

Chapter 3

1. Martin O'Connor (ed.), *Is Capitalism Sustainable? Political Economy and the Politics of Ecology*, Guilford Press, New York, 1994.

2. Jonathan Porritt, *Capitalism as if the World Matters*, Earthscan, London, 2005.

3. J. Braithwaite, and P. Drahos, *Global Business Regulation*, Cambridge University Press, Cambridge 2000.

4. Data derived from the World Bank's *The Little Green Data Book 2007*, World Bank, Washington DC, 2007.

5. IPCC, *Fourth Assessment Report: Climate Change 2007*, 2007, www.ipcc.ch.

6. David Pepper, *Eco-Socialism: From Deep Ecology to Social Justice*, Routledge, London and New York, 1993.

7. Herman Daly, *Beyond Growth: The Economics of Sustainable Development*, Beacon Press, Boston MA, 1996.

8. Thomas L. Friedman, *The World is Flat: A Brief History of the Twenty-first Century*, Farrar, Straus & Giroux, New York, 2005.

9. John Williamson (ed.), *Latin American Adjustment: How Much Has Happened?*, Institute for International Economics, Washington DC, 1990; Jeffrey Sachs (ed.), *Developing Country Debt and the World Economy*, National Bureau of Economic Research, Cambridge MA, 1989.

10. Williamson (ed.), *Latin American Adjustment*.

11. B. Fine, *Development Policy in the Twenty-first Century: Beyond the Post-Washington Consensus*, Routledge, London, 2001; Williamson (ed.), *Latin American Adjustment*.

12. J. Valdez, *Pinochet's Economists: The Chicago School in Chile*, Cambridge University Press, New York, 1995; David Harvey, 'Neo-liberalism and the Restoration of Class Power', in *Spaces of Capitalism*, Verso, London, 2006: 9–68.

13. Eric Hobsbawm, *Age of Extremes: The Short Twentieth Century, 1914–1991*, Vintage, New York, 1994.

14. Stephen F. Frowen (ed.), *Hayek: Economist and Social Philosopher: A Critical Retrospect*, Macmillan, London, 1997; Milton Friedman and D. Rose, *Capitalism and Freedom*, University of Chicago Press, Chicago, 1982.

15. Noam Chomsky, *Profit Over People: Neoliberalism and Global Order*, Seven Stories Press, New York, 1998; Joseph Stiglitz, *Globalization and Its Discontents*, W.W. Norton, New York 2002; Joseph Stiglitz, *Making Globalization Work*, W.W. Norton, New York, 2006; Amatya Sen, *Development as Freedom*, Anchor Books,

New York, 1999; Noam Chomsky, *Hegemony or Survival: America's Quest for Global Dominance*, Metropolitan Books, New York, 2003.

16. Peter Gowan, *The Global Gamble: Washington's Faustian Bid for World Dominance*, Verso, London, 1999.

17. D. Yergin, and J. Stanislaw, *The Commanding Heights: The Battle Between Government and Market Place that is Remaking the Modern World*, Simon & Schuster, New York, 1999.

18. The basic thrust of Third Way thinking was championed most fervently by Anthony Giddens. See Anthony Giddens, *The Third Way: The Renewal of Social Democracy*, Polity Press, Cambridge, 1998. He later became his own critic when he admitted that the Third Way expressed the world-view of the multinational corporate sector. See Anthony Giddens, *The Third Way and Its Critics*, Polity Press, Cambridge, 2000; Anthony Giddens (ed.), *The Global Third Way Debate*, Polity Press, Cambridge, 2001; and Anthony Giddens et al. (eds), *Global Europe Social Europe*, Polity Press, Cambridge, 2006.

19. Michael Novak, *The Spirit of Democratic Capitalism*, Madison Books, New York, 1982.

20. R. Scruton, *The West and the Rest: Globalization and the Terrorist Threat*, Continuum, London, 2002.

21. M. Northcott, *An Angel Directs the Storm: Apocalyptic Religion and American Empire*, I.B. Tauris, London, 2004.

22. Ibid.

23. Joseph Stiglitz, *Globalization and its Discontents*, Allen Lane, London, 2002.

24. Naomi Klein, *The Shock Doctrine: The Rise of Disaster Capitalism*, Metropolitan Books, New York, 2007. See also Amartya Sen, *Development as Freedom*, Anchor Books, New York, 1999.

25. Jonathan Porritt, *Capitalism As If the World Matters*, Earthscan, London, 2006: 88–107.

26. David Held and Anthony McGrew, *Globalization/Anti-Globalization*, Polity Press, Cambridge, 2002.

27. Noam Chomsky, *America's Quest for Global Dominance*, Metropolitan Books, New York, 2004.

28. Klein, *The Shock Doctrine*.

29. See also Herman Daly, 'Population, Migration and Globalization', *Ecological Economics* 59, 2006: 187–190.

30. Klein (*The Shock Doctrine*: 142–68) describes how in August of 1985 Victor Paz Estenssoro had come to power in a 'democratic' election in Bolivia under the 'guidance' of Jeffrey Sachs's blueprint for shock therapy for the country's economic ills.

31. Ibid.

32. Naomi Klein (ibid.: 86) recounts the real story of Chile's economic 'miracle' and points out that by 1988, 45 per cent of Chile's population had fallen below the poverty line, while the richest 10 per cent of Chileans had seen their incomes increase by 83 per cent. In 2007, out of 123 countries in which the United Nations tracks inequality, Chile ranked 116th making it the 8th most unequal country. Central Intelligence Agency, 'Field Listing, Distribution of Family Income, Gini Index', *World Factbook 2007*, www.cia.gov.

33. Mark Weisbrot, 'Doing It Their Own Way', *International Herald Tribune*, 28 December 2006; 'Latin America – The Return of Populism', *The Economist*, 12 April 2006.
34. Daniel Yergin and Joseph Stanislaw, *The Commanding Heights: The Battle Between Government and the Market Place that is Remaking the Modern World*, Touchstone, New York, 1998.
35. Javier Martinez and Alvaro Diaz, *Chile: The Great Transformation*, Brookings Institution Press, Washington DC, 1996.
36. Klein, *The Shock Doctrine*: 85–6. Pinochet never privatized Codelco, the state copper mine company nationalized by Allende. Codelco generated 85 per cent of Chile's export revenues.
37. Nancy Birdsall et al. (eds), *Beyond Tradeoffs: Market Reform and Equitable Growth in Latin America*, Brookings Institution Press, Washington DC, 1998; Nancy Birdsall and Augusto de la Torre, *Washington Contentious: Economic Policies for Social Equity in Latin America*, Carnegie Endowment for International Peace and Inter-American Dialogue, Washington DC, 2001; Pedro-Pablo Kuczynski and John Williamson (eds), *After the Washington Consensus*, Institute for International Economics, Washington DC, 2003.
38. Birdsall and de la Torre, *Washington Contentious*.
39. Bernard M. Hoekman et. al., *Development, Trade, and the WTO: A Handbook*, World Bank, Washington DC, 2002.
40. World Trade Organization, www.wto.org.
41. Bernard Hoekman, 'The WTO: Functions and Basic Principles', in Hoekman et al., *Development, Trade and the WTO*: 41–9.
42. Michael Finger and L.A. Winters, 'Reciprocity in the WTO', in Hoekman et al., *Development, Trade and the WTO*: 50–60.
43. Constantine Michalopoulos, 'WTO Accession', in Hoekman et al., *Development, Trade and the WTO*: 61–70.
44. Valentina Delich, 'Developing Countries and the WTO Dispute Settlement System', in Hoekman et al., *Development, Trade and the WTO*: 71–80.
45. The so-called concessions by the EU and USA in the agricultural negotiations turn out to be empty promises, according to Friends of the Earth. The commitment to eliminate export subsidy credits is missing any substance as no end date is mentioned in the text. On domestic support for agriculture, language in the framework agreement clearly opens the door for the EU and USA to maintain almost their entire level of current subsidies and to use these to continue the dumping of agricultural goods in developing-country markets. At the same time, developing countries could be forced to give up import protections used to achieve food sovereignty.
46. 'Globalization and the Environment in a Reformed UN: Charting a Sustainable Development Path', 24th Session of the Governing Council/Global Ministerial Environment Forum, Nairobi, February 2007.
47. Global Environment and Trade Study, www.gets.org/; see Orin Kirshner, 'WTO Fails to Advance Environmental Agenda at Cancún'. Ministers from WTO member countries decided at the 1996 Singapore Ministerial Conference to set up three new working groups: on trade and investment, on competition policy, and on transparency in government procurement. They also instructed

the WTO Goods Council to look at possible ways of simplifying trade procedures, an issue sometimes known as 'trade facilitation'. Because the Singapore conference kicked off work in these four subjects areas, they are sometimes called the 'Singapore issues'. These areas were originally included on the Doha development agenda. The carefully negotiated mandate was for negotiations to start after the 2003 Cancún Ministerial Conference, 'on the basis of a decision to be taken, by explicit consensus, at that session on modalities of negotiations'. There was no consensus, and the members agreed on 1 August 2004 to proceed with negotiations in only one subject area: trade facilitation. The other three were dropped from the Doha agenda.

48. See L. Shalated, *Allies or Antagonists? Investment, Sustainable Development and the WTO*, Heinrich Böll Foundation, Washington DC, 2003, www.boell.org/docs/boell_allies_or_antagonists.pdf.

49. See Friends of the Earth, www.foe.co.uk/resource/press_releases/wto_deal_endangers_environ_02082004.html.

50. David Held and Anthony McGrew, *Globalization/Anti-globalization*, Polity Press, Cambridge, 2002: 58–76.

51. Martin Khor, 'How the South is Getting a Raw Deal at the WTO', in Robin Broad (ed.), *Global Backlash: Citizen Initiatives for a Just World Economy*, Rowman & Littlefield, Lanham MD, 2002.

52. Bhagwati, meanwhile, maintains that there is still a greater tariff protection on manufacturing and agricultural production in poor countries. See Jagdish Bhagwati, 'From Seattle to Hong Kong', *Foreign Affairs* 84(7), 2005: 3–22.

53. The Third World Network, www.twnside.org.sg/pos.htm.

54. Jagdish Bhagwati, *In Defense of Globalization*, Oxford University Press, Oxford, New York, 2004.

55. W. Antweiler, B.R. Copeland and M.S. Taylor, 'Is Free Trade Good for the Environment', *American Economic Review* 9, 2001: 877–908; OECD, *Economic Globalization and the Environment*, OECD, Paris, 1997.

56. In most developing countries, the 'choice' of commodity specialization was imposed by colonial rule. Between 1880 and the First World War, Africa and major parts of Asia were colonized and functioned to serve the 'mother country' with raw materials, foodstuffs, labour and/or access to markets. The infrastructure was developed to move basic export commodities for shipment to Europe and to import manufactured goods from the same. The physical infrastructure developed under colonial rule carried over into the post-colonial era, and many developing countries today experience as a result ongoing economic dependence through import and export relationships with the Western world. Many former colonies remained highly dependent on outside trade relationships after independence even though the formal economic and political ties with the 'mother country' had ended. See Andre Gunder Frank, *Capitalism and Underdevelopment in Latin America*, Monthly Review Press, New York, 1967.

57. S. Dinda, 'Environmental Kuznets Curve Hypothesis: A Survey', *Ecological Economics* 49, 2004: 431–55; D. Stern, 'The Rise and Fall of the Environmental Kuznets Curve', *World Development* 32(8), 2004: 1419–39.

58. S. Shin, 'Economic Globalization and the Environment in China: A

Comparative Case Study of Shenyang and Dalian', *Journal of Environment and Development* 13(3), 2004: 263–94.

59. P. Fearnside, 'Soybean Cultivation as a Threat to the Environment in Brazil', *Environmental Conservation* 28(1), 2001: 23–38; C. Gfissler and E. Penot, 'My Oil Palm versus Your Forest: Deforestation and Farm Concession Policies in West Kalimantan, Indonesia', *Bois et Forêts des Tropiques* 16, 2000: 7–22.

60. W.T. Harbaugh et al., 'Reexamining the Empirical Evidence for an Environmental Kuznets Curve', *Review of Economics and Statistics* 84(3), 2002: 541–51.

61. R. Schmalensee et al., 'World Carbon Dioxide Emissions: 1950–2050', *Review of Economics and Statistics* 80(1), 1998: 15–27.

62. Ibid.

63. E. Neumauyer, 'Pollution Havens: An Analysis of Policy Options for Dealing with an Elusive Phenomenon', *Journal of Environment and Development* 10(2), 2001: 147–77. M. Cole, 'Trade, the Pollution Haven Hypothesis and the Environmental Kuznets Curve: Examining the Linkages', *Ecological Economics* 48, 2004: 71–81.

64. E. Neumayer, *Greening Trade and Investment: Environmental Protection without Protectionism*, Earthscan, London, 2001.

65. K. Gallagher, *Free Trade and the Environment: Mexico, NAFTA, and Beyond*, Stanford University Press, Stanford CA, 2004.

66. H. Daly, 'Globalization versus Internationalization – Some Implications', *Ecological Economics* 31, 1999: 431–55.

67. J. Boyce, 'Green and Brown? Globalization and the Environment', *Oxford Review of Economic Policy* 20(1), 2004: 105–28.

68. 'Rushing on by Road, Rail and Air', *The Economist*, 16 February 2008: 30–32.

69. WTO Aid-for-Trade Initiative, launched at the 2005 Hong Kong Ministerial Declaration in 2005. For a summary of Lamy's comments at the Aid-for-Trade Conference in Manila, Philippines, 19–20 September 2007, see www.wto.org.

70. World Bank and Public–Private Infrastructure Advisory Facility, *Private Participation in Infrastructure Database* (2007), www.ppi.worldbank.org. The resources include toolkits on how to design PPI schemes, websites that contain papers discussing PPI issues or transaction information, and selected reading lists of papers dealing with private participation in the different infrastructure sectors, and reviewing country- or project-level experiences.

71. World Bank, *Private Participation in Infrastructure: Trends in Developing Counties in 1990–2001*, World Bank, Washington DC, 2003.

72. Ada Karina Izaquirre, 'Private Infrastructure: A Review of Projects with Private Participation, 1990–2000', World Bank, *Public Policy Journal* 246, June 2002.

73. Neil Roger, 'Recent Trends in Private Participation in Infrastructure', *Public Policy Journal* 196, September 1999.

74. Ada Karina Izaquirre, 'Private Participation in Energy', *Public Policy Journal* 208, May 2000.

75. Ada Karina Izaquirre, 'Private Power Projects: 'Annual Investment Flows Grew by 44 percent in 2003', *Public Policy Journal* 281, December 2004.

76. Ada Karina Izaquirre, 'Private Participation in the Transmission and Distribution of Natural Gas – Recent Trends', *Public Policy Journal* 176, April 1999.
77. Gisele F. Silva, 'Private Participation in the Airport Sector – Recent Trends', *Public Policy Journal* 202, November 1999.
78. Doug Andrew and Silviu Dochia, 'The Growing and Evolving Business of Private Participation in Airports: New Trends, New Actors Emerging', *Gridlines Public–Private Infrastructure Advisory Facility (PPIAF)*, September 2006: 15.
79. Gisele F. Silva, 'Toll Roads: Recent Trends in Private Participation', *Public Policy Journal* 224, December 2000.
80. Dirk Sommer, 'Private Participation in Port Facilities – Recent Trends', *Public Policy Journal* 193, September 1999.
81. Nicola Tynan, 'Private Participation in the Rail Sector – Recent Trends', *Public Policy Journal* 186, June 1999.

Chapter 4

1. 'Multinational' and 'transnational' are used interchangeably throughout the book. Whereas many transnational corporations conduct business in several countries – and are therefore technically multinational corporations – among United Nations reporting agencies and in other statistical sources the entity is referred to as a transnational corporation.
2. Herman E. Daly, 'The Perils of Free Trade', *Scientific American*, November 1993: 50–57.
3. D.C. Korten, *When Corporations Rule the World*, Kumarian Press, West Hartford CT, 1995.
4. Yda Schreuder and Christopher Sherry, 'Global Corporations in the Greenhouse: Developing Equitable Accounting Measures', *Bulletin of Science, Technology and Society* 19(6), December 1999: 511–20.
5. Aharoni Yair, 'World Investment Report 2004: The Shift towards Services', *Transnational Corporations* 14(1), April 2005: 158–67.
6. UNCTAD releases statistics that are relevant for the analysis of international trade, foreign direct investment and commodities, and more explicitly for understanding the economic trends of developing countries over the past decades, particularly in the context of globalization. The statistics are based mostly on existing national and international data sources. See www.unctad.org/templates/Page.asp?intItemID=1584&lang=1; www.unctad.org/Templates/Page.asp?intItemID=3198&lang=1. Detailed statistics on FDI and operations of TNCs in selected countries are available at the World Investment Directory online.
7. FDI stock for associate and subsidiary enterprises is defined as the value of the share of their capital and reserves (including retained profits) attributable to the parent enterprise plus the net indebtedness of the associate or subsidiary enterprise to the parent firm. This is normally the equivalent of the value of fixed assets and the value of current assets and investments, excluding amounts due from the parent, less liabilities to third parties. See www.unctad.org/Templates/Page.asp?intItemID=3202&lang=1.

8. L. Eden, 'Transfer Pricing, Intra-firm Trade and the Bureau of Labor Statistics', Bureau of Labor Statistics Working Paper, January 2001: 334.
9. Definition derived from UNCTAD; see www.unctad.org/Templates/Page. asp?intItemID=3146&lang=1.
10. For UNCTAD definition of TNC, see www.unctad.org/Templates/Page. asp?intItemID=3148&lang=1.
11. About the 1997 Southeast Asia crisis, see David Harvey, *Spaces of Capitalism*, Verso, London, 2006: 96–110.
12. UNCTAD, *World Investment Report* 2007, www.asiaing.com/world-investment-report-2007.html.
13. UNCTAD, *FDI in Least Developed Countries at a Glance, 2005/2006*, United Nations, New York, 2007, www.unctad.org/en/docs/iteiia20057 _en.pdf.
14. See UNCTAD statistics, www.unctad.org/templates/Page.asp?intItemID= 1584&lang=1.
15. UNCTAD, *World Investment Report 2007*, Country Fact Sheet: China, www. unctad.org/sections/dite_dir/docs/wir07_fs_cn_en.pdf.
16. Michael P. Todaro, *Economic Development in the Third World*, Longman, New York, 1981; Arthur McCormack, *Multinational Investment: Boon or Burden for the Developing Countries?*, W.R. Grace, New York, 1980; Orville L. Freeman, *The Multinational Company: Investment for World Growth*, Praeger, New York, 1981.
17. Stephen H. Hymer, *The International Operations of National Firms: A Study of Foreign Direct Investment*, MIT Press, Cambridge MA, 1976. For a Marxist and dependency perspectives on multinational corporations and development, see Fernando H. Cardoso and Enzo Faletto, *Dependencia and Development in Latin America*, University of California Press, Berkeley, 1979.
18. For an overview see, Theodore H. Moran, 'Multinational Corporations and the Developing Countries: An Analytical Overview', *Multinational Corporations: The Political Economy of Foreign Direct Investment*, D.C. Heath, Lexington MA, 1985.
19. According to UNCTAD rules a threshold of 10 per cent of equity owned by a parent company is sufficient to qualify as an affiliate or associate enterprise. Because the definition of a TNC does not specify majority control, it is possible for an enterprise to be an associate of more than one TNC.
20. As an example, Indian steel conglomerate ArcelorMittal has grown into one of the largest global TNCs in a short period of time; see 'Face Value: Lakshmi Mittal Built the World's Biggest Steel Firm from Scratch', *The Economist*, 16 February 2008: 76.
21. UNCTAD examined the magnitude of the phenomenon and looked at the economic forces that determined the patterns of investment on the part of developing countries TNCs. UNCTAD, *World Investment Report 2006: FDI from Developing and Transition Economies: Implications for Development*, UN, New York, 2006.
22. Peter Dicken, *Global Shift: Mapping the Changing Contours of the World Economy*, Guilford Press, New York, 2007: 13–27, 524–53.
23. M. Gross, 'Intra-firm Trade with ASEAN Countries by Japanese and U.S. Multinational Corporations', Working Paper No. 273, Kiel Institute for World Economics, 1986.

24. For a review of the main issues related to FDI and intra-firm trade and data collection efforts, see, Ralph Kozlov and J. Steven Landefeld (US Department of Commerce's Bureau of Economic Analysis), 'Globalization, Off-shoring, and Multinational Companies: What Are the Questions, and How Well Are We Answering Them?', paper presented at the American Economic Association Allied Social Science Associations annual meeting, Boston MA, 6 January 2006, see www.bea.gov/.

25. L. Eden 'Transfer Pricing, Intra-firm Trade and the Bureau of Labor Statistics', Bureau of Labor Statistics Working Paper, January 2001: 334, see www.bls.gov/.

26. Seattle to Brussels Network, *The EU Corporate Trade Agenda: The Role and the Interests of Corporations and their Lobby Groups in Trade Policy-making in the European Union*, Brussels and Berlin, November 2005, see www.s2bnetwork. org.

27. K. Fukasaku, 'Economic Regionalization and Intra-industry Trade: Pacific–Asian Perspectives', Technical paper No. 53, OECD Development Centre, Paris, 1992, see www.oecd.org.

28. C. Oman, *New Forms of Investment in Developing Country Industries: Mining, Petrochemicals, Automobiles, Textiles and Food*, OECD Development Centre, Paris, 1989, see www.oecd.org; Michael Borrus et al. (eds), *International Production Networks in Asia: Rivalry or Riches?* Routledge, London and New York, 2000.

29. OECD, 'Intra-Industry and Intra-Firm Trade and the Internationalization of Production', *OECD Economic Outlook* 71, 2002: 161–2, Table VI.1. For example, in the Czech Republic, Hungary and Slovakia the largest exporting firm is owned by the German Volkswagen group.

30. Cross-border trade between TNCs and their affiliates, referred to as intra-firm trade, accounts for a large and growing share of international trade in goods, although aggregate data are only sparsely available. See, J.H. Lowe, 'An Ownership-based Framework of the U.S. Current Account, 1982–1998', *Survey of Current Business*, January 2001.

31. OECD, 'Intra-Industry and Intra-Firm Trade and the Internationalization of Production'. For anecdotal information, see 'China Makes, the World Takes', *Atlantic Monthly*, July/August 2007; 'Multinationals: Are They Good for America?', *Business Week*, 10 March 2008.

32. D. Hummels et al., 'The Nature and Growth of Vertical Specialization in World Trade', *Journal of International Economics* 54(1), 2001.

33. D. MacCharles, *Trade among Multinationals: Intra-Industry Trade and National Competitiveness*, Croom Helm, London, 1987.

34. M. Bonturi and K. Fukasaku, 'Globalization and Intra-firm Trade: An Empirical Note', *OECD Economic Studies* 20, Spring 1993: 145–59.

35. OECD, 'Intra-industry and Intra-firm trade and the International of Production', *OECD Economic Outlook* 71, 2002: 166, Table VI.5.

36. Naomi Klein, *The Shock Doctrine: The Rise of Disaster Capitalism*, Metropolitan Books, Henry Holt, New York, 2007.

37. Paul Knox and J. Agnew, *The Geography of the World Economy*, Edward Arnold, New York, 1995; Peter J. Taylor and N. Thrift, *Multinationals and the Restructuring of the World Economy*, Croom Helm, London, 1986.

38. Vicente Paolo B. Yu III, 'Briefing Paper: WTO Committee on Trade and Environment', February 2005, www.tradeobservatory.org/library.cfm?refID =25583.

39. See WTO Committee on Trade and Environment, www.wto.org/english/tratop_e/envir_e/envir_req_e.htm.

40. G. Fields and G. You, 'Falling Labor Income Inequality in Korea's Economic Growth: Patterns and Underlying Causes', *Review of Income and Wealth* 46(2), 2000: 139–60; B. Lin, 'Economic Growth, Income Inequality and Poverty Reduction in the People's Republic of China', *Asian Development Review* 20(2), 2003: 105–24.

41. UN Economic Commission for Latin America and the Caribbean (ECLAC), *A Decade of Social Development in Latin America, 1990–1999*, UN, Santiago, Chile, 2004.

42. G. Schneider, 'Globalization and the Poorest of the Poor: Global Integration and the Development Process in Sub-Saharan Africa', *Journal of Economic Issues* 37(2), 2003: 387–94.

43. UNDP, *Making Global Trade Work for People*, Earthscan, London, 2003.

44. B. Sutcliffe, 'World Inequality and Globalization', *Oxford Review of Economic Policy* 20(1), 2004: 15–37.

45. I borrowed the term 'Atmospheric Commons' from several research papers published by colleagues at the Center for Energy and Environmental Policy at the University of Delaware; John Byrne, *Equity and Sustainability in the Greenhouse: Reclaiming our Atmospheric Commons*, Parisar, Pune, 1997; John Byrne et al., 'An Equity and Sustainability-Based Policy Response to Global Climate Change', *Energy Policy* 26(4), 1998: 179–84; John Byrne and Leigh Glover et al., 'Reclaiming the Atmospheric Commons: Beyond Kyoto', in V. Grover (ed.), *Climate Change: Five Years after Kyoto*, Science Publisher, Enfield NH, 2004: 429–52.

46. Paul Knox and J. Agnew, *The Geography of the World Economy*, Edward Arnold, New York, 1995; Peter J. Taylor, and N. Thrift, *Multinationals and the Restructuring of the World Economy*, Croom Helm, London, 1986.

47. Yda Schreuder and Christopher Sherry, 'Flexible Mechanisms in the Corporate Greenhouse: Implementation of the Kyoto Protocol and the Globalization of the Electric Power Industry', *Energy and Environment* 12(5/6), 2001: 487–98.

48. See Chapter 5 below, and Yda Schreuder, 'EU Emissions Trading Scheme in the Corporate Greenhouse: A Predicament for Power Intensive Industries', *Forum on Public Policy: Special Issue on Trade and the Environment* 1(1), 2005: 190–204.

49. D.C. Esty, *Greening the GATT: Trade, Environment, and the Future*, Institute for International Economics, Washington DC, 1994; D. Vogel, *Trading Up: Consumer and Environmental Regulation in a Global Economy*, Harvard University Press, Cambridge MA, 1995.

50. For a review of trade and environmental issues under NAFTA, see John J. Audley, *Green Politics and Global Trade: NAFTA and the Future of Environmental Politics*, Georgetown University Press, Washington DC, 1997; P.M. Johnson, *The Environment and NAFTA: Understanding and Implementing the New Continental Law*, Island Press, Peterborough ON, 1996.

51. M . Munasinghe (ed.), 'The Sustainomics Trans-disciplinary Met-Framework for Making Development More Sustainable: Applications to Energy Issues', *International Journal of Sustainable Development* 5(1/2), 2001: 125–82.

52. American Iron and Steel Institute, 'Environmental Aspects of Global Trade in Steel: The North American Steel Industry Perspective' 3: www.steel.org/AM/ Template.cfm?Section=Articles8&CONTENTID=20532&TEMPLATE=/ CM/ContentDisplay.cfm.

53. Bin Shui and Robert C. Harriss, 'The Role of CO_2 Embodiment in US–China Trade', *Energy Policy* 34, 2006: 4063–8.

54. American Iron and Steel Institute, 'Environmental Aspects of Global Trade in Steel'.

55. G. Eskeland and A. Harrison, 'Moving to Greener Pastures? Multinationals and The Pollution Haven Hypothesis', *Journal of Development Economics* 70, 2003: 1–23; M.S. Mani and D. Wheeler, 'In Search of Pollution Havens? Dirty Industry in The World Economy, 1960–1995', *Journal of Environment and Development* 7(3), 1998: 215–47; E. Neumayer, *Greening Trade and Investment: Environmental Protection without Protectionism*, Earthscan, London, 2001; D. Wheeler, 'Beyond Pollution Havens', *Global Environmental Politics* 10(3), 2002: 1–10.

56. Jonathon Porritt, *Capitalism as if the World Matters*, Earthscan, London, 2005.

Chapter 5

1. The EU Commission and the European Parliament presented a proposal for establishing an emissions trading scheme on 23 October 2001. For a history and discussion of the EU ETS, see Bernhard Hillebrand et al., *CO2 Emissions Trading Put to the Test*, LIT Verlag, Munster, Hamburg and London 2002.

2. Christian Egenhofer, and Noriko Fujiware, *Reviewing the EU Emissions Trading Scheme: Priorities for Short-term Implementation of the Second Round of Allocation*, Report of the Centre for European Policy Studies Taskforce, July 2005; Christian Egenhofer et al., *The EU Emissions Trading Scheme: Taking Stock and Looking Ahead*, European Climate Platform: A Joint Initiative of the Center for European Policy Studies and the Climate Policy Research Programme of the Swedish Foundation for Strategic Environmental Research, July 2006; Christian Egenhofer and Noriko Jujiware, *Shaping the Global Arena: Preparing the EU Emissions Trading Scheme for the Post-2012 Period*, Center for Policy Studies Task Force Report 61, March 2007. The European Climate Platform is a joint initiative by Climate Policy Research Programme and the Center for European Policy Studies, established in 2005. See Center for European Policy Study, http://shop.ceps.be.

3. At the time this was a rather surprising outcome since the EU had long been critical of market mechanisms and preferred regulatory measures. Environmental groups, in general, preferred regulatory measures, while industry and their lobbyists preferred voluntary approaches. Eco-taxation was considered but thought to be too costly, and thus emissions trading became the preferred scheme to deal with greenhouse-gas emissions reductions.

4. One tonne of CO_2e = one AAU. Officially designated as MT CO_2e: Metric Tonne Carbon Dioxide Equivalent.

5. The 'Linking Directive' (see p. 234) awards credits obtained with Joint Implementation and the Clean Development Mechanism. CDM credits have been available since 2005, whereas Joint Implementation credits may only be used from 2008 onwards.

6. The 'EU Bubble' agreement, in which EU member states' individual emissions-reduction targets are explained, is the so-called EU Burden Sharing Agreement for the Kyoto Protocol.

7. The Scheme is based on Directive 2003/87/EC, which entered into force on 25 October 2005.

8. For a critical review of the EU ETS Phase I, see Climate Action Network Europe, 'National Allocation Plans 2005–2007: Do They Deliver: Key Lessons for Phase II of the EU ETS', July 2006; see www.climnet.org. The recommendations included: (a) more ambitious caps for the phase 2008–2012, (b) use of product-benched benchmarks and auctioning as the principle means by which allowances are distributed; (c) greater transparency and verification by which member states draw up their National Allocation Plans.

9. Egenhofer et al., *The EU Emissions Trading Scheme*.

10. Point Carbon, *Carbon Market Europe*, 22 June 2007, a report released by Point Carbon, a leading provider of analysis, advisory services and news information for emissions trading and energy markets. Point Carbon has offices in Oslo (Head Office), Kiev, Malmö, London, Tokyo and Washington DC. See www.pointcarbon.com.

11. Technically, JI project partners are listed in Annex B.

12. Climate Action Network Europe 'National Allocation Plans 2005–2007', July 2006; 'Assessment of Key National Allocation Plans for Phase II of the EU Emissions Trading Scheme', November 2006; see www.climnet.org.

13. Ibid.

14. Point Carbon, *Carbon Market Europe*.

15. E. Woerdman, 'Hot Air Trading under the Kyoto Protocol: An Environmental Problem or Not?' *European Environmental Law Review* 14(3), 2005: 71–7.

16. Climate Action Network Europe, 'Assessment of Key National Allocation Plans': 5–6; for Poland: 19–20.

17. A study funded by *New Scientist* magazine polled 1,500 people, asking whether they would prefer the government to implement standards, emissions taxes or cap-and-trade as the main instrument in its climate-change policy in the electricity and transportation sectors. In June 2007 new standards for increased fuel efficiency in cars (Corporate Average Fuel Economy or CAFE standards) were introduced.

18. The draft bill presented by Barbara Boxer, chair of the Senate's environment committee, Joe Lieberman (Independent) and John Warner (Republican) follows the recommendations outlined by the United States Climate Program (USCAP), a group of businesses (including car makers Ford and Chrysler) and environmental groups.

19. Clean Air Watch argues that free allowances will result in windfall profits for

those utility companies that can pass on increased energy prices resulting from emissions trade to customers regardless of their actual investment in trade or increased energy efficiency as was the case with the EU ETS during the first phase of trading (2005–07).

20. Most states under RGGI have announced their intention to auction 100 per cent of the allowances assigned to them. This would transfer the windfall profits from industrial companies and utilities to state governments. States that pursue a 100 per cent auction will realize new revenues worth hundreds of millions of dollars per year through 2019. See Regional Greenhouse Gas Initiative, www.rggi.org. For ICF Consulting, see *ICF Perspectives*, Spring–Summer 2005, www.icfi.com.

21. Point Carbon, *Carbon Market Europe*: 22–3.

22. Ibid.: 19–20.

23. Ibid.: 17–20.

24. Raimund Bleischwitz et al., 'The Sustainability Impact of the EU Emissions Trading System on the European Industry', Bruges European Economic Policy Briefings 17, September 2007, www.coleurop.be/eco/publications. htm.

25. International Emissions Trading Association, 'Building a Global Carbon Market: Report pursuant to Article 30 of the Directive 2003/87/EC', Brussels, 13 November 2006, see www.ieta.org; Egenhofer et al., *The EU ETS*.

26. Carbon Trust, *The European Emissions Trading Scheme: Implications for Industrial Competitiveness*, Carbon Trust, London, 2004; Carbon Trust, *Allocations and Competitiveness in the EU Emissions Trading Scheme: Options for Phase II and Beyond*, Carbon Trust, London, 2006. See www.carbontrust.co.uk/carbon.

27. Yda Schreuder, 'EU Emissions Trading Scheme in the Corporate Greenhouse: A Predicament for Power Intensive Industries', *Forum on Public Policy* 1(1), 2005: 190–204.

28. Alliance of Energy Intensive Industries, 'Energy Intensive Industries Call upon EU Decision-makers to Pay More Attention to the Impact of Emissions Trading upon Their Competitiveness', January 2004. See www.eula.be.

29. Alliance of Energy Intensive Industries, 'The Impact of EU Emission Trading Scheme (ETS) on Power Prices: Remedial Action Urgently Needed 10 Months after Start of ETS', November 2005; 'Contribution to the EU Energy Strategic Review: Urgent Measures Are Required to Improve the Functioning of Electricity and Gas Markets', September 2006.

30. Communication from the Commission to the Council and the European Parliament on the Competitiveness of the Metals Industries, Commission for the European Communities, Brussels, 22 January 2008, http://ec.europa. eu/enterprise/steel/comm_pdf_com_2008_0108_f_en_acte.pdf#page=1.

31. Alliance of Energy Intensive Industries, 'The Impact of EU Emission Trading Scheme (ETS) on Power Prices'.

32. European Commission, *Green Paper: A European Strategy for Sustainable, Competitive and Secure Energy*, Brussels, 8 March 2006, www.ec.europa. eu/energy/green-paper-energy/index_en.htm.

33. 'Hot air' trading would occur under the Kyoto Protocol if the emissions ceiling in a country is higher than its business-as-usual emissions level. This

would allow the country to sell emissions rights without having to reduce emissions. Hot-air trading might also occur when Russia or the Ukraine start trading their surplus carbon credits during the second commitment period of the EU ETS (2008–12). Woerdman, 'Hot Air Trading under the Kyoto Protocol'.

34. European Commission, *Green Paper: A European Strategy*.

35. The Alliance for a Competitive European Industry was formed in 2004 by eleven major European industry sector associations and UNICE, the Confederation of European Business. The industry sectors concerned represent the interests at EU level of some 6,000 large companies and 1.7 million SMEs with a combined output of nearly €5,000 billion and a turnover of €1,300 billion value-added. The companies employ at least 23 million people in the EU.

36. Christian Egenhofer et al., 'Business Consequences of the EU Emissions Trading Scheme', Center for European Policy Studies, Task Force Report 53, February 2005; Bleischwitz et al., 'The Sustainability Impact of the EU Emissions Trading System on the European Industry'.

37. Confederation of European Paper Industries (CEPI) website: www.cepi. org.

38. Confederation of European Paper Industries, *Bio-energy and the European Pulp and Paper Industry*, CEPI, Brussels 2007. See www.cepi.org.

39. European Cement Association, www.cembureau.be.

40. Alliance for a Competitive European Industry, 'Cases for a Competitive European Industry: The New European Industrial Policy – From Commitment to Results', paper presented at workshop, Brussels, 15 September 2006: 8–9.

41. European Cement Association Activity Report 2005, Brussels, 2006; see www. cembureau.be.

42. McKinsey and EcoFys, *EU ETS Review: Report on International Competitiveness*, European Commission, Directorate General for Environment, Brussels, December 2006; Misato Sato et al., 'Differentiation and Dynamics of Competitiveness Impacts from the EU ETS', 12 April 2007, www.electricitypolicy. org.uk/TSEC/2/differentiationdynamics.pdf.

43. Carbon Trust, *Allocation and Competitiveness in the EU Emissions Trading Scheme*.

44. See European Association of Metals, www.euras.be.

45. Robin Smale et al., 'The Impact of CO_2 Emissions Trading on Firm Profits and Market Prices', *Climate Policy* 6(1), 2006: 29–46.

46. Communication from the Commission to the Council and the European Parliament on the Competitiveness of the Metals Industries: 4–5.

47. CRU has recently released its annual Primary Aluminum Smelting Costs report, which details historical, current and future costs for the global aluminium industry, with detailed costs for more than 170 smelters, including the 57 largest Chinese smelters. See CRU News, 'Higher Power Costs Driving Aluminum Smelter Closures in Europe and the USA', 30 March 2006, http://cruonline.crugroup.com/Default.aspx?tabid=388.

48. See European Confederation of Iron and Steel Industries, www.eurofer.org.

49. www.eurofer.org/publications/pdf/2007–ClimateChange.pdf.

50. Carbon Trust, 'The European Emissions Trading Scheme'.

51. Eurofer, 'Report on the Economic and Steel Market Situation QII/2007 and forecast Q III-IV/2008', June 2007, www.eurofer.org/publications/ pdf/2007–ClimateChange.pdf.

52. In the cement and steel sector, reductions in output are estimated at 5 and 10 per cent respectively, but were accompanied by greater increases in profits as prices rose due to the fact that increased energy costs of abatement are passed on to the customer. See Robin Smale et al., 'The Impact of CO_2 Emissions Trading on Firm Profits and Market Prices', *Climate Policy* 6(1), 2006: 29–46.

53. Sato et al., 'Differentiation and Dynamics of Competitiveness Impacts'.

54. Carbon Trust, *The European Emissions Trading Scheme*; *Stern Review on the Economics of Climate Change*, www.hm-treasury.gov.uk/independent_reviews/ stern_review_economics_climate_change/sternreview_index.cfm; Intergovernmental Panel on Climate Change, www.ipcc.ch/; Communication for the Commission to the Council and the European Parliament on the Competitiveness of the Metals Industries.

55. Climate Strategies was founded in 2006 as a network organization focused on delivering research on climate policy to international policymakers. Its initial work on the EU ETS has had a major impact on the revisions implemented for the second phase (2008–12) ETS. The network aims to assist governments in solving the collective problems of climate-change policy. Sponsors include departments of European governments and other stakeholders, including the UK Carbon Trust. See www.climatestrategies.org.

56. J.P.M. Sijm, K. Neuhoff et al., 'CO_2 Cost Pass Through and Windfall Profits in The Power Sector', *Climate Policy* 6(1), 2006: 49–72.

57. Smale et al., 'The Impact of CO_2 Emissions Trading on Firm Profits and Market Prices'.

58. Sato et al., 'Differentiation and Dynamics of Competitiveness Impacts'.

59. Ibid.

60. Communication from the Commission to the Council and the European Parliament on the Competitiveness of the Metals Industries.

61. Carbon leakage here is defined at the national level, whereas in the jargon of JI/CDM it is defined at the project level, as we will see in the next chapter.

62. Arjan Lejour, 'How Carbon-Proof is Kyoto? Carbon Leakage and Hot Air', Report 99/4, Centraal Plan Bureau, Netherlands, 1999, www.cpb. nl/eng/pub/cpbreeksen/cpbreport/1999_4/s3_2.pdf.

63. J.P.M. Sijm et al., *Spillovers of Climate Policy: An Assessment of the Incidence of Carbon Leakage and Induced Technological Change due to CO_2 Abatement Measures*, Rijksinstituut voor Milieu, Netherlands, 2004.

64. Mustafa H. Babiker, 'Climate Change Policy, Market Structure, and Carbon Leakage', *Journal of International Economics* 65(2), March 2005: 421–45. For a review and evaluation of the different CGE models, see J. Weyant (ed.), 'The Costs of the Kyoto Protocol: A Multi-Model Evaluation' *Energy Journal* 1999: 1–398.

65. T. Rutherford and M. Babiker, ' Input–Output and General Equilibrium Estimates of Embodied Carbon: A Dataset and Static Framework for Assessment', Working Paper 97–2, University of Colorado, Boulder 1997. For a detailed explanation of the GTAP-E model, see Jean-Marc Burniaux and Truong Truong, 'GTAP-E: An Energy-Environment Version of the GTAP Model', GTAP Technical Paper 16, 2002.

66. Nicholas Stern, *The Economics of Climate Change: The Stern Review*, Cambridge University Press, Cambridge, 2006. The concern about the impact of the Kyoto Protocol on the US economy was clearly expressed in the Byrd–Hagel resolution in the US Senate in 1997, which opposed the ratification of the Kyoto Protocol.

67. Babiker, 'Climate Change Policy, Market Structure, and Carbon Leakage'.

68. Hiroshi Hamasaki, 'Carbon Leakage and a Post-Kyoto Framework', Working Paper 287, Fujitsu Research Institute, Tokyo, April 2007. In this study, it is estimated that as a result of the Kyoto Protocol CO_2 emissions may be reduced by as much 50 per cent in some countries with reduction targets established or agreed to under the Kyoto Protocol, but that CO_2 emissions will increase in countries without reduction targets.

69. O. Kuik and R. Gerlagh, 'Trade Liberalization and Carbon Leakage', *The Energy Journal* 24(3), 2003: 97–120.

70. Ibid.; M. Scott Taylor and Brian R. Copeland, 'Free Trade and Global Warming: a Trade Theory View of the Kyoto Protocol', *Journal of Environmental Economics and Management* 49(2), 2005: 205–34; Sijm et al., *Spillovers of Climate Policy*.

71. The 'Factor-Endowment' hypothesis rests on the traditional factor endowment theory of Heckscher–Ohlin, which states that a capital-abundant country will export capital-intensive goods while a labour-abundant country will export labour-intensive goods. James Harrigan, 'Factor Endowments and the International Location of Production: Econometric Evidence from the OECD, 1970–1985', *Journal of International Economics* 39(1–2), August 1995: 123–41. For a review of the argument see, Donald R. Davis and David E. Weinstein, 'Do Factor Endowments Matter for North-North Trade?' Working Paper 8516, National Bureau of Economic Research, October 2001.

72. Sijm et al., *Spillovers of Climate Policy*: 145–87, Appendix C.

73. Peter Dicken, *Global Shift: Mapping the Changing Contours of the World Economy*, Guilford Press, New York, 2007: 542–6; Z.K.Wang and L.A. Winters, 'Carbon Taxes and Industrial Location: Evidence from the Multinationals Literature', in A. Ulph (ed.), *Environmental Policy, International Agreements, and International Trade*, Oxford University Press, Oxford, 2001: 135–51.

74. M. Fujita, P. Krugman and A. Venables, *The Spatial Economy: Cities, Regions and International Trade*, MIT Press, Cambridge MA, 1999; C. Elbers and C. Withagen, 'Environmental Policy, Population Dynamics and Agglomeration', *Contributions to Economic Analysis and Policy* 3(2), 2004: 1–21.

75. J. List, W.W. McHone and D.L. Millimet, 'Effects of Air Quality Regulation on The Destination Choice of Relocating Plants', *Oxford Economic Papers* 55, 2003: 657–78; T. Jeppesen and H. Folmer, 'The Confusing Relationship between Environmental Policy and Location Behaviour of Firms: A Methodological

Review of Selected Case Studies', *Annals of Regional Science* 35, 2001: 523–46; T. Jeppesen, J. List and H. Folmer, 'Environmental Regulations and New Plant Location Decisions: Evidence from a Meta-Analysis', *Journal of Regional Science* 42, 2002: 19–49.

76. Stern, *The Economics of Climate Change*: 282–301.

77. M.H. Babiker, 'Sub-Global Climate-Change Actions and Carbon Leakage: The Implications of International Capital Flows', *Energy Economics* 23, 2001: 121–39.

78. David Harvey, *A Brief History of Neoliberalism*, Oxford University Press, Oxford, 2005: 120–51.

79. Statement by Yasheng Huang, 'Is China Playing by the Rules? Free Trade, Fair Trade, and WTO Compliance', Congressional-Executive Commission on China, 24 September 2003.

80. Harvey, *A Brief History of Neoliberalism*: 120–51.

81. 'Rushing on by Road, Rail and Air', *The Economist*, 16 February 2008.

82. Dwight H. Perkins, 'China's Recent Economic Performance and Future Prospects', *Asian Economic Policy Review* 1, June 2006: 15–40, Table 2.

83. E. Ianchovichina and Will Martin, 'Trade Impacts of China's World Trade Organization Accession', *Asian Economic Policy Review* 1, June 2006: 45–65.

84. Barry Eichengreen and Hui Tong, 'How China is Reorganizing the World Economy', *Asian Economic Policy Review* 1, June 2006: 73–97.

85. S. Lall and M. Albaladejo, 'China's Competitive Performance: A Threat to East Asian Manufactured Exports?' *World Development* 32, 2004: 1441–66.

86. Harvey, *A Brief History of Neoliberalism*: 139.

87. Kam Kiu Newsletter, www.kamkiu.com/english/news.asp.

88. Peng Cheng Aluminum Zhong Wang Group, www.pcaus.com.

89. www.alcan.com/web/publishing.nsf/Content/Insights+on+the+Global +Aluminum+Industry, www.alcoa.com/locations/china_beijing/en/home. asp. See also Warren H. Hunt, 'The China Factor: Aluminum Industry Impact', www.tms.org/pubs/journals/JOM/0409/Hunt-0409.html.

90. International Aluminum Institute, 'Primary Aluminum Production', 20 May 2008. see www.world.aluminium.org/statistics.

91. *11th Five year Plan of National Economic Development*: http://en.ndrc.gov. cn/hot/t20060529_71334.htm.

92. www.greenpeace.org/raw/content/china/en/press/reports/energy-revolution. pdf.

93. National Development and Reform Commission, People's Republic of China, http://en.ndrc.gov.cn/brief/default.htm.

94. Stern, *The Economics of Climate Change*: 546–47.

Chapter 6

1. Larry Lohmann (ed.), *Carbon Trading: A Critical Conversation on Climate Change, Privatization and Power*, Dag Hammarskjöld Foundation, Durban Group for Climate Justice and The Corner House, Sturminster Newton, 2006. See www. thecornerhouse.org.uk.

2. The examples are all from ibid.: 22–5.

3. Most of the discussion concerns CDM. Compared to CDM activity, JI activity lags behind and concerns only a minor share of joint implementation projects.

4. Yda Schreuder and Christopher Sherry, 'Flexible Mechanisms in the Corporate Greenhouse: Implementation of the Kyoto Protocol and the Globalization of the Electric Power Industry', *Energy and Environment* 12(5/6), 2001: 487–98.

5. See Michael See, *Greenhouse Gas Emissions: Global Business Aspects*, Springer Verlag, New York 2001: 8–9.

6. Anne Arquit Niederberger and Raymond Saner, 'Exploring the Relationship between FDI Flows and CDM Potential', *Transnational Corporations* 14(1), April 2005: 1–40.

7. For unilateral CDM projects the initiative lies with the host country. Usually the unilateral projects are much smaller than Annex-I country initiated projects and occur in countries that are typically not targeted by the international CDM investors community. See Joris Laseur, 'Unilateral CDM: Addressing the Participation of Developing Countries in CDM Project Development', M.A. thesis, International Economics and Business, University of Groningen, Netherlands, July 2005.

8. UNFCCC COP6, The Hague, the Netherlands, November 2000; http://unfccc.int/cop6/ and COP6 – Part II, Bonn Germany, July 2001; http://unfccc.int/cop6_2/index.html.

9. Frank Jotzo and Axel Michaelowa, 'Estimating the CDM Market under the Marrakech Accords', *Climate Policy* 2, 2002: 179–196.

10. 'Shell and the CDM', presentation at China's Business Council for Sustainable Development, www.cbcsd.org.cn/themes/Clean_Development_Machanism/download/GarthEdwardbeijing_IETA.pdf.

11. UNFCCC COP7 2002, Marrakesh Accords to the Kyoto Protocol, http://unfccc.int/cop7/.

12. Ben Pearson and Yin Shao Loong, 'The CDM: Reducing Greenhouse Gas Emissions or Relabelling Business As Usual?' Third World Network and CDM Watch, March 2003.

13. UNFCCC COP7 2002, Marrakesh Accords to the Kyoto Protocol,.

14. PROBASE briefing note on additionality, quoted in Pearson and Yin, 'The CDM'.

15. CDM PDD, Version 1, 3.7.02; quoted in Pearson and Yin, 'The CDM'.

16. Guidelines for completing Project Design Documents, CDM PDD, www.unfccc.int/cdm.

17. Jane Ellis et al., 'CDM: Taking Stock and Looking Forward', *Energy Policy* 35, 2007: 15–28.

18. In fact, it is doubtful if HFC$_{23}$ projects belong in the CDM; they should perhaps be listed under the Montreal Protocol.

19. Jane Ellis et al., 'Taking Stock of Progress under the Clean Development Mechanism (CDM)', OECD, Geneva.

20. Othmar Schwank, 'Concerns about CDM Projects based on Decomposition of HFC$_{23}$ Emissions from HCFC$_{22}$ Production Sites', June 2004, cdm.unfccc.int/public_inputs/inputamooo1/Comment_AMooo1_Schwank_081004.pdf.

HFC$_{23}$ is a byproduct of HCFC$_{22}$, which is used as refrigerant and as feedstock for the production of Teflon.

21. G. Lu, 'Incineration of HFC$_{23}$ Waste Streams CDM projects in China: Opportunities in the Project Development and Cooperation', referenced in Ellis et al., 'CDM: Taking Stock and Looking Forward'.

22. Heidi Bachram, 'Climate Fraud and Carbon Colonialism: The New Trade in Greenhouse Gases', *Capitalism, Nature, Socialism* 15(4), December 2004: 1–16.

23. Michael Wara, 'Measuring the Clean Development Mechanism's Performance and Potential', Working Paper 56, Program on Energy and Sustainable Development, Stanford University, July 2006, www.pesd.stanford.edu/publications/cdm/; and Michael Wara, 'Is the Global Carbon Market Working', *Nature* 445(8), February 2007: 595.

24. Wara, 'Measuring the Clean Development Mechanism's Performance and Potential'.

25. International Emissions Trading Association, www.ieta.org. Until recently, ExxonMobil was noticeably absent from this organization!

26. International Emissions Trading Association (2006), 'EU ETS Review – Building a Global Carbon Market: Report pursuant to Article 30 of the Directive 2003/87/EC', paper presented to the European Commission, Brussels, 13 November 2006, www.ieta.org.

27. International Emissions Trading Association (2007), *State and Trends of the Carbon Market*, 2006 and 2007, www.ieta.org/ieta/www/pages/index.php.

28. Sijm et al., *Spillover of Climate Policy – An Assessment of the Incidence of Carbon Leakage and Induced Technological Change due to CO$_2$ Abatement Measures.*

29. Ibid.: 22–5.

30. Ellis et al., 'CDM': 19, Figure 5. Official Development Assistance is development aid from industrialized countries (OECD countries) to developing countries for economic development and welfare assistance. ODA has a grant component of at least 25 per cent.

31. Sijm et al., *Spillovers of Climate Policy*: 22–5.

32. The Institute for Global Environmental Strategies (2006), 'CDM and FDI: Comparative Analysis', paper presented at CDM/JI Programme, Institute for Global Environmental Strategies, Kayo, Ikeda, Japan, 30 March 2006, www.iges.or.jp/en/cdm/pdf/activity_regional01/05.pdf.

33. Ellis et al., 'CDM': 17–18.

34. Pearson and Yin, 'The CDM'.

35. Ellis et al., 'CDM': 17.

36. Mike Jackson et al., 'Greenhouse Gas Implications in Large Scale Infrastructure Investments in Developing Countries: Examples from China and India', Program on Energy and Sustainable Development Working Paper 54, March 2006, http://iis-db.stanford.edu/pubs/21061/China_and_India_Infrastructure_Deals.pdf.

37. National 11th Five-Year Plan, www.gov.cn/english/2006–04/05/content_245566.htm.

38. Office of National Coordination Committee on Climate Change, 'Measures for the Operation and Management of CDM Projects', http://cdm.ccchina.

gov.cn/english/NewsInfo.asp?NewsId=905.

39. Fei Ten and Alun Gu, 'Climate Change: National and Local Policy Opportunities in China', CCMP-Climate Change Modeling and Policy, Fondazione Eni Enrico Mattei, July 2007, 4: www.feem.it.

40. Carbon Trust, www.carbontrust.co.uk/energy; Climate Strategies, www.climate-strategies.org; Netherland Research Program on Climate Change,www.ciesin.org/TG/HDP/netgcrp.html; Joint Implementation Network, www.jiqweb.org; Climate Action Network Europe, www.climnet.org.

41. Climate Action Network Europe, www.climnet.org; Green Peace International, www.greenpeace.org/international/.

42. See, for instance, John Byrne and Leigh Glover, *Climate Shopping: Putting the Atmosphere up for Sale*, TELA, Melbourne, 2000; The Corner House, www.thecornerhouse.org.uk; see Larry Lohmann, *Carbon Trading*, International Durban Group for Climate Justice: www.carbontradewatch.org/durban/.

43. Heidi Bachram, 'Climate Fraud and Carbon Colonialism: The New Trade in Greenhouse Gases', *Capitalism, Nature, Socialism* 5(4), December 2004: 1–16.

44. Jackson et al., 'Greenhouse Gas Implications'.

45. Sinks Watch, www.sinkswatch.org.

46. For a discussion about Shell's investment in Canada's tar-sand oil extraction, see Elizabeth Kolbert, 'Unconventional Crude: Canada's Synthetic-Fuels Boom', *The New Yorker*, 12 November 2007: 46ff.

47. 'Shell and the CDM', presentation at China's Business Council for Sustainable Development: www.cbcsd.org.cn/themes/Clean_Development_Machanism/download/GarthEdwardbeijing_IETA.pdf.

48. www.emissierechten.nl/india.htm 30 July 2007.

49. Shell in India, www.shell.com/home/content/in-en/about_shell/dir_about_shell_india_0204.html.

50. Anne A. Niederberger and Raymond Saner, 'Exploring the Relationship between FDI Flows and CDM Potential', *Transnational Corporations* 14(1), April 2005: 1–40.

51. Frank Lecocq and K. Capoor, *State and Trends of the Carbon Market 2003*, http://conserveonline.org/docs/2004/01/StateandTrendsofCarbonMarket2003.pdf.

52. Price Waterhouse Coopers, 'Responding to a Changing Environment: Applying Emissions Trading Strategy to Industrial Companies', Price Waterhouse Coopers, March 2005, www.pwc.com/extweb/pwcpublications.nsf/docid/.

53. Carbon Trust, www.carbontrust.co.uk/.

54. William Megginson and Jeffry M. Netter, 'From State to Market: A Survey of Empirical Studies on Privatization', *Journal of Economic Literature* 39, June 2001: 321–89.

55. Energy Information Agency, *Privatization and the Globalization of Energy Markets*, Energy Information Agency, Washington DC, 1996, www.eia.doe.gov.

56. Schreuder and Sherry, 'Flexible Mechanisms in the Corporate Greenhouse': 496.

57. Marc Morano, 'Enron and the Clinton Administration: Ties that Bind', CNS News, 2002, www.newsmax.com/archives/articles/2002/3/18/83918.shtml.

On the real intentions of Enron's Dabhol power plant, see, Subodh Wagle, 'TNCs as Aid Agencies: Enron and the Dabhol Power Plant', *The Ecologist* 26(4), July/August 1996: 179–84.

58. Morano, 'Enron and the Clinton Administration'.

59. See US Initiative on Joint Implementation, 'CAPEX Power Generation Project', project summary, www.gcrio.org/usiji/; and El Paso International, www.epenergy.com.

60. Christopher Sherry, 'Economic Globalization, the Environment, and the Electric Power Industry: U.S. Direct Investment in the Greenhouse', M.A. thesis, Energy and Environmental Policy, University of Delaware, 2000.

61. Amy Ridenour, 'Enron and the Environmental Movement: Global Warming Politics Makes for Strange Bedfellows', *National Policy Analysis*, January 2002, see www.nationalcenter.org/NPA384.html. For a list of members of the Business Environmental Leadership Council of the Pew Center for Global Climate Change, see www.PewCenter.org.

62. Christopher C. Horner, *The Politically Incorrect Guide to Global Warming and Environmentalism*, Competitive Enterprise Institute, Washington DC, 2007.

63. Magdalena Muir, 'European Energy Liberalization and the Integration of Eastern Europe with EU Energy Markets and Environmental Initiatives', written remarks prepared for ENERGEX 2002 conference, 19–24 May 2002, Krakow.

64. Pinsent Masons, 'Energy Privatization in Romania', December 2005, www.pinsentmasons.com/media/119220455.htm.

65. See www.cleanedge.com/story.php?nID=4854.

66. See Gazprom, www.gazprom.com/eng/articles/article8925.shtml.

67. www.eaqua.com/pages/eea_en/Media/Press_releases/Latest_press_releases/Pressemitteilung.htm?id=267872.

68. E.ON Ruhrgas, www.eon-ruhrgas.com/cps/rde/xchg/er-corporate/hs.xsl/426.htm?rdeLocaleAttr=en.

Chapter 7

1. Alliance for Climate Protection, www.climateprotect.org/about #ourmission.

2. International Conference on Climate Change, 2–4 March 2008, New York, organized by the Heartland Institute, a Chicago-based group whose anti-regulatory philosophy has long been embraced and supported financially by various industries and conservative donors; www.heartland.org/NewYork08/sponsorships.cfm.

3. A Call for Action: United States Climate Action Partnership, www.us-cap.org/about/report.asp; Pew Center on Global Climate Change, www.pew-climate.org/uscap.

4. International Energy Agency, *World Energy Outlook: China and India Insight*, IEA, 2007, www.worldenergyoutlook.org/2007.asp.

5. *Fourth Assessment Report of the Intergovernmental Panel on Climate Change (IPCC): The AR4 Synthesis Report*, November 2007, www.ipcc.ch.

6. J. Byrne et al., 'Undoing Atmospheric Harm: Civil Action to Shrink the

Carbon Footprint', in P. Droege (ed.), *Urban Transition: From Fossil Fuels to Renewable Power*, Elsevier, Oxford, 2008: 27–53.

7. IPCC, *IPCC Fourth Assessment Report: Synthesis Report for Policy Makers*, November 2007, www.ipcc.ch/ipccreports/special-reports.htm.
8. *Energy [R]evolution: A Sustainable China Energy Outlook*, Green Peace and European Renewable Energy Council, January 2007, www.greenpeace.org/raw/content/china/en/press/reports/energy-revolution.pdf.
9. Byrne et al., 'Undoing Atmospheric Harm'.
10. *Stern Review on the Economics of Climate Change*, www.hm-treasury.gov.uk/independent_reviews/stern_review_economics_climate_change/stern_review_report.cfm.
11. International Energy Agency, *World Energy Outlook 2007*.
12. Ibid.: 'Fact Sheet: Global Energy Demand'.
13. Ibid.: 'Fact sheet: CO_2 Emissions'.
14. J. McNeill, P. Winsemius, and T. Yakushiji, *Beyond Interdependence: The Meshing of the World's Economy and the Earth's Ecology*, Oxford University Press, New York, 1991; Shui Bin and Robert C. Harriss, 'The Role of CO_2 Embodiment in US–China Trade', *Energy Policy* 34, 2006: 4063–48.
15. Daniel Altman, *Connected 24 Hours in the Global Economy*, Farrar, Straus & Giroux, New York, 2007.
16. Yda Schreuder and Christopher Sherry, 'Global Corporations in the Greenhouse: Developing Equitable Accounting Measures', *Bulletin of Science, Technology and Society* 19(6), 1999: 511–20
17. W. Zeile, 'U.S. Intra-firm Trade in Goods', *Survey of Current Business*, February 1997: 23–38.
18. Thomas L. Brewer, 'The WTO and the Kyoto Protocol: Interaction Issues', *Climate Policy* 4, 2004: 3–12.
19. Herman, E. Daly and R. Goodland, 'The Perils of Free Trade', *Scientific American*, November 1993: 50–57.
20. Byrne et al., 'Undoing Atmospheric Harm'.
21. See Chapter 2 above.
22. Whereas a serious effort has been under way to establish a global greenhouse-gas accounting system (see the Greenhouse Gas Protocol Initiative, a decade-long partnership between the World Resources Institute and the World Business Council for Sustainable Development), the dramatic change in the global economic accounting called for here is of a different order. See World Resources Institute, *The Greenhouse Gas Protocol: A Corporate Accounting and Reporting Standard*, March 2004, www.ghgprotocol.org.
23. China's position was expressed through the National Development and Reform Commission in June 2007, in advance of the G8 meeting. See http://en.ndrc.gov.cn/.
24. S. Dunn, 'Can the North and the South Get in Step?', *World Watch Magazine* 11(6), November/December 1998: 19–27.
25. Michael Woodin and Caroline Lucas, *Green Alternatives to Globalization: A Manifesto*, University of Michigan Press, Ann Arbor, 2004.
26. Article 4.5 of the UNFCCC states that developed countries shall take all practicable steps to promote, facilitate and finance as appropriate the transfer

of or access to environmentally sound technologies and know-how to developing countries to enable them to implement the Convention provisions.

27. 'Clash over Technology Transfer almost Derails Bali Climate Talks', Third World Network, Bali News Update, 6 December 2007, www.twnside.org.sg; 'Collapse on Technology Talks sours Bali Climate Conference', Third World Network, Bali News Update, 13 December 2007, www.twndise.org.sg.

28. 'Trade Ministers Propose More Intensive Trade-climate Engagement, Third World Network, Bali News Update, 11 December 2007, www.twnside.org. sg.

29. 'Developing Countries Face Pressure, Threats at Climate Talks', Third World Network, Bali News Update, 15 December 2007, www.twnside.org.sg.

30. Al Gore, 'Moving Beyond Kyoto', *New York Times*, 1 July 2007.

31. Research conducted since the mid-1990s at the Center for Energy and Environmental Policy at the University of Delaware referred to in Chapter 2; Byrne et al., 'Undoing Atmospheric Harm'.

32. Paul Baer et al., 'The Right to Development in a Climate Constrained World: The Greenhouse Development Rights Framework', Heinrich Böll Foundation, 24 September 2007, www.ecoequity.org/docs/TheGDRsFramework. pdf.

33. For a review of the various burden-sharing commitments, see, Marcel Berk and Michel den Elzen, 'Options for Differentiation of Future Commitments in Climate Policy: How to Realize Timely Participation to Meet Stringent Climate Goals', *Climate Policy* 52, 2001: 1–16; Baer et al., 'The Right to Development in a Climate Constrained World'.

34. Baer et al., 'The Right to Development in a Climate Constrained World'.

35. Jonathan Porritt, *Capitalism as if the World Matters*, Earthscan, London, 2005.

36. Michael Shellenberger and Ted Nordhaus, 'The Death of Environmentalism: Global Warming Politics in a Post-Environmental World', paper presented at the October 2004 Meeting of the Environmental Grantmakers' Association, New York.

37. US Climate Action partnership, www.us-cap.org.

38. 'German's Social Democrats Move Left', *International Herald Tribune*, 28 October 2007. One of the issues in the decision to change the party strategy for the next general election – scheduled for 2009 – concerned the issue of reducing speed limits on German highways in order to reduce CO_2 emissions and to privatize the Deutsche Bahn (German railroads).

39. Yda Schreuder, 'The Polder Model in Dutch Economic and Environmental Planning', *Bulletin of Science, Technology and Society* 21(4), August 2001: 237–45.

40. Jared Diamond, *Collapse: How Societies Choose to Fail or Survive*, Penguin, London, 2005: 486–525.

41. Ibid.: 519–20.

42. A.W. Wyckoff, and J.M. Roop, 'The Embodiment of Carbon in Imports of Manufactured Products: Implications for International Agreements on Greenhouse Gas Emissions, *Energy Policy* 22, 1994: 187–94.

43. R. Schaeffer and A.L. de Sá, 'The Embodiment of Carbon Associated with Brazilian Imports and Exports', *Energy Conversion and Management* 37,

1996: 955–60; J. Munksgaard and K.A. Pederson, 'CO$_2$ Accounts for Open Economies: Producer or Consumer Responsibility? *Energy Policy*, 29, 2001: 327–34.

44. Shui Bin and Robert C. Harris, 'The role of CO$_2$ Embodiment in US–China Trade', *Energy Policy* 34, 2006: 4063–8.

Index